THE
BLUE
HOUR

THE
BLUE
HOUR

A Portrait of Jean Rhys

LILIAN PIZZICHINI

BLOOMSBURY
LONDON · BERLIN · NEW YORK

First published in Great Britain 2009

Copyright © by Lilian Pizzichini 2009

The right of Lilian Pizzichini to be identified as the author of
this Work has been asserted by her in accordance with
the Copyright, Designs & Patents Act 1988

No part of this book may be used or reproduced in any manner
whatsoever without written permission from the Publisher except
in the case of quotations embodied in critical articles or reviews

Every reasonable effort has been made to trace copyright
holders of material reproduced in this book, but if any have been
inadvertently overlooked the Publishers would be glad to hear
from them. For legal purposes the copyright acknowledgements
on page 309 constitute an extension of the copyright page

Bloomsbury Publishing Plc
36 Soho Square
London W1D 3QY

www.bloomsbury.com

Bloomsbury Publishing, London, New York and Berlin

A CIP catalogue record for this book is available from the British Library

ISBN 978 0 7475 9740 7

10 9 8 7 6 5 4 3 2 1

Typeset by Hewer Text UK Ltd, Edinburgh
Printed in Great Britain by Clays Ltd, St Ives plc

Mixed Sources
Product group from well-managed
forests and other controlled sources
www.fsc.org Cert no. SGS-COC-2061
© 1996 Forest Stewardship Council
FSC

For Dolly and Rita

CONTENTS

'Like' is of all the words the most ridiculous with which to express the love that I have for this place, love that has something almost physical about it so that in moments of pain I have quite literally lain full length and drawn solace from the ground.

Elizabeth Garner, *Duet in Discord*

There is nothing unusual in all this, except to those who live like exiles in grey shadows.

Phyllis Allfrey, *The Orchid House*

Foreword

In the summer of 1912 the French parfumier Jacques Guerlain concocted a scent from musk and rose de Bulgarie with a single note of jasmine. He intended his new scent, which he called L'Heure Bleue, to evoke dusk in the city. The blue hour is the time when heliotropes and irises in Parisian window boxes are bathed in a blue light and the well-groomed Parisienne prepares for the evening.

For the novelist Jean Rhys, the blue hour was also the hour when the lap-dog she saw herself as being during the day turned into a wolf. Dogs hunt best during twilight. Underneath our surface sophistication lurks a predator. Jean Rhys was always concerned with what lay beneath the top notes. In *Quartet*, her first novel, set in Paris, a young female character, smarter and bolder than her heroine, is wearing L'Heure Bleue by Guerlain. Rhys's heroine absorbs the woman's scent as though in breathing it in she can capture her rival's self-possession.

The scent itself is dusky, as though bought from an old-world apothecary on a forgotten street in Paris. Its hints of pastry and almonds make L'Heure Bleue a melancholic fragrance, as though in mourning for a time passed by. The curves of the Art Nouveau bottle, the stopper, in the form of a hollowed-out heart, allude to the romance of the years leading to the First World War. The story Jean Rhys told in *Quartet* describes the last days and weeks of a relationship, the loss of love and safety, and, implicitly, the death of old Europe. L'Heure Bleue was her favourite perfume, and *The Blue Hour* is an attempt to re-capture her life.

Chapter 1:

LE REVENANT

On 25 February 1936, Jean Rhys boarded a French ship called the *Cuba* at Southampton dock. The ship was bound for Dominica, her childhood home, which she had left twenty-nine years previously. Since then, she had lived in London, Paris and Vienna; she had married twice and given birth to two children (the first died in infancy, the second was living with her ex-husband). She had published a volume of short stories entitled *The Left Bank*, a translation of a French thriller, *Perversity*, and three novels, *Quartet*, *After Leaving Mr Mackenzie* and *Voyage in the Dark*. She had received critical acclaim, albeit somewhat guarded, and very little financial reward.

Going home was a matter of urgency: she had to go home to keep writing. She had moved through scenes of Parisian and London life like a sponge, soaking up the atmosphere and detail, yet so absorbed in her own travails that she was unable to connect with external reality. She had met famous people and been the lover of two English gentlemen, one a famous novelist. She had been disappointed and cast aside. She had been cut adrift from her roots, and had found no haven. Dominica was calling her home.

Jean was accompanied by her second husband, Leslie Tilden

Smith, an occasional literary agent and publisher's reader. The couple's families came to see them off at Southampton: Leslie's daughter Anne, Jean's sisters, and her long-lost brother Owen, who had recently returned from a failed fruit farm in Australia. He was as feckless as herself. Everyone brought flowers for the happy couple and everyone was happy for Jean. So was she; at forty-six years old, she was going home.

But the journey was hindered by the sea: the Sargasso Sea, where the *Cuba* seemed to flounder for long, dreary days in a mess of weed and wreckage. The sea itself was blocking her way.

The *Cuba* had a French crew and French and English passengers. Jean and Leslie had a table on the French side of the dining room. Jean liked French people. Unfortunately, the reality of being surrounded by people overcame her initial delight at their nationality. And they were not all French. Sitting next to her at the dining table was a voluble Italian woman with two noisy children and a thunderous husband. The woman's chatter enraged Jean. Words were exchanged, the Italian glowered, an atmosphere poisoned the nightly meal.

Close proximity to other people wiped her out, erased her. It is so hard to get what you want in this life. Everything and everyone conspires to stop you. This was how it seemed to Jean. She could not voice her feelings, and her life, as she told it to others, seemed unreal. She often found that when she told people her story, they looked at her with disbelief in their eyes. So she stopped telling them. Instead, she told it to herself in her novels. That way, she at least could believe it. As a writer, this strategy worked well for her; as a woman, it did not.

Jean put on different guises for different phases, becoming a different person depending on whom she was with; there was no continuity to her idea of herself. When surrounded by others, it was a battle to preserve even the most subtle sense of who she might be.

Jean created her own world as protection from this one, with its infuriating chatterboxes, selfish drama queens, and arrogant upstarts. When she argued with her neighbours, as she would for the rest of her life, it was not merely a matter of winning or losing an argument, it was a struggle to prove that she existed.

The *Cuba* stopped at St Lucia for a week. The last time Jean had stayed on this comparatively sophisticated French island was for her Uncle Acton's wedding. Acton was dead now. His widow, Evelina, and her two daughters Lily and Monica Lockhart, were running the Hotel St Antoine outside Castries. There had been a son, Don, who had shot himself. Volatility was not unheard of in Jean's family. On both her mother's and father's sides there were instances of consuming despair and depression. Jean recognised something of her younger self in her cousin Lily, who was a bit of a loner. She went for walks by herself in the moonlight, and edited a self-published magazine for which she wrote all the stories. Leslie, an experienced man of letters, 'could see no merit' in Lily's magazine, Jean wrote in a letter to a friend. But Jean liked it. She struck up a friendship with the girl, a rare instance of mutual sympathy in Jean's family.

The couple's stay in St Lucia was pleasant. They were waited on by a woman dressed in the old style, the *foulard* and *madras* of the *gwan' wobe* (*grande robe*) of the French Antilles. The woman brought in Jean's afternoon tea on a tray. It was, she said, 'the past majestically walking in'.

But there were too many familiar faces here, too many conversations to be had and too many demands on her waning energy. Jean wanted to write. Towards the end of March they arrived in Roseau, Dominica, her birthplace. She wrote to Mother Mount Calvary, her favourite nun at the convent where she had been educated. She had come home, she wrote; she wanted to see the Good Mother. But she was afraid Mother might have forgotten her.

'How could I forget you, Gwen?' was Mother Mount Calvary's reply, using Jean's real name. She invited Jean to visit for tea.

Going back is difficult because everything always changes. Mother Mount Calvary looked old and sombre though she smiled and kissed Jean affectionately. She had sad news for Jean. Mother Sacred Heart, another beloved nun, was dead. The convent was faced with closure. One consolation was a photograph in Mother's office of Jean's father. He had been a doctor to the convent, and a favourite son of the parish. Jean visited his grave in the nearby graveyard. She was grateful to be away from the anxious, ageing nun, who had gamely tried to conceal her worry about her future. But her anxiety betrayed itself, and Jean found it painful to countenance.

Jean sat by her father's grave with its Celtic cross, almost obscured by weeds and neglect, and wept for the past. Her father, apart from the nuns, had been forgotten. His good works, his kindness to the poor, were as though they had not happened. No one tended his grave. His life had been *temps perdu*, a waste of time. Nature had confirmed that, wiping out the traces of his endeavour with senseless fertility.

Jean still loved her island. For her, it was the loveliest place that could be imagined. It was so conducive to sleep. The hot weather, the steady rainfall, the lushness, made sleep irresistible. She felt the usual delicious sinking sensation she always felt when tired, as though she were dying of opened veins in a hot bath. Her thoughts were of death, and Dominica was a beautiful place to die in.

A friend of Jean's dead mother offered her the use of a

remote estate called Hampstead in Portsmouth, on the Atlantic side of the island. The familiar English names of the locations belied the dramatic rainforest colours that ran through the gardens encasing the house. Much to her relief, this was not the suburban England that felt so suffocating to her. The colours enlivened her. She felt confident enough to make a joke about several years of hard drinking not making her calm enough to face cockroaches. She had sea on one side and mountains on the other. She had a beach with white sand, a good pool in the river, and a nice girl to look after her and Leslie. Most important of all, there was no one to interrupt her writing or her recovery of her self.

'The wonderful thing is to wake up and know that nobody can get at you – nobody,' she wrote to a friend.

Jean in Dominica

This contentment did not last. Leslie tried to blame it on the heat but Jean sank further into a misery born of anger and paranoia. There were too many people around. She sensed hostility. The servants preferred Leslie to her. Her father had been kind to the blacks, she wanted to tell this new generation of black Dominican. Not all the whites were oppressive, she wanted to explain. But no one was in the mood to appreciate her sensitivity to the past and her need to repair the losses she and her family had incurred. When she asked for dishes that Francine, her family's cook, had prepared, the servants looked at her in disbelief as though such dishes had never existed. When she asked drivers to take her to the places of her childhood, they shook their heads in stupefaction. These places were no longer there, not even the Imperial Road which had been opened by the great Mr Hesketh Bell whom she had danced with at the celebratory ball and to whom she had once been so unpardonably rude. The road was just a track now, covered with forest. Genever, the family estate, was a burnt-out wreck covered in ferns. She walked round it, trying to remember the honeysuckle and the jasmine. There was nothing left.

Chapter 2:

DOMINICA

On 10 January 1882 William Rees Williams, aged twenty-nine, and Minna Lockhart, aged twenty-nine, married in Roseau, Dominica, a colony of the British Empire. He was Medical Officer and Health Officer to the Port of Roseau. She was a third-generation white Dominican Creole and a Welshman. Over the next thirteen years they would have six children: William Edward, Owen Lockhart, Minna Sophia, Brenda Gwenith Maxwell, Ella Gwendoline and Brenda Clarice.

Jean Rhys was born Ella Gwendoline Rees Williams on 24 August 1890 on the Windward Isle of Dominica. Nine months before she was born her mother had lost a cherished baby – Brenda Gwenith – to dysentery, and many years before that, a beloved sister called Ella, so Ella Gwendoline was named after two dead girls. For a long time – almost the entire duration of her childhood – Jean Rhys felt as though she were the ghost of her mother's baby. She would carry this feeling of insubstantiality with her into adulthood. As she grew, her mother's inattentiveness and mournful demeanour had far-reaching effects. As far as the young Jean could see, nothing could compensate her mother for her loss.

There were other, more tangible reasons for her sense of separateness from others. Ella Gwendoline, or Gwennie as her family called her, was fair and delicate. Her siblings were strong and dark. There was William Edward, who was seven when she was born, Owen Lockhart, who was five, and

Minna Sophia, who was four. Jean was her mother's fifth
baby and would always feel lost in the crowd. She did not
fit in: she was pale where the others were swarthy, she was
timid where the others were confident. Nor was she like the
black girls who lived on Genever, her family's estate. They
ran, swam and sweated as a matter of course. She was a well-
brought up little white girl, the descendant on her mother's
side of a wealthy slave-owner for whom blacks were possessions. She would never be accepted as one of them. To make
matters worse, her mother was fond of remarking that black
babies were prettier than white babies.

Gwennie desperately wanted to please her mother. So
each night she prayed to God that the colour of her skin
might change. But each morning when she looked in the
mirror, she was disappointed. When she was told that
Gwendoline, as well as being so close to her dead sister's
name, meant 'white' in her father's native tongue, she felt
doomed to an invisible existence. She was strangely languid
– her inactivity was often commented upon. Perhaps she was
gathering her energy for the long journey ahead that would
take her from the Caribbean, across the Sargasso Sea, into
the cold, grey stretches of the North Atlantic and deep into
Europe's capital cities. Here she became a wanderer, never
belonging, haunted by a sense of loss. Dominica, she would
say many years later, was 'the only home I ever had'.

Dominica: at the centre of the Lesser Antilles, 15 degrees
north of the Equator, its colours more vibrant than anywhere
else on earth, its rains more sudden and heavier, its nights
that fall faster and blacker. Like its neighbours – Grenada, St
Vincent, St Lucia and Martinique – Dominica is a volcanic
island with high peaks and deep ridges. But Dominica is
the epicentre of the force that lifted the Antilles out of the
ocean. Hot springs spout plumes of water from the soft, red

earth. As if marking its special provenance, a rainbow almost perpetually hangs its arch over the island.

There is a wild and melancholic beauty to Dominica. Viewed from the deck of a sailing ship its brooding mountains, lush vegetation and tumbling streams intoxicate the keen-eyed traveller. In 1856, Anthony Trollope wrote: 'To my mind, Dominica as seen from the sea, is by far the most picturesque of all these islands. Indeed it would be difficult to beat it either in colour or grouping. It fills one with an ardent desire to be off and rambling among those green mountains.' Inland, Dominica is even more alluring: like a siren, she draws you in partly because of what she withholds. Even though the island is small, there are impenetrable spots deep in the forest that resist exploration or cultivation. It is easy to lose one's way there.

The caprice of fecundity has thwarted many a planter's ambitions. Coconut, cocoa, lime and rubber crops have all been tried and, largely, failed. Things can go badly wrong: families' fortunes run dry, their plans go awry, rare plagues devastate their crops, and rains flood the harvest. Jean remembered her mother's complaints in the drenching heat: that washed clothes never dried to a crisp; that it was hard to keep a house clean. Despite the beauty that mesmerised her dreamy little girl, for her mother, the privileged daughter of a patrician white, life was hard here.

James Potter Lockhart, Jean's maternal great-grandfather, came to Dominica to manage a sugar plantation in the 1790s. He was a Scot, the grandson of William Lockhart, laird of Birkhill, Lanarkshire, and a prosperous sugar merchant. In 1824 he bought the Genever Plantation at Grand Bay, down in the south of the island. His ledgers declared that he owned 1,200 acres and 258 slaves. By the time Jean was born, 'Old' Lockhart's riches had dwindled and the estate, though still in the family, had fallen into decline. There was a picture of him in the house in Roseau, Dominica's capital, where Jean grew up. As a small girl she loved to hear stories about this serious, heavy man in a powdered wig. Next to his portrait on the dining-room wall was one of his young wife. Her breezy dark eyes and black curls captivated the little girl. Her maiden name had been Jean Maxwell, and she came from Cuba. Family legend had it that she was originally a Spanish countess. This may have been a blind to cover up a Cuban heritage which would suggest that black blood was passed to Lockhart's children. A person of European descent born in the Caribbean is known as a white Creole. But when Jean repeated the family legend that her great-grandmother had been a Spanish countess to her father, he simply said: 'Spanish? I wonder,' before adding: 'Who's white? Damned few.' Whatever the case, on reaching adulthood, Jean would give the name of her spirited great-grandmother a new lease of life.

In her memoir, *Smile Please*, written at the end of her life, Jean recalls visits to her great-aunt, Jean Maxwell's daughter, still living at the old estate, Genever. Great-aunt Jane, with her green parrot sitting on her shoulder, would tell the little girl stories about Old Lockhart and his wife. He was said to be very jealous, not of other men, but of his wife's love of priests and Catholicism. On their marriage he had made her convert to Protestantism. One day, she told him with a loving smile, 'There was a lovely priest in my room yesterday.' A terrible row ensued. It eventually transpired that what she had meant to say was, 'There was a lovely breeze in my room.' Jean loved to hear this story of verbal slippage, with its implications of flouting authority.

The stories Jean heard about the master of Genever were bewildering. She would visit the estate every summer with her family. There, she would listen to the servants ruminating on the old days. They told her that Lockhart had had many mistresses amongst his slaves, and consequently, many children running around the estate. Wills, deeds and land rights were fiercely guarded by his legitimate offspring and contested just as fiercely by the illegitimate. In Dominica's version of Victorian society, boundaries had to be maintained between what was right and respectable, and what was not. Lockhart was not respectable, and so he became notorious. The plantocracy disapproved. But he was lord of his plantation and as such, he could do as he liked. When he tired of his black mistresses he freed them. If he was feeling kind, he would give them a hut with a little garden. If he could never remember the names of all his children, at least he tried, sporadically, to help them.

All the while Jean was growing up, she grew increasingly aware of ancient resentments and old grudges against his profligacy and the seeming injustice of it all. If some of the blacks, to whom she might be related, eyed her and her family suspiciously, so did the white planters, who feared loucheness more than anything.

Lockhart's legitimate children were Richard, the eldest son and heir, who disappeared, Cora, who married but had no children, Edward, Jean's grandfather, and Sophia who remained unmarried. No one knew what happened to Richard. Stories circulated that he had been disinherited for beating a slave or that he ran away with the family silver. But these are familiar stories from Victorian families with black sheep. There again, years later, Jean would talk about an aunt who was 'peculiar' and 'shut away'. Jean used the name Cora in her last novel.

In 1837 James Potter Lockhart died, leaving his lovely Cuban wife with four children still living at home. Genever, like most estates in Dominica, was difficult to manage and remote – a two-hour ride on horseback to Roseau. Jean's great-grandmother managed the estate with an overseer until 1844, when rumours started circulating that the Emancipation Act was about to be revoked. The freed slaves rioted and burnt down the estate house. Jean Maxwell's eldest son, Edward Lockhart, was by now a magistrate, and with his wife, Julia Matilda Woodcock, he took over the estate and rebuilt the house. They presided over the gradual decline of Genever. Their first child, Ella, died aged thirteen. Minna and her twin, Brenda, were born in 1853. When Edward died in the early 1880s, Acton, the girls' younger brother, took over the estate. The price of sugar was falling, and it was hard to get labourers to work as though they were slaves. Acton did not really have a chance.

As young, well-bred ladies in Dominican high society, the twins Minna and Brenda had a sheltered and constricted life. They lived at Genever; took well-worn walks though the gardens and tea on the lawn. They were poorly educated. They received visitors always dressed in white, in case they should meet their fate, in other words, the man they were to marry. Minna was the younger and smaller twin, 'Miss Petit' the servants called her. At twenty-nine years old, she was well into womanhood by the time her fate appeared.

In 1881 William Potts Williams, the new Medical Officer to the Stowe District, sailed up river in a canoe to Genever. Minna and Brenda met him at the landing post. They took him to the estate house, called Mitcham, and gave him tea. Many years later, in *Wide Sargasso Sea*, Jean would write about a young Englishman arriving in the Caribbean and falling ill with fever. When William landed at Genever he, too, fell ill with fever. The twins nursed him back to health and as soon as he recovered he married Minna. She was 'the more angelic of the two – a beautiful sweet nature', he said. After dinner they would sit on the *glacis* (verandah) at Mitcham and William would play his flute.

'Oh, don't play that again,' Minna would say. 'It's too sad. Play something gay.'

'Typical Dominica,' people say when things go wrong on the island and nothing is done about it. It is easy to be indolent there, something Jean learned early on, and something she shared with her father. It was that very indolence that drove her mother mad. Yet the earth itself was so busy, and the island was crawling with strange creatures, so that sometimes all Jean wanted to do was sit and watch – a snake, the *diablotin* – from which the mountain, Morne Diablotin, takes its name – and the devil bird, black as a raven, swooping and soaring around its peak. Jean would listen, too, to the *siffleur montagne* or mountain whistler, whose call of two mournful notes echoed across the cloud forest. This was the only place on earth where you could hear that song. Higher up, in the rainforest, there is a giant toad called the *crapaud*, which tastes like chicken when roasted in a *calabash* – a pot. There was so much to marvel at, and the little girl, left to her own devices by a busy mother and kind but remote father, was entranced by her island home and its stories.

But, as Jean said, 'There are places which are supposed to be hostile to human beings,' and this was one of them. Hurricanes are common and ruinous in Dominica. The sugar trade diminished when she was a child and that generation of planters was ruined. Trouble came from every quarter, and still people tried to build new lives in Dominica.

★   ★   ★

For Jean Rhys's father, Dominica was an escape. William was the youngest son of an Anglican clergyman, William Rees Williams of Cardiganshire, south Wales. Whilst at Cambridge, William senior had made friends with the famous mathematician Robert Potts, whose translation of Euclid's *Elements* enjoyed an immense circulation throughout the British colonies and America; later, William senior married Robert's sister, Sophia.

By the time William Rees Williams married Sophia Potts, he was rector of Bodelwyddan in North Wales. They had three children. At the age of fourteen, their youngest, William, ran away to sea. He was caught at Cardiff and sent home to his father's rectory. At a more suitable age, William junior's desire for flight was given heed by his father who sent him away to sea. But by then he did not want to go. His father insisted, refusing to invest in his younger son's education. William eventually qualified as a first mate and sailed the world. But more significant to him was another encounter with authority. He passed this down to his daughter, too. During one sea voyage, a captain ill-treated the young first mate, taunting him with the words, 'I'll teach you to think you're a gentleman.' This insult was William's spur to leave the navy. He followed his older brother to London to take up medicine. But he could not settle in the Victorian society he found so stifling. His brother distinguished himself as a doctor. William was a rebel and turned to drink.

The little girl loved to hear stories of her father's acute awareness of injustice, his scepticism of authority, and his kindness to impoverished patients. The few remarks that she has handed down to us from her father conjure a man who was weary of social niceties, and who expressed this resentment through irony. He was a puzzle to Jean. His remoteness made him all the more heroic; his witty asides on his family's conformity made her complicit in an ironic commentary on their lives.

The interior of Bod Gwilym, the house in Roseau, was an expatriate exercise in Victorian sobriety. Her father's Welshness was very much in evidence. There were pictures of rural Wales on the parlour wall as well as a photo of Jean's Welsh grandfather. Jean never forgot the way her father would shake his fist at the portrait of the old man in a clerical collar. Only the house's clapboard exterior betrayed its Caribbean location. Situated on the corner of Cork and St Mary's streets, Bod Gwilym faced on to a street packed with houses containing other white families.

For centuries, Dominica had been fought over by the French and British. Both had left their mark. As a child, Jean was left to wander the haphazard lanes of the old French Quarter and the British grid of streets which extended from Cork Street to the river bank.

When she looked down Cork Street she could see the jetty and the sea and hear the bellowing hoot of ships approaching. Along St Mary's Street, she would look down a row of other, gaudily painted wooden houses. They all had first-storey *jalousies* and roofs of overlapping wooden shingles. It was a lively, colourful scene, and the nearby street market filled the air with the perfume of spices.

Family meals took place under a row of family portraits and a picture of Mary, Queen of Scots going to her execution. Pewter mugs and silver dishes were arranged on solid mahogany. At the back of the house, the family servant would sit on the pantry steps grinding coffee beans for Jean's father. He insisted on mocha coffee after meals.

Jean's earliest memory was of her pretty mother bending over her crib. She wrote a poem that expressed her delight in her mother's presence:

for I was in a crib
when she bent
down & kissed me
smelling sweet
In a low cut black
dress
I remember
I remember
& the other baby not yet born.

It's a description of a tantalising closeness, an absence wrapped in perfume. Jean's early memories of her mother suggest a paradise that was subsequently lost. But in truth Minna Rees Williams was a harassed mother of three children when Jean was born, and by the time Jean was five, Minna was pregnant again. The angelic 'Miss Petit' of Genever estate was long gone, except in her daughter's imagination. The reality was a forty-two-year-old woman expecting her sixth baby, who did not have the time or energy for Jean. The little girl's ruptured relationship with her mother created a void that she filled with nostalgic yearnings and a dread of future betrayal.

Jean's baby sister, Brenda Clarice, took her place as the youngest in the family. Worse, her twelve-year-old sister, the lively Minna Sophia, was 'given away' to Aunt Edith and Uncle John Spencer Churchill, the Colonial Secretary of the Bahamas, a long way away from Dominica. Equally disturbing, her brothers William and Owen were sent to Wellingborough School in England. The arrival of Brenda Clarice ruined everything.

Jean became convinced her mother did not like her any more. The caresses and the warmth that she sought and that should have come from her mother were no longer even a remote possibility. Almost overnight, her slim, pretty mother became a solid, frowning woman, austere and disapproving. Jean worried that she, too, would be despatched to a foreign country. This fear made her cling to her mother all the more, which in turn exasperated the tired, fractious woman, burdened with cares.

Children brought up in colonies dominated by Victorian codes of conduct generally did not enjoy close physical relationships with their mothers. This intimacy, a bond without words, fulfilled the child's deep need to be understood. But in Jean there remained an unsatisfied longing for this understanding. This was the root of the loneliness that always threatened to overwhelm the little girl and then the woman. It came from an early, irretrievable loss: the loss of her mother.

In Jean's next memory, the family is celebrating her sixth birthday. Her father was doing well and gaining status in Dominican society. He enjoyed the lushness of the landscape and the rituals of lavish meals served by demure, starchy servants. Every summer the family decamped to his estate in Bona Vista as well as paying visits to Minna's family in Genever. But on her sixth birthday, 24 August 1896, Jean writes in *Smile Please* that they were in Roseau. Her brothers William and Owen were home from English boarding school. Jean wore a white dress and a wreath of frangipani, a flower, she noted, whose branches bleed with white blood. She was morbid, even as a child. She sat on an armchair between her mother and father, feeling very important. Her brothers put on a play for her – 'Little Red Riding Hood' – but abandoned it halfway through when they got bored. The party was over. Her mother, fearing that Jean would cry, hastily gave her a book sent by her paternal grandmother, 'Irish granny', Sophia Potts Williams. This lady, the sister of the great mathematician, who lived in Wales, or England, Jean wasn't sure, sent books every Christmas and birthday, as well as boxes of chocolate, Carlsbad plums and jars of Stilton cheese for Father. There was a picture of a little girl in a pink dress on the cover of the book. She was sitting next to a big spider but Jean could not read the words underneath it.

She was confused but she had to have her photograph taken. Mother frowned as her daughter's arm moved when the photographer asked Jean to smile. 'Smile, please,' he kept saying. She did not feel like smiling.

A new baby meant that Meta, a *da*, the Creole word for nurse, took over from Mother. Meta 'always seemed to be brooding over some terrible, unforgettable wrong'; Jean wrote in her memoir that Meta 'couldn't bear the sight of me'. Brenda's birth spelt the end of her childhood in more ways than one. There would be no more visits with sister Minna to Miss Jane's sweet shop to buy lumps of sticky guava jelly, ginger, coconut or lassi mango; Minna had gone. Instead, Meta dragged Jean straight past Miss Jane's and hauled her round the Botanical Gardens for their daily walk, staring darkly and muttering curses all the while. There was no more sweetness to be had. Meta sent her six-year-old charge to sleep at night with tales of zombies and *soucriants*, the Caribbean version of vampires – livid, living corpses with gnashing teeth, haggard lips and terrifying powers – and Jean was convinced they would assault her while she slept. Worst of all was the *loup-garoux*, a fiendish female werewolf. Stories of the *loups-garoux* were brought to Dominica by the French colonists of the eighteenth century. These ghastly apparitions were old women who had made a pact with the devil. In exchange for occult abilities they had to provide him with human blood every night. So at first cock-crow they climbed the steep hill to the mythical silk-cotton tree and unravelled their flesh, which they folded and hid away. The *loogaroo écorché,* as Meta called them, were only visible as a ball of bluish fire. If you woke in the morning feeling sluggish it was because your essence had been sucked from you in the night.

Meta expressed her feelings of fear and fatalism in terms of voodoo and *obeah,* the Caribbean black magic. She ensured that little white Jean was haunted by the same sense of horror. On this tiny, inhospitable but luscious island where 300 white people hid their fears behind the artifice of good manners, the 30,000 black people forced into subservient roles spoke of blood-sucking vengeance. The original inhabitants of the island, the peacable Arawaks, had put a curse on the island as the Caribs, the first colonisers, hounded them to their deaths. The curse was that there would be beauty, gaiety and longing, with corruption, cruelty and dread. The island was filled with 'a kind of lovesick sloth', 'a heavy, languishing drowsiness', which Englishmen, it was said, resented.

Fear, awe and reverence for nature dominated Jean's child-hood. Her relish for Dominica and her awe at its ravines torn out by torrents, its azure sea and green forests never left her. Sometimes, when she was a young woman writing in Montparnasse or Bloomsbury, or an old woman writing in her bungalow in Devon, she must have dreamt of being a child again, paddling in the swirl of water in the lizard-green pool in the forest, hearing from somewhere in the trees above her the lugubrious notes of the *siffleur montagne,* a sound so melancholy it was the perfect emanation of this sad and beautiful place. She must have remembered the river ahead of her running deep into the passage between the swaying trees. These were her moments of pure being, when she imagined herself at one with the world. In *Wide Sargasso Sea* Jean plunges us back into the child's curiosity at all the

marvellous complexities of the world. She invokes the very
earliest period of our lives when sexuality – still exploratory
– pours itself into sensuality. She was a solitary child, so
experiences such as feeling the sun or sea-spray on her skin
were not shared, were not made light of, were not tempered
by another's experience of them. Every natural thing or
function that should give us pleasure became a source of
anxiety to her. So intense was her apprehension of nature
that it brought her closer to a sense of death than anything
the Church or her parents' morality could offer her. Every
moment was irreplaceable, furthermore there were no words
for it. And her inability to convey her anxiety, her joy, made
her a mute.

Jean spent much of her childhood screaming, crying or
collapsing with terror, and taking weeks to recover in bed.
Once there, she would be ministered to with handkerchiefs
drenched in *eau de cologne* by a gentle woman who whispered
soothingly in her ear. It was a way of returning to her
mother's bosom.

Jean's real mother fretted incessantly about cockroaches.
This fretting rang in the little girl's ears. The cockroaches
came out in swarms on a close night, or if there was a shower
of rain they fell from the skies. Meta made her panic – she
said they would bite her on the mouth in the night and that
the scars would never heal. It did not help that her mother
ran from the room if she saw a cockroach scuttling across
the floor. Jean felt close to her mother when her mother
was afraid. It was her link with her.

It helped that there was so much to fear: there were the
bêtes rouges – almost invisible to the naked eye – they swarmed
up your ankles and made you itch intolerably. There were
bright green lizards and yellow-grey lizards, cold and slimy
with pimples and knobs. The lizards were the terror of the

ladies because they moved so quickly and got mixed up in long, trailing skirts and drapes. And in the grass outside on the lawn, under the mango trees, the rattlesnake or *tête de chien* lay in wait. A foot long and vivid red, you could be dead from its bite in a couple of hours. Jean listened breathlessly as Meta explained the horrors that could befall her. Every step she took could be her last.

Others increased her burden of fear. An old man on the Genever estate, who had been born a slave, described to her 'God knew what scenes of lust or cruelty'. On her first day of school, she 'shrieked, clung to my mother and kicked up such a fuss that I didn't go'. Once, a boy who was always teasing her put a cockroach down her back. She 'went nearly mad with horror and disgust' until she became ill with fever. A friend of her father's, hugely tall and with a long red beard, put her on his knee. She never forgot these incidents or how she screamed in an 'agony of terror', and was sent to her room in disgrace. These were incidental frights. She stored them up untill they found their way on to the pages of *Smile Please*.

Meta, who earns herself a significant chapter in Jean's memoir, remained the real terror of her life, Meta and her feverish lectures on zombies, *soucriants* and *loups-garoux*. Meta was the evil witch to Jean's little innocent. Meta wanted to destroy that innocence. Red eyes and black shapeless things waited for Jean each night in the dark. Her mother did little to protect Jean's innocence, instead giving her another thing to fear: God. While she sewed, her mother would lecture Jean about the Bible, the sharp needles glinting in the sun, conflating in Jean's mind the big book of the Bible and the small one of the needlebook.

There was cruelty and there were monsters and an obsession with dirty fingernails and concealing her sweat and being slapped for no reason by her mother simply because she was vexed, and there was the haven of enjoyment – hammocks on the verandah and wicker-work loungers and Father at twilight smoking a cigar and sipping at his sherry sangris. These were the moments of heart–stopping beauty that her father enjoyed. The mountains around Roseau rising in voluptuous mounds and the mail boat pausing at sunset to meet the dug-out canoe carrying its passengers across the water. Flickering lights on the harbour and on the other side the mysterious, blue-green meeting-place of mountains and the little capital of Roseau.

Jean coming up to seven years old played in the quarantine station behind her house, sitting on a swing, and singing, 'Soldier, soldier, marry me / With your musket, fife and drum'. Her elder siblings gone; she was getting used to lone- liness. Her only friend was Willie, the youngest son of Dr Nicholls, the senior doctor on the island. She did not see so much of him now as he had gone to a boys' school. When she did see him, it was cause for celebration. She and Willie had to bathe in a stone bath as big as a room. One day, when she was around nine years old, conscious of his gaze, she slid gracefully down the edge of the bath into the water. She had begun to be a woman.

And as her self-awareness grew more keen, Meta's mocking increased alongside it. She wore carnival masks to frighten the girl, poking out her tongue through a slit and gabbling wildly at her, until Jean broke down in tears. Jean was so easy to break, so easy to reduce to a quivering jelly that she almost invited hostility. She certainly expected it. Meta took out her frustrations on this wreck of a girl. She played tricks on her. She would tell Jean that Willie was waiting on the *glacis* for her, so that she would fly downstairs before she was properly dressed. She would then hear Meta upstairs laughing loudly.

At the age of nine she looked at the photograph taken on her sixth birthday and saw that she was not the same pretty little girl swathed in white flowers; she had lost her curls and dimples. This was the first time she found herself longing for the past. She also noticed that the little girl's finger was raised as though in warning. Jean had become a thin girl, tall for her age, with straight hair. Brenda, the toddler, was the adored and petted child. Jean was forced by her mother to wear ugly clothes. Unlike the black girls who were the children of her family's servants, she had to wear a vest and bloomers under her starchy garments. Unlike the girls at convent school, her black stockings fell untidily around her ankles. When she asked a girl at school how she managed to keep her stockings so tightly stretched, the girl reluctantly told her that her garters were probably too slack. Jean could not understand why the girl was so dismissive of her. But she sewed a tuck into her garters which smoothed out her stockings. She was pleased with the result but her mother disapproved of the tight fit around her knees and demanded she remove the tucks. Another girl at school, Gussie de Freitas, was equally untidy and tried to befriend Jean – Jean's discomfort with her body was beginning to be recognised by others. She spurned Gussie, preferring to be an outcast on her own. She had a creeping sense of the difference between what she was and what she wanted to be.

Her father, Dr Rees Williams, was similarly debilitated by the disconnection between the image he had of himself and the one he presented to the outside world. He was a respected figure in his community and his kindness and liberality helped him achieve this status. He acted the gentleman but his actions were depleting the family's finances. He would not take money from his poor patients, and most of his patients were poor. The grander residents of Dominica insisted on consulting the senior doctor of the island, Dr Nicholls, Willie's father. This trouble with money is one possible reason why Jean's older sister, Minna, was adopted by the childless Spencer Churchills and why Mrs Rees Williams was growing increasingly dissatisfied and her husband correspondingly remote.

Jean's father never learned to moderate his 'reckless, throw-away attitude' to money. As long as cocktails were served at the blue hour, and mocha coffee after meals, his equilibrium was maintained. This attitude was passed down to his daughter Jean and his son Owen. For now, though, Owen was at boarding-school in England and Jean, when she was at Bona Vista, where Father was happiest, was allowed to run free.

Jean lived in the kitchen with the servants. Eating with your fingers from the *calabash* was like being a Negro, like the other women in the kitchen. Here was one of the few places where she felt safe. Watching the rain coming from across the sea, closing the shutters to dim the room, Father and his friends playing Bezique in the dining room, was like being a young girl in a romantic story. The rain falling and abating, and being barefoot afterwards in the grass and feeling the dampness on her skin.

As she grew older, she engaged with books far more than she did with people. People – black, white, coloured, servants, and high society – were so confusing, and generally did not seem to want to speak to her, or to listen. She read Milton's *Paradise Lost*, where she hunted down references to 'Th' infernal Serpent', 'th' Arch–Enemy', 'th' Apostate Angel', 'the Fall'n Cherube', 'the suttle Fiend'. She devoured 'Childe Harolde', Byron's story of an eternal wanderer, who grieves for a lost love and who, haunted by guilt, indulges in 'riot

most uncouth' and 'sin's long labyrinth'. Byron touched a
nerve with her. The Man of Feeling, with his frisson of
erotic diabolism, said things like, 'The great object in life is
sensation – to feel that we exist, even though in pain.' Already
Jean recognised something of what he was saying. She read
the eighteenth-century poets with their freight of irony so
similar to her father's, who shared their humorously grim
despair at social hypocrisy. In 'Pity for Poor Africans', Cowper
writes, 'I pity them greatly, but I must be mum, / For how
could we do without sugar and rum?' These were the writers
who stoked her propensity for detached bemusement.

More conventional reading came in the form of the novels
of Mrs Felicia Hemans. Everything she wrote conveyed a
moral exemplar: her women were calm and moderate, bright
and cheerful. Jean read the classics: *Robinson Crusoe*, *Treasure
Island*, *Gulliver's Travels*, *Pilgrim's Progress*. And, though they
were not her particular favourites, she read the Brontë sisters,
whose classic tropes she would later revise: the orphan, the
friendless girl, the cuckoo in the nest, the woman in the
attic, the wayward men.

Meta did not like her reading. She would creep up on
her from behind, grip her by the shoulders and shake her
violently. Jean would scream: 'Black Devil! Black Devil! Black
Devil!' and Meta would threaten her with 'tears of blood'.
She would threaten her with tears of blood for being dirty,
for tearing her dress, for not doing what she was told. One
thing Jean knew for sure was that one day she would surely
weep tears of blood.

But some of the women from her childhood had a benign
influence on Jean. She spent many hours talking to Cook
who was an *obeah* woman – her name was Ann Tewitt –
and she never forgot her. Unfortunately, she could not focus
on what Ann had once told her with such a significant nod

of the head – her fortune perhaps? Under her bed in the kitchen, Ann kept a large *conarie,* or earthenware jar, containing round balls of earth or clay. Some contained hair and rags and were bound with twine; others were stuck round with human or dogs' teeth and glass beads. But Jean could not hear what Ann was saying when she steadied her eyes upon her. When someone did pay her attention, she was so embarrassed and grateful she could barely take in what they were saying.

Every summer she could escape Meta by visiting Great-aunt Jane at the Genever Estate. From Roseau, through the rainforest towards Petite Savanne (a village inhabited by the descendants of the first French settlers), you pass the ruined Genever sugar mill. The sea lashes at the road. The ruined estate and the neglected garden entranced her, as did the woman she loved most in the world, Great-aunt Jane. The old lady and the little girl would stroll on the lawn among large clumps of bamboo and messy beds of hibiscus, oleander and honeysuckle. They would come to a stop beside the shaddock, the 'tree of life'. In her lazy, lilting West Indian drawl, Great-aunt Jane, who had passed her youth on St Kitts and spoke French beautifully, would sing her songs handed down from her grandmother, Jean Maxwell. It was an afternoon world at Genever – a place where Jean could watch the sea from a telescope and imagine the drowned mountain ranges of other islands. Afternoons were long and languorous and sometimes she would wander alone in the gardens and imagine James Potter Lockhart, his Spanish countess (who possibly wasn't) and their 258 slaves.

Great-aunt Jane was delightfully romantic. She wore her white hair in ringlets that fell from under a lace cap, and captivated Jean with her stories of a gracious society where romance and chivalry, curtseys and quadrilles, lace and finery were the order of the day. She would tell her great-niece tales from the old days, of *beaux* and *belles*, and the slave girl she had once been given for her birthday. Great-aunt Jane was kind and listened to Jean's complaints, and soothed her by sitting her on her knee and embracing her. Jean felt loved and understood sitting on that comfortable lap encased in black silk, the two of them surrounded by the moss-stained walls of the wild and melancholy garden. She adored her great-aunt – loved her more than she loved her mother or even her father, partly because Great-aunt Jane was straightforward and partly because the old lady made a fuss of her. She considered her needs and tried to meet them: she made Jean a cardboard dolls' house with cardboard furniture and little tin plates for meals.

Jean remembered her great-aunt's home, the Genever estate, in *Voyage in the Dark* and *Wide Sargasso Sea*. The 1,200 acres of rotting plantation, the crumbling house and its gardens gone to seed were her lost paradise. The stories that Great-aunt Jane told swirled around Jean's head rendering Genever all the more fantastical. Its heyday was gone, but she remembered every detail her great-aunt told her and nourished them back to life in her books. She even wrote the gardener, Godfrey, who was rumoured to have been born on a slave ship, into her last novel. Her grandmother's parrot became her heroine's. '*Qui est là?*' he cackled, and answered himself: '*Chere cocotte. Chere cocotte.*'

But her mother decided that Jane was spoiling her. Money also became an issue and there was a big family fall-out over Genever. So, quite suddenly, Jean was stopped from seeing Great-aunt Jane ever again. Later in life, she became tormented by the fact that she had never had the chance to tell Jane she loved her. The child she had been had not felt the need to make such a declaration. The adult she became stoked her own torment because she could never find the words to tell the people she loved that she loved them. They simply would not come to her. The feelings were locked up inside her with no escape. Until, as an old lady herself, she poured all her love for Great-aunt Jane and her garden into her last novel.

There were more losses: Jean had a friend, a black girl called Francine, who, like Great-aunt Jane, told her tales that were full of romance, pretty dresses and good meals. Is it significant that the two women Jean loved and lost told her stories? Francine's stories would start with a ceremony. She would say, 'Tim Tim', Jean had to answer 'Bois seche', which was the name of an *obeah* god, then Francine would repeat the magic formula, '*Tablier Madame est derrière dos*' (Madam's apron is back to front). One day Francine disappeared and was never seen again. Jean could not understand why she had not said goodbye.

Jean came to expect neglect, indifference, disbelief and cruelty from people. They were strange, inexplicable objects to which she could not attach herself. Jean's energy, her need for a connection, her nascent libido were re-directed back into herself, into inanimate objects – books, buildings, furniture, paintings – and into nature. As a result, her youthful capacity for love and empathy fell away from her; people – as individuals and in groups – were closed to her, and it was hard for her to find an opening with them, a way of belonging. This conviction she had of not belonging had a profound effect on her. However much others tried to include her, she could not do away with the feeling that certain components of her self, the things that made living in society bearable, had been lost and could not be regained.

In 1903 a riot took place in Roseau between blacks and whites. Thirteen-year-old Jean heard what sounded like animals howling in the night. But Father said that the voices that screamed 'Kill them! Kill them!' were harmless. Mother knew better, or so she said. Jean wondered; she had become wary of blacks. Not ones she knew like Francine, or the housemaid Victoria, who was from the 'English' island, Antigua. She liked Victoria, who was a Methodist, and sang hymns. 'Steal away to Jesus' was her favourite, which she sang while washing up. She was always sad, and Jean felt sorry for her. But blacks like Josephine, another cook, who was Dominican and spoke patois, were different. Jean was afraid of her, as was her mother. Mother and Josephine met on neutral territory in the pantry to discuss the day's meals. Once Jean peeked into the kitchen where Josephine was holding court surrounded by women she had never seen before. These were the women who delivered baskets of fresh bread which they balanced on trays on their heads. It was the blacks she did not know who scared her the most.

One day at school, where most of the girls were black, she happened to be sitting next to an older girl, very tall, very pretty, with noble bearing, aquiline features and flashing eyes. She did not look coloured or Creole, but Jean knew at once that she was. She could not help staring at the splendidly beautiful creature in a silent fit of admiration and curiosity. Finally, the girl turned to return her admirer's gaze. The look of hatred was unmistakable. Jean never tried to be friendly to a black girl again.

Her father persisted in the old traditions of patronage towards blacks. There were regular morning processions of old men who came to his surgery for alms. He gave Jean bread and money to distribute amongst them. One patient, a self-contained and modest man, sang her a song, '*Il y avait une fois . . . un pauvre gars*'. She was touched by his dignity but her mother was dismissive of his guilelessness; she mistrusted it.

Jean had complicated and conflicting ideas about black people. On the one hand she envied them, on the other she feared them. She was entrenched in stereotypes of black physicality, loucheness and aggression. Yet she knew that they hated because they had been hated. Although they laughed loud and long, she noticed they seldom smiled. She saw them (and for her they were always the 'other', as for any white Creole) as being strong and at ease with themselves. She heard them every night as they danced to drums in the jump-ups in Roseau. They were more alive than whites, she felt, more alive than her.

She envied blacks their French priests as well as their colourful clothes. She liked watching the black women walking to mass at the Roseau Cathedral of Our Lady of Fair Haven. She appreciated the fact that blacks sat amongst whites in Roseau Cathedral, rather than in the back pews at the Anglican Church. The worshippers were proud of their cathedral. The women wore sweeping trains to their dresses, heavy gold jewellery and turbans. If the petticoat beneath their gown did not make the 'frou-frou' sweeping sound they liked, they sewed paper into the hems. These women, unlike Jean, did not have to worry about who would marry them. They had many children but seldom bothered to marry the fathers. But Jean knew it would become her duty to receive proposals, and dreaded growing up in case she did not receive any. Despite the fact that Great-aunt Jane and her mother's spinster twin, Aunt Brenda, were perfectly happy (much more so than her own mother) she feared becoming an old maid.

Sex, race and money were minefields. She knew that black people did all the work and white people had all the money, and would often comment on this disparity, hence her family's nickname for her: 'Socialist Gwen'. When she remarked that things were unfair, people laughed. She was possessed with a tremendous feeling of injustice that would leave her with a bitter mistrust of the world and was uncannily sensitive to the subtleties of social distinctions. The one group of people who were hated by blacks and whites alike were the coloureds, the half-breeds, the mulattos. White Creoles, like Jean and her mother, were a notch below pure whites – they were saved by the colour of their skin. But coloureds lived uneasily in the social world, they did not belong to either group and so were rejected by both. One day, Jean would put a coloured woman into one of her stories, 'The Day They Burned the Books'. This woman, whose white husband despises her, and whose eyes were 'wicked, like a soucriant's', would burn the books in her husband's library on his death.

Around 1900, when Jean was ten, two dolls arrived from England. Jean remembered these dolls well into her old age, and describes their arrival in *Smile Please*. One doll was dark, the other fair. Jean wanted the dark one but Mother made her give it to her sister Brenda. When Jean complained, Mother said grimly, 'Nothing is fair.' Jean smashed the fair doll with a stone. The mingled sense of shame and triumph at her own wickedness overwhelmed her. She asked her father why she had done such a wicked thing. The man who she thought knew everything could not tell her.

'I can't imagine what will become of you,' said her mother.

But Jean never forgot that sense of guilty triumph at having performed a wilful, wicked act. If she destroyed the fair doll was she not destroying herself and taking satisfaction in her own destruction? If she was not fair, she would be free to be black and truly at home on her island. It was an act of rebellion against her mother. Her middle-aged, plump, severe mother was no longer – if she ever had been – that beautiful, sweet-smelling woman who Jean remembered in her cot. Jean no longer watched her mother brushing her hair in front of the looking glass. She had loved to watch her mother brushing her hair. Now, there were times when she was afraid of her mother and times when she just disliked her. But she feared her most when she seemed, together with her twin sister Brenda, Jean's Auntie B, to be quietly laughing at her. Brenda had come to live with Jean's parents after the fall-out at Genever and Auntie B strongly disapproved of her dreamy, book-reading niece. She made it clear to the girl that she was turning into a disappointment as well as a nuisance. Jean watched them laughing silently at her father, too, when he talked about English politics. She started to feel protective towards her father and grew to distrust women. Jean simply became indifferent to them, and if her mother and Auntie B thought her untidy, clumsy, and indolent, she started to take a perverse pleasure in proving them right.

Her need to be admired by her mother had been replaced with a burgeoning desire for independence. Her daydreams of future successes in the social world were a defence against her loneliness; security against present disapproval. But this method of defending herself was itself insecure, particularly as she used it so excessively. It was not the true expression of trust in herself but an idealisation of her future, which would inevitably lead to disappointment.

One of their neighbours, a white man, had married a coloured woman, and occasionally Jean and her mother would visit Mrs Campbell for tea. The path to her house was shaded with clumps of feathery bamboos and tufted gru-gru palms. Jean loved the patois names of things. She loved to ride down Mrs Campbell's path on her horse, the deep blue ocean stretching ahead of her in the distance.

One day Jean and her mother sat in Mrs Campbell's garden. Sugared oranges cut in two hung on the posts of the summer-house. They watched as hummingbirds flew above them, hovering, sipping oranges. Jean had never seen such a swarm of colour. Mother started to cry and to tell Mrs Campbell about her money worries. Mrs Campbell continued to smile at the humming-birds. By the time Jean and her mother arrived home, Mother's reserve had reasserted itself. But Jean had glimpsed her distress and it was the end of her comfortable certainty that her father could provide for them. She sensed there was some nameless anxiety behind his recklessness, his insistence on charity, and the cocktail hour. He had tried for so long to present himself as the perfect English gentleman amongst the natives, and to perform the rituals that were expected of him, he had even enjoyed his act, but he was tired now.

Her confidence in her father was shaken and in 1902, she was introduced to a man who would confuse her further. Mr Howard, a friend of the family and a respected member of their social circle, started taking her for rides in his carriage around the Botanical Gardens. She was led to believe that this was a great privilege and she was a lucky girl that such a distinguished gentleman should pay her attention. He was, as she recorded in her diary, 'an English gentleman with a capital G'. On one such occasion they proceeded down Cork Street, following a grey stone wall, before reaching a gate that opened on to the gardens. He talked to her all the while, treating her with the utmost deference as though she were an adult. She was captivated by the intensity of his attention. He asked her old she was.

'I'm twelve,' she said.

'Twelve,' he repeated. 'Quite old enough to have a lover.'

This was how Mr Howard's seduction of Jean began. The lawn rolled in gentle slopes and they came to rest under the cannonball tree which let loose its load with a thud upon the grass. All the while he was telling her a story. He told her that if she lived with him – which she would one day because he was going to kidnap her – he would love her, which meant punishing her, and that she would have to give herself up entirely and hopelessly to him and that he would not allow her to wear many clothes and as he said all this he was touching her twelve-year-old breasts. She was breathless as she listened; at once enraptured and repulsed by his words of seduction, startled and disturbed by the touch of his hand. But Mr Howard was in his seventies so he must be like a grandfather, and she must do as he said. He was abusing her, but she did not know this. What she did know was that *he* knew she was not a good girl. Otherwise he would not have said these things to her. He dropped her off at home and left her feeling guilty. Unlike Francine and Great-aunt Jane, Mr Howard used stories to break through the little girl's reserve and to force an unnatural intimacy.

The second time he called for her she told her mother she did not want to go. But her mother told her not to be so rude, and after that initial reluctance, Mr Howard worked hard to win her over. This, for a neglected girl, was even more entrancing. He found out what sweets she liked and brought them to her. He asked her questions about herself and listened carefully to the answers. 'Mostly he talked about me, me, me. It was intoxicating . . . irresistible.' Then he continued his story. He would take her to his beautiful house on another island, he would dress her:

My arms were covered with bracelets and my hands with
rings. I laughed and danced but I was not happy or unhappy.
I was waiting . . . My bracelets tinkled when I moved and
sometimes quite naked I waited on the other guests.

She wrote her account of Mr Howard in a series of notebooks;
as a grown woman, she returned to this scene of seduction
again and again. Sometimes he told her about his past, but
mostly he told her about love and that it was a tension
between violence and submission. She would be allowed to
rebel against him but only so much as to make it more enjoy-
able when he forced her to submit. She was hooked, and
soon it became clear to others that something was going on
between the elderly man and the child. Her mother became
cold towards Mr Howard; his visits were no longer encouraged. And yet her parents, mired in Victorian codes of
conduct, allowed their young daughter to be alone with this
man. His stories became the bedrock of her sexual fantasies
that involved male cruelty and female submission. She turned
his fantasies into a dialogue; on other trips she would ask
him questions: what exactly would she wear? What would
they have to eat?

'How white your hands are against the grass,' he answered.

He went on, 'Let her naked be, teaching the sheets a
whiter hue than white.'

He said, 'I wouldn't often let you wear clothes you understand.'

This fantasy, in which she grew to be increasingly complicit,
dominated her future relationships with men. She felt complicit
because he was fascinating; charismatic and powerful in the
eyes of society, and he used that power to serve his ends.
Her certainty that no one would believe he was abusing her
is a characteristic response of someone who has been abused,

especially when the young girl, not the old man, became the subject of reproof.

Mr Howard's wife sidled up to Jean and whispered in her ear: 'You are a wicked girl. And you will be punished.'

Mrs Howard's unfair judgement replicated Jean's own mother's misperception. She could only feel that her mother was not concerned for her welfare. Other women, meanwhile, injured her welfare, as did men – except with men, the pain was pleasurable. This realisation came at a crucial time, just as she was beginning to realise her colour was a cause for concern. 'White cockroach', black children would call after her as she walked the streets of Roseau. There was black resentment to deal with, as well as white hypocrisy, the whole messy business of sex, slavery, pain and death, and her growing impatience with her parents' limitations.

Chapter 3:

NEITHER NUN NOR ZOUAVE

In 1904 Dr Rees Williams was given extended leave to return to England with his wife for six months. Fourteen-year-old Jean was sent to board at a convent school in Roseau, while little Brenda Clarice stayed at home with Auntie B. In England, Edward VII, who had acceded to the throne in 1901, was dispelling the solemnity of his mother's reign.

At convent school Jean came under the influence of two nuns, Mother Sacred Heart and Mother Mount Calvary, the Mother Superior. An unusual woman for such a time and place, Mother Mount Calvary liked the French poets Baudelaire and Rimbaud, and through them offered her young charge an ironic critique of Dominican society. In short, the Mother Superior of Jean's convent was a rebel. Her other favourite nun, Mother Sacred Heart, had recently arrived from England, and introduced the girls to English poets like Shelley and Cowper. Jean liked these too, but she loved the French.

There was prejudice against Catholicism on the island so Jean, who was so afraid of disapproval, had been reluctant to go to the convent. But once there, she loved the stories of Purgatory and Hell, and the ritual of Catechism. Nuns made good storytellers. One of the sisters told the girls that they should meditate every day on the Four Last Things: Death, Judgement, Hell and Heaven. When they went to sleep at night, they were told to lie down straight with their arms by their sides and their eyes shut and say, 'One day I shall be dead.' Jean took these stories very seriously.

Stories that the other convent girls told her – about sex and reproduction – she refused to hear. When she found pictures of childbirth she was horrified at the disfigurement of the body it entailed. She cried when she saw her dog, Rex, mating on the street. She blocked the sight from her mind – these things happened – but she would shut them away where she did not have to think about them. The only trouble was that she was constantly thinking about them, remembering them in detail for the rest of her life. She had a vague, persistent feeling that she would always be defeated by biology and society. So she hid in books, where 'fatally', like Madame Bovary, she got her ideas.

The convent was a relatively safe place – reading and quietness were encouraged, and she was allowed to express her ideas even if they were argued against. She decided she wanted to be a nun. She wore stones in her shoes to share Jesus' suffering and wept for his death on every suitable occasion. She felt protected by a benevolent God: the sun was not so terrible and punishing in its harsh light, but only doing as it was told. So were the moon and the stars, the wind and sea. So would she. Life would be simple because God was ruling over everything from His Heaven.

A sermon made an impression on her: 'Faith without works is dead'. When her parents returned to Dominica and she came back from her convent she determined to impress them with her new-found goodness. Her first good work was to help the kitchen girl, Victoria, with the washing-up. But this did not alleviate Victoria's sadness, it only seemed to irritate her. So, once again, Jean felt rejected. Then she turned to the family estate's overseer, John. She decided to teach him to read. They were getting along famously and she had never been happier: feeling useful and needed, like someone good and noble in a book. But John's wife was not quite so comfortable with the arrangement and John, who had been enjoying the lessons, too, acted as though Jean was to blame for this discomfort. Everything gets twisted, she decided: class, race, religion, sex, are all barriers to being good. And then John's friend Emile asked Jean's mother for Jean's hand in marriage. In exchange for a yam.

'You're only worth a yam!' her mother shrieked.

Although the nuns would never have laughed at her and although they had inspired her to read the poets, she began to doubt religion. It was not helping her to feel better about herself or to come to terms with the world. It was complicating things. Actions, even though they were intended to be good, were open to mistranslation. Each night now, instead of praying 'Dear God, let me black' or 'Dear God, let me be good', she knelt by the open window to watch the profusion of stars.

A new secret pleasure was to read books about prostitutes. These were even more intriguing than Baudelaire, and Roseau's library was well stocked with them. *The Sands of Pleasure* by Filson Young was the publishing sensation of 1905. It was set in Paris where, the narrator claims, 'You must get the idea of morality out of your head because it doesn't exist in this world, what's more the consciousness of its absence doesn't exist. That's why everybody is happy.' This was Jean's first encounter with the more louche side of Edwardian society. The women were beautiful, but they wore revealing dresses and presided over the pleasures of men. The women here, she read, were 'admirable, courageous dissemblers'. Their demeanour placed them beyond mother-

hood and domestic happiness into a world similar to the one
Mr Howard had imagined.

What was the young, white Creole girl to make of all
this? That sex outside marriage was a terrible sin; that
women must be pure and men respectful, but that some
women were abandoned in every sense. She started thinking
about life outside Dominica, about morals and English snow,
about frozen water and roaring fires. She hated the sound
of the word 'cold', which she could not imagine being, but
she loved to say the word 'wisteria'. She talked knowledge-
ably with the girls at school about strawberries and cream
although none of them had any idea what they might taste
like. She read Charles Dickens. She knew that Christmas
on the other side of the Atlantic was freezing and snowy;
that people shivered round a fire. England became her vision
of glamour and excitement, of beautiful ladies, Sherlock
Holmes, romantic, swirling fog and sophisticated theatre,
while on her side of the world, bed was at 9 p.m. when
the old gun at the fort was fired. For special treats her
parents took her to musical evenings where Mrs Wilcox,
a neighbour, sang, 'When we are married, why, what will
we do?' Life was dull in Dominica and would be glorious
once she was in England.

Father's sister Clarice, who would eventually escort Jean
away from Dominica, spent winters with them. It was she
who told Jean stories about her father. Jean liked to boast
that her father had been all over the world but Clarice kept
telling her that he was sad. 'Poor Willy,' she would repeat
meaningfully. And there her father sat, oblivious to his family,
under a green-shaded reading lamp on the wicker sofa, hidden
by *The Times* weekly edition, his pipe rack in the gallery. His
red hair, which Jean loved, glinted in the dim light. Jean's
own fair hair had tints of red in it, too, and his melancholic

absence of mind pierced her. She was struck by the fact that he had fallen ill with fever on arrival in the island. Perhaps he had never recovered.

Clarice and Mother disliked each other – perhaps Clarice's affectionate concern for her brother irked his wife. Clarice turned to Jean for company. She told her stories about Aunt Jeanette who lived in Cambridge in England, the wife of the great mathematician. She was such a beautiful woman that once when she entered her box at the theatre everybody stood up spontaneously. Another time, a man complimented her on the street, and he turned out to be someone important from King's College. This fabled man who Clarice crowed about was, she told her niece, a famous wit. Aunt Jeanette liked witty people, she would forgive people anything if they could make her laugh. One day Jean would meet Aunt Jeanette, Clarice promised. And one day Jean did; for a short while she took tea with her weekly at her home on Trumpington Road in wet and windy Cambridge. The last time Jean saw Aunt Jeannette, the old lady embraced her and said 'Poor lamb.' It was as though she knew the young girl's fate.

Her father said a similar thing: 'You poor thing. I do believe you're going to be like me.' She adored her father despite, perhaps or because, she saw so little of him. She tried again and again to remember how he had explained Nirvana. Words were becoming increasingly important to her and had a talismanic power for her – this could be because of her father's rare, gnomic utterances combined with the poetic influence of the nuns. '*Morne*' was her favourite word, it was French patois for 'mountain', which was ugly by comparison. The other words she loved were 'pain', 'shame', 'sea' and 'silence', as well as lines from a Victor Hugo poem. She remembered Mother Mount Calvary reciting them to her in her elegant French voice:

Partons, c'est la fin du jour
Mon cheval sera la joie.
Ton cheval sera l'amour.

At the age of sixteen, Jean was taken out of the convent. Her parents were preparing her for adult life. Despite being shy and awkward, which made people think she was rude, she was entered into high society. In 1906 (she would never forget this), there was a fancy dress party to celebrate the completion of the Imperial Road – the road which she discovered thirty years later, overgrown and forgotten. The road was the crowning achievement of the island administrator, Mr Hesketh Bell, and united the Caribbean and South Atlantic sides of Dominica. Auntie B made Jean's dress. She had wanted to go as a *zouave* because she had seen in the Anglican cathedral once two magnificent black men dressed in the *zouave* uniform with swords dangling from their hips and spurs at their heels. They were bold and reckless, which she wanted to be. Like Queen Victoria, whom she had read about, she fell in love with their uniform. But she was told red and yellow did not suit her colouring – she was too fair – and neither could she go as a gypsy, it was unseemly. She lost interest in the party but let Auntie B decide on a 'yachting' dress, the pattern of which her aunt found in a London magazine called *Glass of Fashion Up-to-Date*. It was blue–green like the sea, and Mr Hesketh Bell asked her for the first waltz. She received lots of compliments. She was happy.

But her contentment did not last: whilst out riding the following afternoon between Canefield and Goodwill estates she saw Mr Hesketh Bell coming towards her in a trap. She was too shy to say hello. A few days later Mother asked her why she had been so rude; apparently, Hesketh Bell had joked about it. She was mortified by Hesketh Bell's reproach, and her mother told her she was peculiar. So the happiness faded and she was miserable under her mother's glowering eye.

Then another terrible faux pas confirmed her mother's disappointment in her. During one of her parents' musical evenings, when the guests were gathered around the piano, she was told to play a duet with a visitor called Mr Gregg. Mr Gregg was furious when she forgot what *da capo* meant. It was all her fault that he left abruptly, her mother told her. Jean felt he would hate her for ever. There was no one to correct her, no one to look after her. But it was too late to be corrected. She was a disappointment.

She was nearly seventeen, and her parents realised she was not quite the adult they wanted her to be. She needed to

complete her education in England in order to take her place
in their society. They took her to Bona Vista for the summer.
In *Smile, Please* she calls it Morgan's Rest. The hills were
like clouds, the clouds were like hills. Regardless of her fear
of ants, she lay down on the earth and kissed it, thinking all
the while 'Mine, mine'. But the earth was indifferent. It
cared not about her departure nor her return. It was yet
another rejection. But she was growing up and must act like
a lady. She was told to fill the parlour with vases of roses –
La France and Maréchal – that her mother had planted. She
was asked to sing Edwardian songs for her parents'guests, and
to play Welsh airs for her father. 'Gwenllian's Repose' was
his favourite. At Bona Vista she describes sunset bringing
sadness and moths. A death-like stillness was pervading her
family home. She found a way to alleviate sadness. She started
writing in an exercise book. On its cover she wrote 'My
Secret Poems' and underneath the motto of the Lockharts:
'I unlock locked hearts.' She felt calmed by writing poems
full of doom and trauma.

  She would write about men and women and mothers and
daughters for the rest of her life; about loss, the fear of loss
and the inability to recover from loss because there is nothing
that will compensate for what is gone. And she would write
about the chaos of non-being that she felt to be her real self
disguised by the masquerade of being a woman. She would
write about make-up, performance and puppetry, about being
born into a script and not being able to find the words to
write yourself out of it. Paradoxically, of course, Jean Rhys
the writer did find the words. But her women never do.
They are doomed to act out a script written before they
were born.

  In 1907, just before she left Dominica, Jean states in *Smile
Please* that her mother was bedridden for weeks. She does

not say why at the point of her daughter's departure, her mother was struck by paralysis. The reader is left to wonder at this and her mother's parting words, 'You haven't seen what I've seen, haven't heard what I've heard.'

'Do you like Aunt Clarice?' her father asked her during their last talk. He was preparing her for England: 'Don't write at the first shock,' he said. 'You must get used to it.'

In *Wide Sargasso Sea*, the stepfather of Jean's heroine says about England: 'The place stinks of hypocrites if you've got a nose. I don't care if I never see it again.' But Jean's father knew his daughter needed to leave Dominica. He sailed to Bridgetown, Barbados, with her. He hugged her tight, breaking her new coral brooch, but she was too happy to notice. He and Mother and the West Indies were the past.

When she came to write about Dominica, her one true home, she wrote about the earth trembling and the colours breathing. Red, purple, blue, gold and all the shades of green. In England the shades of grey were repeated in people's faces. In England she lost her sense of oneness with the colours of the world.

Chapter 4:

LONDON

In autumn 1907 Jean arrived in England, accompanied by her Aunt Clarice. They took a train from Southampton to London, and Clarice booked them into a boarding-house in Bloomsbury. Back in Dominica, Jean's twenty-two-year-old brother Owen also left the island, being 'spirited out' after an affair with a black woman.

Her father had told her not to write at the first shock. Little did he know how long the shock would last. She was numb with it. Nothing could touch her. 'Aunt Clarice doesn't wear her heart on her sleeve,' Jean's father had told her. Jean faithfully recorded his words in her diary. He recommended that she try to make her aunt like her; that the effort would be worth it. But Jean was more interested in her fantasies of a rapidly approaching England than in trying to please a starchy aunt. In her turn, Clarice grew frustrated with this self-absorbed girl who seemed so heedless of others' needs or their attempts to please her. As their journey to England progressed, she could not appreciate how much the change in climate – of mores and temperature – would alienate the girl; that she might need comforting and reassurance.

At first, being on board the ship was like being at a party. Jean could still feel the heat of the Caribbean sun, and there were new experiences to distract her. Breakfast was a lavish display of exotic English foodstuffs, and then there was elevenses, which consisted of a strange, meaty drink called Bovril. She could see that the rules of decorum were important to observe. Even lunch – all five courses of it – had rules. She ate everything that was put in front of her until Clarice explained you were only supposed to take a little of each dish. Tea was another large meal you weren't supposed to eat, and dinner was the largest and most important. The orchestra played at each meal – and this enchanted her. There was one bright spot when she sang as part of an evening's entertainment, and her fellow passengers applauded her. She told her aunt she would go straight on to the stage as soon as they got to London. She was excited by this sudden shower of attention. To add intrigue to excitement, she made friends (briefly) with an exotic lady with a past who had two young men travelling with her in attendance.

The ship's crossing of the Sargasso Sea – a two-million-square-mile ellipse of deep blue water adrift in the North Atlantic – signalled the end of the warmth that Jean had grown up in. Cold descended. The strangeness and excitement were over. All that occupied her now was the grey sky, choppy sea, and thick, scratchy rugs. She could not stop shivering.

The ship docked in Southampton, a drab industrial port, on a damp, grey evening. The place was cold and dark, and Jean's heart sank. But Aunt Clarice hustled her on to the platform of a station where they were to take the train to London. This thrilled her: she had never seen a train before and imagined herself boarding a brightly coloured, wooden contraption similar to the toy trains her brothers had played with as children. She knew so little of the world that when she stood with her aunt on the platform she did not realise the great brown thing in front of her was a train. Clarice opened the door into a dingy, narrow room overhung with racks for bags, where people huddled into corners. Soon the train was submerged in a tunnel and she was plunged into blackness.

She arrived in Edwardian London. Edward VII dominated English society, rather as his mother had done before him, only Edward was not an aged widow. He was not a liberal either, but he was licentious. He enjoyed having mistresses, betting on horses, and going to the theatre. His subjects enjoyed him enjoying these things, too. The theatrical entertainments of the time reflected his passion: gaiety girls, these pretty young things were called.

Jean had her preconceptions of what London would be like; she had seen photographs of 'bits' of streets, buildings and bridges. She had a vague idea of a bulbous St Paul's, of Nelson's Column and the Monument, of the Houses of Parliament and Buckingham Palace – all hazily united into one 'view' by a river Thames as green and leafy as Dominica's. Now she saw that the city was full of workers jammed into newly installed electric trams that took them to their places of work.

Clarice found a room for herself and her niece in a boarding house in Upper Bedford Place, Bloomsbury. The area was respectable but shabby, an irregular series of squares and roads, filled with smog because of nearby small industries and factories. Jean woke up early. She wanted to see what London was like and walked out into a surprisingly dreary street. The smog was still low, and the pavements were empty, like a vast mausoleum that no one visited. It was half past six in the morning. Instead of the familiar view of London she had nurtured in Dominica she saw a quiet, anonymous Georgian street. She saw long, broad streets, no variety, no traffic, no people. She walked down Great Russell Street where at number 62, Sir Edward Poynter, esteemed

Academician, would one day paint her. She walked the entire length – nearly a third of a mile – of Gower Street, as straight as a rule, the repetition of Georgian houses overwhelming. Not even a solitary pedestrian or horse-drawn carriage could detract from what Ruskin described as Gower Street's 'depth of ugliness in street architecture'. She kept on walking – surely something grand would offer itself up to her when she turned the next corner? – down the busy commercial thoroughfare of New Oxford Street – the sound of distant traffic slurring through London's mud and where she was confronted by stuccoed fronts and High Victorian kitsch – and on to ancient High Holborn. All Jean could see was another endless procession of office blocks: sombre Georgian houses with panelled rooms inhabited by firm upon firm, in floors one above another, of solicitors, architects, money lenders, and journalists. At number 30 she passed the Royal Exchange Assurance, one of England's oldest insurance companies, and next to it, the business offices of Pears, the soap manufacturers, whose product her face would one day advertise. The faint rays of the sun illuminated stains and dirt in the paving stones. She could see more clearly now the rigid rows of streets all of blackened bricks, grimy windows and enamelled-iron advertisements. London was disappointing. She could not see her future in its smog-smudged streets.

She writes about her first morning in London in *Smile Please*. On returning to the boarding-house, she noted that its occupants were still asleep. She decided to run a bath.

When the bath was half full I undressed and got in, thinking it very pleasant. I began to feel rather happy and thought that when the water got cool I would turn the hot tap on again. I began to sing.

A loud voice interrupted her – a voice telling her to turn the tap off immediately.

The landlady was furious and Clarice had to explain another set of rules. Bathing has its rituals, which involve consulting the needs of other people. There was not an endless supply of hot water. Her aunt informed her that she had noticed 'that you are quite incapable of thinking about anyone else but yourself.' Her aunt's disapproval turned Clarice into another version of her mother. Jean turned in on herself even more.

The landlady was still angry with Jean at breakfast; in *Smile Please* she recalls that the woman glared at her so hard she could not swallow her egg and bacon. Clarice rushed her off to the Wallace Collection. It had been opened as a national museum seven years earlier by the then Prince of Wales. Here Jean sat on a bench while her aunt inspected the various galleries, and fell asleep. She ignored Mme Pompadour. She closed her eyes to Boucher's myths and maidens. She vaguely noted Sir Joshua Reynolds' soft-eyed girls, and Fragonard's coquettes. She was not interested in what these exhibits were telling her. They added up to an elaborate code of etiquette and an ensuing appetite for sexual intrigue that would always bemuse her.

Her aunt took Jean to all the sights, and expected her to enjoy them. She did not. She found the exterior of Westminster Abbey quite pleasing but once inside she complained that it was too crowded, a muddle of statues and people. Clarice was appalled at this show of non-conformity and expected her niece to back it up with argument. But she could not – it was more a feeling than a criticism, although others supported her instinct for form. The Victorian architect Augustus Pugin, for example, speaks of 'the incongruous and detestable monuments' that visitors such as Clarice no

doubt venerated. John Ruskin decried 'the ignoble, inco-
herent fillings of the aisles' and William Morris said it was
full of 'monstrous and ghastly pieces of perversity and bluntness
of feeling'. But Jean knew nothing of Pugin, Ruskin or
Morris and felt alone in her appraisal. As for St Paul's, it was
too cold and remote. The interior's cool perfection did not
impress her.

Her aunt was by now exasperated. Here was white marble,
chiselled into monuments, and yet Jean remained unimpressed.
She must have been very irritating to Clarice, refusing to
respond with the grateful enthusiasm of a young colonial.
What Jean wanted was warmth and colour. What she got
was a series of confusing impressions.

The twentieth century brought to London penny buses,
gramophones, bamboo furniture, Glory Songs, tennis, picture
postcards, miraculous hair-restorers, and prize competitions.
Madame Helena Rubinstein, the 'Viennese Complexion
Specialiste', had produced a complexion corrective that
restored clearness and whiteness of skin to city-dwellers. Jean
was not enlivened by any of this. Often Clarice would turn
round to find that her niece had melted into the crowd
behind her, dazed and stilled by the hurried mêlée of the
street.

There was nothing here to confirm Jean's Dickensian idea
of foggy London town decked with holly and ivy. Motor
traffic threw up clouds of dust from soft roads designed for
horse traffic. There were none of the pretty frocks she had
seen in her Auntie B's fashion magazines. The outfits of the
ladies were suited to dirty skies and damp weather. Kate
Croy in Henry James's *The Wings of the Dove* was described
by one reviewer as 'the contemporary London female, highly
modern, inevitably battered'. Even though women were
mobilising themselves – the second reading of the Women's

Suffrage Bill was passing through the House of Commons –
to Jean they looked worn down by the stresses of urban life.
In *Voyage in the Dark*, her third novel, she writes of a young
white Creole girl newly arrived in London. She says of Anna
Morgan, her heroine, that she did not know that white
women could look so poor and drab.

Even high fashion – the idea of which thrilled her – was
low-key. A big velvet bow on a brown or navy hat would
invariably be in a dusky shade. Topaz brulée was the colour
that season: a bronzed yellow with deep golden tones that
did not startle or offend. Pleated skirts (the hem eight inches
from the ground) were popular in wine and mulberry – deep
colours to blend into the dingy streets. Evening gowns were
in delicate biscuit colours with folds of grey tulle flowing
from the décolletage. Tea gowns were in dusty pink with
cream lace trimmings. Everyone was more restrained here.
Everyone respected the rules and knew their place.

She did not understand London's history but she sensed
its ruthlessness. Ford Madox Ford, who would be her lover
in interwar Paris, commiserated: 'London loves nobody, needs
nobody; it tolerates all the types of mankind. It has palaces
for the great of the earth, it has crannies for all the earth's
vermin. Palace and cranny, vacated for a moment, find new
tenants as equably as the hole one makes in a stream – for,
as a critic, London is wonderfully open-minded.' This is what
Jean could not stand: the impersonality of the city; its pitiless
disregard for individuals.

Clarice took her to see the animals at London Zoo – a
museum of live creatures, an invention of the early nineteenth
century, a symbol of knowledge and civilisation. In a series
of brick terraces overlooking the Regent's Canal, animals
were displayed for the benefit of the paying public. She saw
the lion pacing its cage; its majesty gone, its eyes haunted.

Her aunt made a special effort to find the Dominican parrot, a grey bird hunched on its bar. It refused to return Jean's greeting and would not look her in the eye. The humming-birds in their cage – their colours dimmed – were hurtling themselves against the bars as though looking for a means of escape. Such uncomprehending despair finished her off, yet when Clarice asked her if she had enjoyed it, she said yes. She had at least learnt one of the rules.

Only one sight impressed her. From the top of an omnibus she spotted a well-dressed, lavishly hatted lady walking in the park. She appeared to be everything an Englishwoman should be; rich, respectable, and protected from the messiness of life. She wanted to be her. This was the London of her imagination, not the long, dark streets of Bloomsbury.

Finally, Aunt Clarice took her to Swan and Edgar's to buy some clothes. Jean was drawn to a wine-coloured suit with a fur collar. She was convinced that not only would she look nice in it, as the saleswoman assured her, but she could also be a different girl in it. But Clarice considered it too expensive. Instead, she bought her niece starched blouses, woollen combinations, and a scratchy blue suit with brass buttons. Jean was heartbroken. Clarice was preparing her niece for the next chapter in her life: an education at an exclusive girls' school in Cambridge. But her idea of preparation – of what was practical and appropriate for the daughter of an impoverished colonial doctor – was very different from her niece's notions of elegance and deportment. It would be a long time before Jean achieved the exalted state of being to which she aspired, and when she did, it would not last long.

Chapter 5:

PERSE SCHOOL, CAMBRIDGE

Jean, or Gwendoline Williams, dressed in a shapeless blue suit with brass buttons, entered Form Va of Perse School for Girls in the Autumn term of 1907. In Dominica, Jean's brother Owen returned from exile. Shortly afterwards, his daughter, Ena Williams, the result of his liaison with a black woman, gained a 'half-caste' half-sibling. There would be one more before he left the island for good in 1914.

Miss Kate Harding Street was headmistress of Perse School. She had begun her teaching career at the age of sixteen, as a student teacher in London. The new girl would have found an imposing, stout woman who wore her hair in a braided crown that stood high above a stiff, lacy collar. But the manners of a primly correct Edwardian matron were softened by deep-set, kind eyes. The school itself was on the outskirts of the town centre in a large, brick house with wings on either side converted into dormitories and classrooms. Perse was a prestigious school with a serious mandate that was relatively new and radical to this society. Miss Harding Street wanted to educate girls for academia rather than just the domestic sphere.

Jean, or Gwen as she was known at Perse, was not the only new girl Miss Harding Street welcomed that term; Myrtle Newton was a spirited English girl far bolder than the shell-shocked girl from the lazy tropics. On first arriving at Perse, Myrtle took to the regime swiftly. Jean, however, was stunned by the rules with which she had to comply. They seemed more concerned with what girls could not do, rather than what they could. For example, she was not allowed to run or walk abreast with another girl around the school or on the grounds. She was not allowed to speak between lessons. She was forbidden to leave the premises without gloves and hat. She could not undertake an outing with another girl unless they both had written permission. Not only was England cold and damp, but school was like a prison. Jean was intimidated by the crowd of confident, academic girls filed into ranks around her. She was puzzled by the teachers' insistence on academic excellence and their indifference to beauty. She was constricted by rules that had to be remembered and she was continually reminded of them by Hiss Hannah Osborn, deputy head and Miss Street's lifelong companion.

Miss Osborn never left Miss Street's side, having lived with her 'in an attic' while Miss Street attended university lectures; Miss Osborn had encouraged the sixteen-year-old Miss Street to pursue academic studies, and Miss Osborn disliked Jean from the start. The girl refused to overcome her initial timidity. She did not attempt to disguise her insecurities; expecting others, perhaps, to take pity on her. Miss Osborn was not in the business of dispensing pity – or even compassion. Towards the end of her life, Jean would write a short story describing this period of her life. In 'Overtures and Beginners Please', she depicts a woman, Miss Born, based on Miss Osborn, who is the culmination of all the disapproving maternal figures who would populate Jean's life.

'Miss Born represented breeding and culture and was a great asset to the school,' she wrote. A sinister shadow to the kind and patient Miss Street, Jean could find no escape from her looming, dark presence. Myrtle decided Miss Osborn was a snob. Jean was not comforted. Miss Osborn was fast to become her living nightmare.

It was not just Miss Osborn who felt irritated by the new pupil; Jean was also at a disadvantage with the other girls. She dressed inelegantly and she could not understand the tenor of their conversations. The current between these girls was clipped and sharp. They had no time for dreamers. She could not join in their barked conversations, nor could she show off her slim figure in the clothes her aunt had chosen for her.

School in England epitomised an English society that Jean came to fear and dread. It was strict, correct, conventional. There was no Mother Mount Calvary here, nor suggestive recitals of enigmatic French poetry. The solid, worthy curriculum repelled her. Besides 'religious instruction in accordance with the principles of the Christian Faith', the girls were instructed in 'Reading, Writing, and Arithmetic; Geography and History; English Grammar, Composition, and Literature; Latin; French and German; One or more branches of Natural Science; Mathematics; Needlework; Domestic Economy and Laws of Health; Drawing; Music; Drill, or other physical exercises'.

Every day she woke to a freezing dormitory in a creaky old house and went downstairs to a small, square classroom where the gloom was reinforced by wood-panelling and the smell of boiled cabbage. Food came drenched in lard. Tea was stewed. Porridge was lumpy. The teacher stood in an elevated pew at the front of the class and droned for hours. The girls sat in dark wooden benches that were arranged in rows on bare floorboards. They silently noted down every word being dictated to them. Jean, meanwhile, started to think of herself as a ghost, and all she could see were desks full of ghosts. Through the window, she could see the grey-yellow sky of Cambridge, its muddy colours replicated on walls like smoke, the colours of hopelessness. She knew that no one would see things the way she did. They were too busy joining in.

She writes about herself standing out at Perse for being foreign, and, simply by not being like the others, she was implicitly and unconsciously critical of the school and its rules. Miss Osborn, devoted to the cause, could not forgive this. Miss Street, however, did not make heavy weather of her authority. Although she was always 'Madam' to her pupils, she referred to them as 'my children'. They were in her care, and the young Jean Rhys would have warmed to this strong, compassionate woman.

She was put in Miss Street's boarding house along with five or six other girls. When the wind blew through sashed windows, Miss Street told the maid to give the girl from the West Indies extra blankets and hot milk. Every night, warm in her blankets, she tried to reassure herself: it was only for eighteen months. But she was distressed to discover that she could not recall the scent of her favourite flowers, the sight of Dominica's mountains, or the sea.

She was ignorant of all the things the other girls took for granted, such as bicycles and hockey sticks and homework. They could not understand that a bicycle is no use on a vertiginous island, hence her lack of familiarity with the strange contraption. The other girls did not care that they did not know what a rainforest was. When she tried to tell them, they winked at each other and asked her to sing 'coon songs'. If they would not listen to the truth she would make up stories. So every night, after supper, when they were sitting around the fire in the library, she would regale the mocking girls with stories of exploding volcanoes, wild savages and heroic governors.

Academically she coped well enough. Jean was a clever girl and here she was given a chance to develop that cleverness.

Miss Umfreville Wilkinson taught Grammar and Shakespeare, even if it was bowdlerized. More importantly, she encouraged Jean to develop a logical argument. Miss Blanche Paterson taught Classics, which would give Jean a chance of cultivating the illusion of being cultured. Since she was pretty and graceful, Miss Paterson was Jean's favourite. The fact that Miss Street could never find satisfactory language teachers does not seem to have bothered Jean, although learning French, her favourite language, might have helped her overcome her shyness. She would never lose her West Indian accent; its lilting rhythms and French patois appealed to her more than the clipped English correctness of an Establishment she felt rejected her. The girls at Perse mocked her accent, calling her a 'coon', and describing her voice as 'sing-song'. It was at Perse that she decided to stop speaking.

Although she would often complain of the heavy presentiment that bore down on her, as cold and clinging as the sky, as having set in at Perse School, and although she knew she would never belong in its large, draughty dormitories or wood-panelled classrooms, she gained quite a lot from the experience. She was not as defeated as she maintained. The dark corridors and heavy curtains found their way into her imagination and were transformed into Antoinette Cosway's attic in *Wide Sargasso Sea*. She moulded the objects and the people around her to speak to her in a way that they themselves never could. She had the last word, after all. And, besides, some aspects of life at Perse nourished her. She would recover enough from her initial fright to benefit from the well-meaning intentions of Miss Street and her teachers. She spent many lamp-lit evenings reading romantic novels in the cosy library. She came to feel comforted by the dresser full of Wedgwood, the rugs on the stained floor and the flowery wallpaper.

But her enduring impression was of the flat land and flat sky of Cambridge – a mess of mottled pinks and glaucous greens. The east wind comes straight from the Urals to East Anglia. It rolls over a wide plain heavy with clouds. She had never known the bite of coldness. So conscious was she of her constant physical discomfort she could not enjoy the wild, marshy beauty of 'the Backs'. When she did get permission to leave the school's premises, she had to sidestep pools of brackish water, stick to muddy tracks with the wind bearing down on her.

One particularly wintry day, Miss Paterson, so pretty and graceful, tried to teach Jean to ride a bicycle. They set off for Newnham College, Jean wobbling fearfully behind her teacher. She fell in a ditch just before reaching the town centre. Miss Paterson glanced over her shoulder and without even stopping asked if Jean was all right. Jean was amazed that she should ask such a question. It was clear to see that she had torn her stocking and bruised her knee. But Miss Paterson, pretty though she was, was made of sterner stuff, and expected her charge to get on with it. She did not offer words of comfort. By the time they reached the long, flat strait of Trumpington Road, however, she told the drooping girl to get off her bicycle. There was no encouraging her. So Jean wheeled her bicycle back to the school in shame.

Trumpington Road, dismal and draughty, was where her father's aunt, Jeanette, lived. She and Mr Potts, the translator of Euclid's *Elements*, were the 'Beauty and the Beast' in family legend. Jean was now able to acquaint herself with her father's family. She was invited for afternoon tea every Saturday. Great-aunt Jeanette lived alone in a large, comfortable town house. She was gracious, kindly and composed. Over tea served in bone china, she told Jean about Cambridge in the old days, and the famous academics she had known. This was her weekly opportunity to reminisce and instruct a young person ignorant of English mores. She felt it especially incumbent upon herself to stress upon this young girl the importance of religion. 'Poor Darwin. He threaded the labyrinths of creation and lost his Creator,' she mused. She was also insistent upon the point that 'the Song of Solomon is an allegory of Christ and His Church'. This was very important. It was not a song about a woman, or about sex or love. It was about Christian duty. Having told Jean this, in a strangely revealing non sequitur, she told the girl of the time she had nearly left her absent-minded, professorial husband. She had packed and was ready to leave. She looked in the mirror to adjust her hat, and saw the Devil grinning over her shoulder. Jean was not stupid. She picked up on the unconscious association and put it in 'Overtures and Beginners Please'. She wrote about herself asking the old woman if she was sure it was the Devil she had seen. She was learning about logic in English composition. After all, she pointed out, Aunt Jeannette could not know what the Devil looked like. Aunt Jeannette did not answer.

No one ever did answer the important questions. They just dropped hints that they then brushed aside and carried on as normal. But Jean did not forget their slippages. However, there were more pressing problems to consider. She could not ride a bicycle and she could not play hockey. She talked like a nigger, and the other girls mocked her for it. For a long time she had felt that she was 'a dead girl . . . a drowned girl'. The feeling was confirmed by school. She was different, and yet she would not relinquish that difference.

In the summer term of 1908 Miss Paterson, head of the school's architectural society and Jean's putative cycling teacher, took the girls to see Ely Cathedral. This was the first time Jean felt a sense of wonder in England. There were no pews or chairs, she recalls in *Smile Please*. There was only a space with an altar and stained-glass windows looking down on the emptiness. The pillars on either side of this empty space were like a stone forest. She began to tremble. Half an hour later, at the home of a friend of Miss Paterson's, where the girls had been taken for refreshments, Jean's hands were still shaking when she was given a cup of tea. Miss Paterson, her friend and the girls were sitting on the verandah when Jean dropped her cup and it smashed. She was overcome with shame and humiliation. To make matters worse, Miss Paterson, whose prettiness should have somehow made her more sympathetic, made a sarcastic comment. Jean was mortified; she so wanted to please her.

She did not go to Aunt Clarice's for Christmas 1907 because Clarice said she was ill. Her schoolmates soon disabused her of that; the ones who were left to board over Christmas had grown quite used to neglect. Some of them felt they had been sent to Perse simply to keep them out of the way. They made light of their situation, but Jean could not recover from the disappointment of being left to languish in a draughty school for her first Christmas in England. During these long, un-festive weeks, she got chilblains from the constant cold and damp. When, one night, she saw hail battering the window, she did not ask the girls what this strange substance was; she was frightened they would laugh at her. Every evening of that Christmas holiday felt like a punishment to Jean. Miss Osborn made her read Charlotte Yonge's novels aloud after supper. Yonge, a household name amongst middle-class families with school-age daughters, maintained that the best education for young women was Home Education. The importance of self-discipline, high morals and character could not be impressed upon young women enough. Perhaps this is why the grimly conformist

Miss Osborn made Jean read her work aloud every night in Miss Street's parlour. It was a painful experience for Jean and she did not hide the fact; her lilting Caribbean voice – foreign and thus inferior – halted and stammered over the words. Meekness can be so aggressive. Kindly Miss Street, slumbering in her easy chair with an embroidered shawl covering her shoulders, did not mind. She allowed Jean's faltering voice to waft her to sleep. But Miss Osborn would not take her disapproving eyes away from Jean's face. One can only assume this woman, who made the girl read out loud yet could not bear the sound of her voice, had some unresolved conflict towards girls like Jean. 'Your voice,' she would say every night, 'drop it. An octave at least.' The other girls sat there, not minding, or like Miss Street, they were stupefied by the heat of the fire. This was a private battle between Miss Osborn and the foreign girl. When Jean failed to follow her instructions, Miss Osborn would say: 'That will do, don't go on. I really can't bear any more tonight.' Jean often had this effect on women; she called forth the bully in them.

During the first term, the fifth and sixth forms put on 'Scenes from *The Winter's Tale*'. Miss Street chose her to play Autolycus. It was the perfect role for Jean. But Miss Osborn had to spoil it for her. She pointed out, 'He's a rogue,' which nearly stopped Jean taking the part. Miss Street smoothed over the awkwardness by assuring her that Autolycus was a charming rogue. Then she sat her down and played his songs for her on the piano. Jean was charmed. Autolycus the pedlar – a wanderer and bohemian, a 'snapper-up of unconsidered trifles', like the girl who played him – lives in a world of his own. His spirits are raised and depressed by changing circumstances; he is irresponsible and flighty. But he has sharpened his wits and so has an eye for the main chance. An intelligent rogue who excites admiration and provokes laughter, slightly sinister and untrustworthy, with a bag full of thievish tricks – Jean would fall for two men just like him.

'I would not be a serving man . . . and no work would I do,' she declared on the stage at Perse School. She was dressed in green tights, brown boots, a cap with a feather, and had smeared burnt cork on her eyebrows. Jean's confidence had increased. She was more alive to her surroundings. Her growing friendship with sparky Myrtle assuaged her loneliness. Her performance elicited a round of applause that was 'splendid' to hear. Even the maid who brought her an extra blanket at night expressed her admiration. She had a dead, white face, this scuttling little maid, and a lifeless manner, but her eyes were like 'sparks of blue fire'. The night of her triumphant performance, the maid brought her a hot water bottle and shut the window for her. This was against the rules but the maid saw that Jean was suffering from the cold. She told Jean that she had liked her in the play. That she too had once appeared on the stage. Jean was mesmerised by this woman whose eyes were alight with fire. It was one of those encounters that produced a sensation of something that could not be articulated. The maid, her eyes, and her fragment of a story, were hints of a loneliness that, years later, Jean would recall and make sense of in her short story. Miss Osborn, Miss Street and the maid would all come to life in 'Overtures and Beginners Please'.

And all the while she was haunted by the fact that she still could not remember the trees and flowers of her homeland. Jean was mourning what she had lost, but she could not articulate her loss out loud. She would only be able to do that in novels.

In Jean's second term the Board of Education decided a younger headmistress was needed. Miss Osborn left with Miss

Street, and Miss Bertha Lucy Kennett took over in Spring 1908. Miss Kennett was a mathematician from Girton. She set more exacting standards and was keen to establish a higher academic reputation. She would not tolerate the second-rate. She wanted the school to stand out and be noticed, and for parents and governors to witness this new seriousness of intent. Debates were held on 2 April 1908, and the Old Perseans were invited. Parents of present Perseans were also there. It was an important day in the school's calendar. The motion was: 'The popularity of modern literature, to the exclusion of standard works, is unreasonable and deplorable.' It was proposed by K. Coates in a 'forcible' speech, and opposed by L. Clarkson, who 'handled a difficult subject tactfully'.

D. Kennett (no relation, one assumes), speaking for the motion, spoke of the injurious effects of cheap magazines. Against the motion were the two new girls, M. Newton and G. Williams – Jean. Myrtle, it was reported in the school magazine, had 'the makings of a good speaker but needs to take a less flippant view of matters in general'. Gwen Williams' maiden speech was most welcome, the reporter continued. She 'expressed her views fearlessly'. However, there was a caveat: 'daring and originality are always welcome in a speech, but they must not be confounded with exaggeration'. Jean and Myrtle lost the day. The motion was carried by a majority of five votes. Jean would always be sensitive to the accusation of exaggeration by the temperate English.

At the end of the summer term of 1908 Jean sat the Oxford and Cambridge Higher Certificate in English Literature and Roman History. Jean, as her speech may have indicated, was more interested in popular fiction than English Literature. Possibly because of the failure of the debate, her determination to defend the modern novel was undimmed. She certainly read a lot of them.

G.K. Chesterton called the popular fiction of his day the 'Hammock school', as in 'I read this book in a hammock; half asleep in the sleepy sunlight.' This suited Jean down to the ground. She was in a permanent state of dissociation – emotionally so removed from her surroundings it was as if they were no longer there. She could take comfort in heavily embroidered fantasies. For her English Literature exam she chose her favourite novel, *The Garden of Allah* by Robert Hichens, as an example of a 'modern' novel. Night after night she had shivered under her bedclothes immersed in this heady story of a Russian monk who inevitably yields to the call of passion against the backdrop of African deserts. She did not do well in her English Literature exam. Miss Wilkinson, who had coached her for the debate and had encouraged the young girl to express herself with verve and élan, in the expectation that she would shine, was disappointed.

'I was so sure of you,' she said sadly.

When Jean explained that she had chosen *The Garden of Allah*, she threw up her hands in despair: 'That explains it!'

Myrtle did badly too and for the same reason. The two girls egged each other on in their rebellion against the school's stuffiness. It was an act of self-sabotage typical of Jean.

However, another exotic novel that had swept across Europe, bringing its writer instant, momentary fame, helped Jean win the Ancient History prize. *Quo Vadis* by Henryk Sienkiewicz gave a broad, theatrical picture of Roman life in all its splendours and horrors. The Apostles Peter and Paul make an appearance alongside a variety of Roman characters, but sexual passion dominates the story. As Vinicius declares his love to Lygia: 'It seemed to her at moments that [he] was singing a wonderful song, which was instilling itself into her ears . . . he was telling her something which was in her before, but of which she could not give account to herself. She felt that he was rousing in her something which had been sleeping hitherto . . .'

Yes, Jean could relate to that.

On Speech Day the Ancient History Prize was given to G. Rees Williams by W.L. Mollison, Esq. A year after entering Perse School, the timid Caribbean girl took her rightful place in the school's annals. She was now a prize-winning History scholar, and one of Perse's best actresses. When she could rouse herself, she had a lively, inquisitive mind that she used to interrogate every authority on every subject. On Saturday 5 December 1908, she starred in a performance of Goldsmith's *She Stoops to Conquer*. The school magazine reports 'The leading parts were all admirably taken; but perhaps Gwen Williams, as Tony Lumpkin, carried off the palm. "Tony was a triumph" was a remark made by one of the audience, most of whom we expect would quite agree with her.' Again, the sound of applause rang sweetly in her ears. Whoever was casting the young Jean Rhys in these school plays saw something in her that most people missed: her waywardness and wit.

A letter came during the Christmas holidays from her only friend, Myrtle. Jean would carry this letter around with her until it crumbled into dust. She reproduced it in her short story:

Dear West Indies,

I have been thinking about you a lot since I came to Switzerland, perhaps because my mother is getting divorced. I see now that a silly lot of fools we were about everything that matters and I don't think you are. It was all those

words in *The Winter's Tale* that Miss [Osborn] wanted to
blue pencil, you rolled them out as though you knew what
they meant. My mother said you made the other girls look
like waxworks and when you dropped your cap you picked
it up so naturally, like a born actress. She says that you ought
to go on the stage and why don't you? I like Switzerland
all right. There are a lot of English here and my mother
says what a pity! She can be very sarcastic. Let me hear
from you soon. I felt I simply had to write this.

It was a letter that changed her life. It was like an act of
God, an external authority telling her her vocation. She wrote
to her father and told him she wanted to study at the Academy
of Dramatic Art in Gower Street, London. She was happier
than she had ever been when her indulgent, unorthodox
father agreed. But first she had to pass the entrance examination. This meant extra lessons in elocution and singing. A
clergyman taught her audition pieces: 'Once more unto the
breach, dear friends' and an American piece to suit her accent.
She travelled down to London. There is no record of what
she was wearing but she must have been feeling confident
to be able to recite her pieces to 'two sarcastic gentlemen'
and a lady, who all seemed very bored. They stopped her
before she had finished. To her surprise she was accepted.
But 'the place wasn't Royal then' she wrote in her story, so
perhaps 'it wasn't so choosy'.

The other girls were envious or laughed when they heard
that she had passed. Miss Wilkinson, who had not forgiven
her for doing badly at English Literature, was distant. Perhaps
she felt Jean's new career was a rejection of what the school
had to offer. It did not matter to Jean. Nothing could touch
her.

Chapter 6:

TREE'S SCHOOL

On 16 January 1909, Gwendoline Williams, of Bod Gwilym, Roseau, Dominica, West Indies, entered the Academy of Dramatic Art, colloquially known as Tree's School. It was founded by Sir Herbert Beerbohm Tree, the leading actor manager of the day, in 1904. Tree's Managing Council for the School boasted Sir Arthur Wing Pinero, Sir James Barrie, W. S. Gilbert and George Bernard Shaw. Fees were twelve guineas a term, except for the children of actors, who paid half. Clarice found Jean a room close to Tree's, in a boarding house in Upper Bedford Place, near Gower Street.

This was real independence, and at first, the faded wallpaper and scruffy wainscotting, the brass bedstead and marble-topped washstand with chipped jug and bowl, did nothing to dampen her spirits. Clarice bought her more hideous clothes. She seemed deliberately to frustrate her niece's ambitions, as though she resented spending the family's money on girlish whims. This time she bought Jean a cheap cotton skirt that was several inches too long. Jean tucked the extra material into the waistband of her knickers. She could not afford to have the skirt altered. She managed to wangle some cheap furs and a hat or two from her aunt's strict budget, but it was all very discouraging. Again she would have to face a potentially hostile group of strangers inadequately prepared for their judgement. How could she present an image of urbane elegance when all she had was a skimpy cotton skirt and wilting furs? It was clear to her that Clarice did not approve of her plans but at least her aunt did not have the energy to talk her out of them.

First, second and third-year students at Tree's were known as As, Bs and Cs. The As were the new students, the Bs were one year above, and the Cs were too grand to mix with those below. There were thirty-five As in Jean's year, so she was not alone. But, of course, she felt every slight and snub as if she was. Classes took place in the mornings and Jean attended assiduously. Miss Gertrude, the mistress of drama, took her craft very seriously. The first lesson she gave was in how to laugh on stage. She assembled her students on wooden chairs and gave them a demonstration by singing 'doh re me fah soh lah ti doh' very quickly up the scale in a trilling falsetto – this was laughter on the Edwardian stage. Back at the boarding-house, Jean practised avidly – but she was not convinced. The next morning, when Miss Gertrude called upon her class to perform laughter, Jean's note-perfect performance still managed to convey her scepticism. This was not a method of acting that suited her.

In the next lesson Miss Gertrude announced that she would teach the As to cry. She turned her back to the class for a few moments and when she swung round to face them, tears were running down her impassive face.

'Now you try,' she said.

Jean tried very hard to think of something sad. She looked around her, hoping for inspiration, commiseration, or at least someone as equally dumbfounded. All she could see was the agonised faces of the other. As as they tried to squeeze the tears out, she could not stop laughing – real laughter this time. Miss Gertrude did not approve.

Every week the students would act a scene from a well-known play before Miss Gertrude. Jean played Juliet in *Romeo and Juliet*, Celia in *As You Like It*, Francesca in *Paolo and Francesca* by Stephen Phillips, and Lady Macbeth. She loved being given romantic roles to play, relishing the anguish. Miss Gertrude would then dispense judgements on the various interpretations, and told each actor, 'who was right and who was wrong'.

There were no stunning triumphs as there had been at school or on the boat from Dominica when people had cheered or praised her one performance. She found Miss Gertrude's stern approach to raw emotion bewildering. In the face of competition, her talent shrivelled up. She lost interest. At nineteen years old, she found it hard to summon the belief in herself to stick to something. She wanted instant results, and instant acclaim. Without constant reassurance, she had no sense of worth. She was confident enough in her acting abilities to be able to join in the larky, student fun. But she was still quick to take offence. Lunchtimes were spent in the canteen where she noticed the Bs seemed 'conceited and unkind'. In 'Overtures and Beginners Please', her heroine leaves her fur jacket behind in the canteen. When she goes back to fetch it, she hears someone say, 'Is this goat or monkey?'

But she did make friends. The other exotic girl of her year – a glamorous half-Turkish girl – asked her to her rooms for tea. She wanted to tell Jean about a complicated love affair she was having. Jean listened dutifully, not really sure what she was supposed to say. When her new friend took out her darning, she said, 'I expect you are very surprised to see someone like me darning stockings.'

Jean wasn't, and asked why she should be. There was a puzzled silence on the part of her new friend. Jean left shortly afterwards. She was not invited to tea again.

Her other friend was Honor Grove, whose father was a

baronet and whose mother was a society beauty. They had a grand town house in Bedford Square. Jean learnt a lot from Honor about snobbery. The most important lesson concerned pronunciation. This was a live issue for a white Creole girl with 'a nasty sing-song nigger's voice'. She knew that the King's English must be spoken, and here was Honor speaking it every day. Honor's mother, Lady Agnes Grove, wrote essays on the correct pronunciation of words in *Cornhill* and the *Westminster Review*. In 1907 she had published a book on the matter, *The Social Fetich*, designed 'to amuse, not seriously to instruct'. Jean could see through disingenuousness. She knew that Lady Agnes Grove was serious. The English, she decided, are at their most serious when they are being flippant. It was yet another mask, like Meta's, with cruel eyes and tongue behind the smiling surface.

So she took Lady Grove at her word when she wrote that 'couch', 'mirror' and 'mantel' must be condemned as Cockney aberrations. In their place, one should say 'sofa', 'looking glass' and 'chimney piece'. Jean felt like the mermaid in the fairy tale who comes ashore in order to win the love of her prince. She is given feet to replace her tail but every step she takes is like walking on broken glass. Jean was crippled and constrained by English society and its rules, out of her element.

But Lady Grove also wrote 'Seventy-one Days Camping in Morocco'; she was a leading member of the Union of Women's Suffrage Societies and the Anti-Vivisection League. Lady Grove was an interesting woman who perhaps had a talent for self-mockery – something Jean could not comprehend. At this stage in her life, she considered deportment and social graces crucial to her survival. She did not have the confidence to laugh at herself.

Mr Heath, the elocution master, was one of the few

teachers to encourage Jean, or indeed to take any notice of her at all. So she was especially saddened when Honor, whom she also liked, quarrelled with him over the pronunciation of the word 'froth'. She wrote about this crucial dispute in a chapter of her memoir, entitled 'First Steps'. This is how important these lessons were to her. She was observing Honor closely because she knew that she had to be like her in order to survive.

Mr Heath asked Honor to give a short 'o' to the word 'froth'.

Honor insisted, however, on saying 'frawth'.

They shouted the word back and forth until Honor exploded: 'I refuse to pronounce the word "froth". "Froth" is cockney and I'm not here to learn cockney.'

Jean noticed that under her freckles Honor had turned white. Mr Heath, meanwhile, was 'red as a beet'. He asked Honor to leave the class.

Honor left the school. Mr Heath was dismissed. Two years later the young debutante married an officer of the Imperial Russian General Staff. No one knows what happened to the elocution master but Jean said 'sofa', 'looking glass' and 'chimney piece' until the end of her days.

Jean was, despite her anxiety and resentment, in demand. Men were attracted to her, women befriended her. Harry Bewes was the first English gentleman to want to rescue the young drama student. She must have told her classmates at Tree's that she was being bullied by her landlady because Harry wrote her a letter saying that he had heard from mutual friends about her unpleasant landlady, and that she had better get away from her. Soon Harry asked her if she would marry him. As Jean recalls it in her memoir, Harry must have been very sensible, because he went on to talk about money. He had lots and would like to meet her aunt to discuss the matter. Harry liked her because he had seen her standing up to a group of Bs in the canteen.

'You're always trying to make a big envious thing of a small mean thing,' she had told the Bs after yet another instance of unspecified petty snobbery.

Harry cheered and bought her a coffee.

Jean liked Harry because he didn't give a damn about anybody, and suggested crossing Africa from the Cape to Cairo for their honeymoon. But receiving a proposal was enough. She did not need any more than the fact of his asking, so she declined. She explained that she wanted to be a 'great' actress, which she quickly revised to 'good'. Harry left Tree's to go travelling in Africa. His early departure, like Honor's, was put down to illness.

The dancing teacher suggested they all go to see Maud Allen at the Palace Theatre. Maud Allen danced barefoot and decked herself out in Grecian tunics in the vague hope of resembling Isadora Duncan. The whole of London was shocked when, in one of her dances, she carried the head of John the Baptist on a plate. She had to cut that scene, though it was talked about for a long time afterwards. Jean was very impressed by the freewheeling movements of this daring woman.

But the dancing teacher said, 'Maud Allen is *not* a dancer. She doesn't even begin to be a dancer. But if I told her to run across the stage and pretend to pick a flower she would do it, and do it well. I'm afraid I cannot say the same of all the young ladies in this class.'

Jean was enjoying her independence, so Clarice rented a flat in Baker Street to check on her niece. It was an elegant mansion block on the bustling street, above the oldest underground station in the city. She asked Jean for tea. Full of enthusiasm for her studies, Jean demonstrated in her aunt's sitting-room how to fall when you have been stabbed in the back, when you have been stabbed in the front, and when you have stabbed yourself. It was a different fall each time.

A bemused Clarice asked if this was it. No, replied her niece, she was taking classes in fencing, ballet, elocution, and *gesture del sarto*. Clarice wanted more solid signs of industry and application. Had her niece not appeared in any plays? Jean avoided the issue by quoting Francesca:

> Now I am free and gay,
> Light as a dancer when the strings begin,
> All ties that held me I cast off . . .

An unimpressed Clarice interrupted the gaiety.

'You'll find that very expensive,' she said.

By the second term Jean had lost her enthusiasm for fencing, ballet, elocution and *gesture del sarto*. Her friends Honor and Harry had left Tree's. She continued to enjoy playing tragic roles, but what little conviction she had had in the teaching methods of Tree's tutors started to falter. She would always be dismissive of anything that lacked emotional truth or authenticity.

During the summer holidays in July 1909 she paid a visit to Uncle Neville Williams, her father's older brother, in the northern spa town of Harrogate. Uncle Neville was everything her father was not: he was the son in whom money had been invested. He had lived with the expectations of his family and had risen to meet them. Her father had been left to shift for himself. If her father was the rebel, his brother was replete with respectability. He had conformed, and he sensed his brother's resistance to conformity in his niece. They would never understand each other: he would always disapprove of her, she resented his authority, his complacency and his pride.

It was in Neville's solid, square house that she heard from her father for the last time that counted. He wrote that he would not pay for her to return to Tree's for the autumn term. He had received a letter from the Academy:

2 July 1909
W. Rees Williams Esq

Dear Sir
In answer to your letter of 15th June I write to say that your daughter is slow to improve with her accent which in my frank opinion would seriously affect her chances of success in Drama. I fear it would take her a considerable time to overcome this accent which in my judgement would only fit her for certain parts and those perhaps few and far between.
Believe me, dear Sir
Yours faithfully

She cried bitterly. She walked, disconsolate, around the streets of Harrogate. She writes in 'Overture and Beginners Please' that the streets were filled with music – concertinas, harpists, barrel organs, and a man singing, 'It may be for years and it may be for ever.'

She could not stop crying; everything, the music, the lyrics, were expressing her despair over the fact that her father had taken her dream from her – he had withdrawn his approval and his belief in her.

In the story she writes that it was the news of her father's death that caused her to walk the streets of Harrogate crying. But her father did not die until June 1910. Whatever the reason for her tears, the emotion was real. Furthermore, she added that her mother had demanded she return to Dominica.

But no one ever demanded that she go home. It was simply assumed that she had no other option.

Jean knew that Clarice had asked for the report from Tree's. She already suspected Clarice of conspiring against her. But she could not accept her father joining forces in letting her down. She perceived his rejection of the self she had conjured in her fantasies, the rejection of the brilliantly successful and wildly acclaimed tragic actress she might have been, as a kind of death. In doing this to her, he might as well, in fact, be dead himself.

Uncle Neville did not want a weeping girl in his upholstered parlour in Harrogate. She was sent to St Asaph in Wales to stay with Clarice. The family hoped she would come to terms with her failure at Tree's and make her return to Dominica. She brooded for several months in the quiet Welsh countryside. Her 'nasty nigger's voice' had let her down, and she had learnt nothing except how to be a snob. She was bitter, and for the time being, defiant.

'You cry without reticence,' said Clarice the day after Jean's arrival from Harrogate. 'You watch me without reticence,' wrote Jean several years later in the story that summed up this period of her life.

The two women were sitting in Clarice's garden. The River Elwy, a calm, slow-moving stretch of water, ran at the bottom of it, and contributed to this peaceful scene with its steadying and sedative effect. Clarice grew tired of the girl's tears and, trying to distract her from bitter lamentations over her failure, her disgrace, her humiliating return to the island where she would be a laughing stock, suggested that Jean take up writing. For all her coldness and exasperation she was a perceptive woman, and she was trying to encourage the girl. But Jean was so overwhelmed by her needs that small acts of kindness, these quietly practical suggestions, were never enough for her.

She did take Clarice's advice, though, and wrote her first story. She sat in Clarice's garden and wrote about a young white man who makes love to a coloured girl. Then he leaves her without saying a word. She is left alone on the island. Clarice was dismissive of the plot's melodramatic tendencies. Even though she knew that a young girl such as Jean had an unquenchable appetite for self-dramatisation, she could not help but be impatient. She did, however, like the descriptions of the flowers and the poetry of the songs that the lonely girl sings. She sent the story to a magazine. It came back with a list of criticisms and a note of dismissal headed, 'Very unlikely'.

Jean wanted to throw her story into the river Elwy. Clarice wanted her to keep it. Though Jean never liked to admit it, the woman whom she felt to be so very unsympathetic had understood her. Clarice had encouraged her to write and to continue writing, despite the initial rejection.

'I'm too miserable to write,' said Jean.

'The nightingale sings sweetest when its breast is pierced by a thorn,' countered her aunt.

Clarice gave her further flowery presentiments of the future: 'Out of the ashes of your failure on the stage will arise the phoenix of a great novel.'

Under the shadow of having to return home a failure she came to know Wales, her father's country. St Asaph is Britain's second smallest city and its cathedral is the most diminutive. Next to it, Jean would have been aware, was her father's birthplace, Bodelwyddan. From Clarice's house on Roe Plas, the River Elwy goes there in a long, undulating line. Jean must have walked along it. Clarice would have promoted daily exercise. Jean talks about the calmness of the River

Elwy in 'Overtures and Beginners Please'. Written towards
the end of her life, she calls the Elwy the river 'Afon',
which is the Welsh word for river. Its waters had made their
impression on her.

By its side, she planned her next move, knowing that
her family were not putting much thought into her future.
Her parents merely expected their daughter's return. Her
mother was probably absent-mindedly looking for an eligible
suitor.

In preparation for a tropical climate, Clarice took her niece
on a shopping trip to London to buy new clothes. She was
relieved that this troublesome, emotional young girl was about
to be taken off her hands, and she was gratified to find that
the girl's tears had dried. Jean was mutely obedient as they
trudged through the department stores that sold reasonably
priced clothes. But while Clarice attended to her own business, Jean sneaked off to Blackmore's theatrical agency in the
Strand. She was going to get a job in the chorus line of a
musical comedy.

Back in the scramble of London she realised there was no
way she was going back to a sleepy island and an inevitable
fate. She climbed the stairs to Blackmore's office above a
tobacconist's, and gave her audition in a shaky voice and
with hesitant dance steps. The stout, weary gentleman ran
his eyes up and down her body. He glanced across at another
gentleman sitting behind a piano, who nodded. He then
turned to her and said she would do. A contract was produced.
She signed it.

Clarice was furious and wrote to Father. But he agreed
with Jean's decision – let her dream. She'll wake soon enough.
He was dead by the time she did.

Despite her annoyance at being deceived, Clarice
accompanied her niece to the first rehearsal of *Our Miss*

Gibbs, the biggest show in Edwardian London. Theatre of this kind was expensive to produce because of the large choruses and flouncy costumes. However, it could be financially rewarding. Success depended on long runs, with provincial tours at the end. This was what Jean was rehearsing for, though she probably did not know it. *Our Miss Gibbs* was about to hit the provinces, having completed its run on the West End stage.

The other girls in the chorus line could not understand their new friend's seeming indifference towards her aunt. 'But she's lovely,' they argued when they met the elegant woman. Clarice chaperoned her niece throughout those first few weeks of rehearsals and sent a telegram on the opening night and the opening nights after that. But Jean persisted in seeing her as a spoilsport. In later life, when she had brought forward her father's death by a year, she liked to say that she had been left alone in the world. She implied that she had had little choice but to go into the chorus. She concealed how determined and dynamic she had been, how much she had wanted it. The truth is she rejected the tedious life her family expected her to undertake. Her parents had not seen her perform or debate, and their lack of ambition for her must have seemed like a betrayal.

But at this stage in her life, she simply did not care. She was going to earn her living on the London stage.

Chapter 7:

GAIETY GIRL

In August 1909 Sir George Dance's Number Two company began a summer tour of *Our Miss Gibbs* at the Pavilion, in Ramsgate. Jean appeared as a chorus girl under the stage name of Ella Gray. On 24 August, she celebrated her nineteenth birthday in Worthing.

Jean went into the tour as though it were a fantasy. The image she had of herself participating in this great theatrical event was based on pictures she had seen in a magazine. An elegant, poised maiden in a frothy frock, gliding across the stage, singing a siren song. She saw herself as a picture of innocence spliced with guile. But the reality was dispiriting: hand-me-down gowns, biting chilblains and relentless hoofing on the splintered boards of provincial theatres in dreary towns in an England she disliked already and grew to loathe.

She forgot the poetry of Crabbe and Cowper she had learnt as a schoolgirl. Then, she had been an intelligent girl focused on books. In 'The Village' Crabbe had depicted the hard graft of labour in blasting heat or cold that lay behind the picture of rural bliss. This was not just the lot of the peasant. It was the lot of the loose-limbed, precision-built chorus girl as she traversed the 'frowning fields' of England. It may have seemed as though she was not paying attention, but from August 1909 when she first joined the chorus line until January 1914 when she wrote her first book, she would be unconsciously absorbing every detail, every conversation she witnessed.

Her favourite of her novels, *Voyage in the Dark*, would be based on this period of her life. Numerous short stories would chronicle the hardships, the saucy chorus girls, the oafish men. Some of the girls exploited her, others tried to give her advice. Men were there to be flirted with, held at bay, or taken material advantage of – it all depended. She did her bit and vamped it up when necessary, and retreated wounded when she was bitten.

Our Miss Gibbs opened at the Gaiety in January 1909 with George Grossmith as the feckless young man about town, and Gertie Millar as Mary Gibbs, a shop girl from Yorkshire, who repeatedly tells the audience, 'They never do that in Yorkshire'. Their fame was unreachable to the likes of a humble bit player like Jean. Like Gertie, Jean – or Ella Gray as she was then known – could activate an alluring smile that lit and elongated her slanting, blue-green eyes. She may not have had Gertie's full bosom, but her legs were long and slender, and her lithe and fluid frame was perfect for the job. There is no mention in her memoir, diaries, or notebooks, and no allusion in her novels or short stories, of an audition process. One assumes she floated through the dreary necessities without taking them too seriously. She got the job, and that was all that mattered.

The show began for Jean at the Pavilion theatre in the Kentish coastal town of Ramsgate. Millar and Grossmith were no longer in the cast of *Our Miss Gibbs*. Their roles had been taken by lesser lights. The Pavilion was a smaller, more down-cast version of the Gaiety. The girls did their own make-up in a stingily lit room, crammed around dusty old mirrors. Jean would have smeared a thin layer of cold cream on her face before applying greasepaint, face powder and finally cochineal lipstick and rouge.

She made her entrance on the rough wooden boards of the draughty stage as part of 'a pretty group' in the opening chorus. The stage was got up to resemble the most exclusive department store in England, Harrods. And so she sang her lines: 'Garrod's! Garrod's! All things are there! / Brooches, Coaches, Tresses of Hair! / Rosies, Cosies, Silk Underwear'. She was dressed as a shop girl in an ankle-length, A-line skirt, a V-necked, tight-waisted bodice with brocade flaps over the bust.

The customary pose was head tilted against hands pressed together in supplication, a dreamy look in the eye, a smile playing on the lips.

The actress who played Miss Gibbs, shop girl par excellence, sang her signature song, 'Moonstruck', dressed in a loose, pale blue Pierrot costume with huge pompoms and a quaint little cap, with Jean and the other girls all around her. Years later, Jean (still calling herself Ella) would wear the same outfit to a fancy-dress party. Standing in a courtyard under a full moon with a man she had just met she would receive a dazzling proposal of marriage. She would be moonstruck. But that was ten years in the future.

For now, the show was popular – the Gaiety Girls displayed their charms. The men gazed at the girls flashing their ankles, the women at the frocks that covered their legs. Sometimes Gaiety Girls made front-page news by marrying peers of the realm and becoming members of the 'actress-ocracy'. Mostly, they were sacked when they had passed their prime.

Next stop was The Royal, Worthing, where Jean celebrated her nineteenth birthday. Along with the other, more lowly cast members she had taken the train from Ramsgate along the coast to Sussex and another coastal town. Again, there is no direct reference to individual performances, towns or people in her writings, but one element in the life of a chorus girl struck her forcibly: she was cold. The approach of winter shrouded the landscape. She could not get warm. Her chilblains, which she had first developed at Cambridge, flared up again. She was earning thirty-five shillings per week plus extra for matinees. She was staying in a seedy lodging house run by a surly landlady who mistrusted the girls who were paying to stay in her damp, dark rooms. England's coastal resorts seemed to Jean to be full of gloom, grey sea and sky and suspicious landladies.

One thing Jean had noticed on arrival in England was how the landscape was parcelled up: even the sea had a side to it, a long, steel-grey pier pointing to the horizon and dividing the broad expanse of sluggish water. The sea, here, did not go on for ever. It did not sing and play in the sun. In the seaside towns that she was touring she had plenty of time to gaze at this sad, tamed sea.

The gap between winter and summer tours was difficult to fill. There was simply no work so most of the girls went home to rest. If they did not have a home they stayed at the Cats' Home, a chorus girls' hostel in London. Jean must have been enjoying this life sufficiently not to run home to Clarice because in December 1909, she stayed there. The Cat's Home was well placed for an exploration of London – close to Leicester Square and its theatres. Of course the other girls would be available for outings too. But it was not an entirely carefree existence. The girls were treated with yet more suspicion, no doubt intended to protect them. But the effect was to make them feel policed. They had to come down for prayers every morning before breakfast, and before long Jean was calling the place 'ghastly'. The name suggests much about its residents – how these young women saw themselves, and how others saw them. This was not what she had expected. What kept her going was the company of the other girls. They were a doughty lot, great fun and full of bitchy witticisms at which Jean marvelled.

Some of the girls took her out and introduced her to men, so she was learning how to enjoy her freedom. In London, if she was lucky she would be taken by an admirer to dinner at the Ritz. At a supper-party at the Greyhound in Croydon a man showed her how to kiss. But it depended on the man, and how generous he was feeling, what kind of fun she would get. The Café Royal had a reputation for *à la carte* dinners and an excellent grill room. The Berkeley, quiet and comfortable, had a moderately priced *table d'hôte*. The White Horse Cellar served a cheap dinner. At Lyon's Popular Café, every meal was a bargain.

January 1910 and the winter tour commenced – one after the other, all the towns were the same: Doncaster, Grimsby, Accrington, Rochdale, Wigan, Dewsbury, Barnsley, Darlington, Wolverhampton, Wakefield, Derby, Hanley, Blackburn, Bury, Oldham, Leeds, Halifax, Huddersfield, Harrogate . . . It was cold, cold, cold, and the show was getting staler with every performance. The chorus dressing room was always the coldest in the house. In February, the bleakest month of all, she got pleurisy. But she hoped things would change. Something would turn up. A man perhaps. A fortune teller told her she saw something 'noble' in her hand. She was not in the least surprised.

The girls dreamed of living out the plot lines of their favourite musical comedies. But they dreaded the tragedy of *The Girl Who Went Astray*, *The Woman Always Pays*, and *Her Road to Ruin*. Tragedy and comedy followed radically contrasting arcs: chorus girl marries peer / chorus girl becomes fallen woman. Both ends of the spectrum shaped Jean's ideas about the fate of women. There simply was not much scope if you were a girl in her shoes. But she liked to imagine she was not. Nancy Erwin from the same touring company as Jean became Lady Dalrymple-Champneys. Jean would read *Tatler* and the *Sketch* for the rest of her life to follow Nancy's career.

Jean's parents, by now, had given up protesting at her choice of career, perhaps delegating this responsibility to Clarice. For her part, Clarice tried to be supportive, if at a distance. This raffish world was too far from her own experience, and she must have realised she had no power over her niece. In her turn, Jean was enjoying the life of a chorus girl, though gradually feeling less and less a part of that world – if, that is, she ever had been part of it.

The slang – which she loved – and the atmosphere increased her sense of alienation. She was entranced, listening to these girls talk. But it was impossible for her truly to belong to a troupe of cockney fun-loving, seen-it-all-before wannabes. She could pretend she was one of them but she could not sustain the performance.

They were a mixed lot of girls in the chorus line of *Our Miss Gibbs*. Between shows she got to observe them in the dressing room, in seaside cafés and in the gloomy boarding-houses that ate into her soul. She wrote them into *Voyage in the Dark*. One girl was the rebellious daughter of a famous Labour politician. Whenever the Conservatives won a by-election she would cheer louder than all the rest. The girls were all staunch Conservatives – espousing the values of the class they aspired to enter. Jean mentions another girl whose claim to fame was that she was the daughter of a woman who had 'stood up in public for Oscar Wilde'. Nothing escaped Jean's notice, and details such as this, which speak of lives shaped by defiance, find their place in her slim novels. And there were so *many* girls, it was hard to stand out and be noticed. There were girls aged sixteen and girls aged forty. Some were married, some were engaged to be married, some were determined to make a good marriage, some even had ambitions to get on in the theatre. But girls falling into this latter category were few and far between.

There was always one girl who was designated the 'company tart'; people would say of her, 'She has a lot of friends.' She was the one who managed to avoid the long, grim train journeys. A man would be sure to take her to the next town by car. These girls most impressed Jean; their savoir faire, their disregard for the opinions of others. In *Smile Please*, she describes one of these girls failing to show up for rehearsal call on a Monday. The stage manager's face when he opened her telegram was a picture of bewilderment: '*Contretemps* – what the devil does she mean, *contretemps*?'

Although the work was gruelling, the routine provided some security. Every Thursday a man collected the theatrical baskets and the scenery, and took them to the nearest railway station. The girls travelled with the props on the Sunday. Jean herded together with the other girls in what they liked to call 'steerage'. They each had just enough room for a small suitcase packed with toiletries, toothbrush and lipstick. A joke went the rounds with them: two railway men are chewing the fat. 'What have you got there, Bill?' 'Fish and actors.' 'Oh, shove them on a siding.'

In May 1910 Jean changed her stage name to Olga Gray. Perhaps Olga was more exotic than Ella, and therefore better suited to her smoky eyes, high cheekbones and sphinx-like smile. She was part of 'Liska's Troupe' in *Chanteclair, or Hi Cockalorum, a Feathered Fantasy in Three Fits*. *Chanteclair* was an imitation of a Paris hit by Edmond Rostand, the author of *Cyrano de Bergerac*. It was an appalling show. The killer gag was a girl in tights walking across the stage, dropping an egg and clucking loudly. The troupe was badly rehearsed. Jean was dismayed that only one of her colleagues in the troupe was attractive – a speciality dancer who was haughty and aloof, and as befitted one of her caste, carried a miniature dog with her. The other girls sneered that she kept it for sex. Was it the fact that she was 'special' that incurred their resentment? Or that she assumed airs and graces that were inappropriate? Jean thought they were being unfair but did not voice her reservations. She enjoyed watching her dance. She enjoyed the spectacle of femininity. But she did not understand the rules.

Chanteclair opened in the north and in her memoir Jean describes herself shivering in the wings. She was waiting to go on when she heard a loud tramping noise. The audience seated in the gallery had walked out en masse. She was shivering with fear as she entered stage left. The mockery and contempt coming up from the audience that remained was palpable. She looked at the girl next to her. Her face was just as fearful but was also grimly determined that the show must go on. Jean was on the end of the chorus line, near the wings. After a few minutes, she crept off. She went back to her lodgings, unhappy at being so cowardly.

'She stuck it, why couldn't I?' she kept thinking.

She decided that the next night she would stick it out, even if the audience threw things.

The following evening while she was making up in the dressing room the call-boy announced that Miss Gray was wanted in Mr Peterman's office. Joe Peterman was the producer.

He was livid.

'Why did you walk off stage in the middle of the act last night? Were you ill?'

In a moment of supreme recklessness she told him the God's honest truth. She told him she was frightened.

'What of?' he demanded.

She dug herself further into a hole with her reply.

'The audience.'

His response was that she could get the hell out of his chorus line and find her own way home. He wanted nothing more to do with her.

She saw his point, but insisted that he pay her fare home. He refused.

But she was desperate – she had not a penny. Whenever the underdog was threatened she fought back. She stood her ground magnificently. She knew there was a Society for the Protection of Chorus Girls. She told him she would report him to them.

He growled like a dog and gave her the money for her ticket home.

On 19 June 1910 Jean's father died. Clarice intimated that enough was enough and it was time to give up the stage and go home. Her mother, however, seemed to have washed her hands of Jean. Neither would Clarice take it upon herself to assume full responsibility for the impossible girl. Jean did not return to Dominica for her father's funeral.

In August 1910, the third tour of *Our Miss Gibbs* commenced. Despite her earlier poor show, Jean was promoted to playing a part above the chorus. She would be one of 'Three Irish Colleens'. But she fluffed her lines and was put back in the chorus.

She did, however, gain an admirer in one of these northern towns. His name was Colonel Mainwaring and he gave her a bracelet. He wrote her love letters which followed her from theatre to theatre.

The chorus girls were pleased for the new recruit. They even tried to teach her how to exploit her charms. But even amongst these reckless outsiders she felt different. She was not plucky, like them. All she knew was that she liked pretty things and handsome men, nice dinners and soppy songs. What is clear is that she was attractive and popular, and at times, had great fun. But it is hard to gain a sense of the physical presence she made. It is as though she was a phantom watching from the shadows. This at least is how she 'writes' herself: as an absence on which others projected their desires and anxieties, rather than the attractive, fun-loving young woman she must have been.

It was precisely during this time that Jean lost her love of books – she threw herself into being a chorus girl; she went to parties, she gossiped and complained that she could not even read a newspaper. The company tart, whom Jean liked very much, would sometimes lend her a book but she would never read it and would often lose it. It was as though books and brains were not going to help her through this minefield, but standing still and being pretty might so she may as well not waste her time on books. Her indifference to literature lasted for years. Only books about sex made an impact on her. In 1909 she read *Nana* by Zola and the newly published sensation, *The Forest Lovers* by Maurice Hewlett, who promised:

My story will take you into times and spaces alike rude and uncivil. Blood will be spilt, virgins suffer distress, the horn will sound through woodland glades.

Jean the chorus girl, dreaming of marrying a knight in shining armour, lapped up the sub-Malory mythologizing, the borrowing from Sir Walter Scott. *The Forest Lovers* is the story of a knight and the peasant girl he rescues. It was a story that would dominate her fantasy life for years. As for the other girls, they were more interested in the fact that the knight and his peasant girl slept with his sword between them. They weren't stupid.

After two and a half tours of dreary towns Jean got sick of the theatre, sick of *Our Miss Gibbs* and sick of wearing patched-up gaiety dresses. She was becoming more attuned to the weary cynicism of the old theatrical hand. By 1910, she was sharing rooms with a friend called Maudie. In *Voyage in the Dark*, she describes herself reading *Nana* as she lies on the sofa in their room on her mornings off. *Nana* is the story of a prostitute who gets money from men and is punished by dying of the 'pox'. Zola's endless succession of words describing the sexual merry-go-round left her feeling 'sad, excited and frightened'. Maudie was more dismissive: 'I bet you a man writing a book about a tart tells a lot of lies one way and another.'

Maudie was twenty-eight years old and very experienced in the ways of the world. Late at night, when they were in bed after the show, she would tell Jean some of her adventures. 'You've only got to learn how to swank a bit,' she would say. 'Then you're all right.'

But Jean was not listening.

One night after a show in Southsea she met her first, great love at a supper party. It was just as the books had told her it would happen. His surname was Smith, he told her. 'Go on,' she reports herself saying in *Voyage in the Dark*. She is acting the part of the cynical chorus girl. But his middle name was Grey, he told her, just like the stage name she had chosen for herself. Most important of all, his first name was Lancelot.

Jean was going places. In December she and Maudie left Sir George's company to join the chorus of a pantomime at the Old Lyceum in London. She was on the glittering West End stage now, simpering her way through *Cinderella*. When the curtain lifted, the audience was treated to a gauzy representation of 'The Realms of Fancy'. The actors progressed through a glade in the forest to 'dreamland'. After a brief interlude in the 'Haunted Heath' a wedding takes place in 'Fairyland'. There were live monkeys, giraffes and lions on the stage.

Life on stage was glorious, but Jean was losing her enthusiasm for the fakery of the Edwardian theatre. Back in the dressing room, Maudie told her she had seen a rat. All Jean could think about whilst floating around Fairyland was the rat in the chorus dressing-room.

When her first real affair started, the curtain lifted on a dream world of her own making, and it was much more inviting. The fantasy of theatreland would be entirely eclipsed. But her lover was convinced that she should get on in the theatre, so she went through the motions of being a Gaiety Girl. He arranged singing and dancing lessons for her. She attended them to please him. Most of the time, however, she was looking out of the window of her boarding-house in Bloomsbury – just as Aunt Clarice had done before him, Lancelot Grey Hugh Smith had installed Jean in a room in central London. So she sat by the window, watching the street, waiting for the messenger boy to bring her lover's letters.

Chapter 8:
LANCELOT, PART ONE

In 1910 Jean met Lancelot Grey Hugh Smith at a supper party in Southsea. A businessman in his forties, Lancelot supported Jean financially for the duration of their relationship and beyond. In May 1911, she appeared in the chorus line of *The Count of Luxembourg*, which opened at Daly's Theatre in Leicester Square. It had one of the shortest runs in the theatre's history. In Dominica, her brother Owen was working on a lime plantation owned by L. Rose and Sons. He was training to be an orchardist. His three illegitimate children, Ena, Mona and Oscar, were causing consternation to the rest of the family. It is unknown where Jean's elder sister Minna was living at this point, but her mother, Auntie B and Brenda were still in Dominica.

At first, Jean disliked him. He was aloof and faintly dismissive. He called her 'My dear child' when she told him she was eighteen (she was twenty). She was tired of men who patronised her because she allowed them to pick her up. But her cynicism did not last long, and she came to worship him. She called him Lancey.

'He was like all the men in all the books I had ever read about London,' she wrote in her memoir. When he walked by her side she felt safe. When he talked to her she felt as though the might of the British Empire was on her side. The space, the comfort that spread around him, was like an aura. He was a dream come true and 'one doesn't question dreams, or envy them'.

Lancey was related to the great banking families of England. His father had been governor of the Bank of England. He had five brothers, and whether they were in banking or the navy they rose to pre-eminence. The eldest became Lord Bicester and chairman of Morgan Grenfell. Another brother was an admiral, a KBE, and had commanded the guard at Queen Victoria's funeral. His sisters made spectacular marriages.

He was born in 1870 at the family's Georgian home, Mount Clare, set in thirty-five acres of park and farmland in Roehampton, which made him forty-two when he and Jean first met. He went to Eton and Oxford, where he read History but did not bother taking a degree. His father wanted him to go into banking but Lancey, with his eldest brother's support, chose to be a stockbroker. After a brief struggle, his father relented and in the mid-1890s Lancey entered the Stock Exchange, joining a small, newly founded firm, Rowe & Pitman.

Using his family contacts and his innate know-how, Lancey made Rowe & Pitman a large, established firm, in fact, the leading 'old-boy brokers' of the City. Their clients included the richest families in Europe, its aristocracy, and Queen Victoria. By the time Lancelot met Jean Rhys he was very rich, and would get richer. He had a house in Charles Street, off Berkeley Square, and spent his weekends with his mother and unmarried brothers at Mount Clare. He was shy of intimacy.

Five years previously he had wanted to marry Violet Hambro, the daughter of an enormously rich family friend. He knew that she was being pursued by his cousin, the similarly well-placed Everard Martin Smith, but she encouraged Lancey's advances. Perhaps she was playing a clever game to egg on his rival, because just as Lancelot was about to propose, she announced her engagement to Everard. Lancelot felt

cruelly slighted. Although her family maintained his motivation for marriage with Violet had been mercenary, he
insisted this was not the case. Maybe it wasn't. But throughout
his life he had difficulties identifying what he wanted. Wealth
and status he had, beautiful pictures and ornaments graced
his houses, he went to the best tailors and he wore the finest
shirts. He was stylish, but he was not at ease. He liked lively
company but remained detached. Like Jean he had a deep
well of unfulfilled needs at the centre of his being; a well
that remained empty. At any rate, he never tried the Violet
type of girl again. He settled into a routine of attending
restaurants and parties with his banking friends where they
were entertained by subtle and knowing chorus girls and
actresses. His affairs usually lasted six months, and Lancelot
became known throughout the theatrical demi-monde as a
profligate and inconsistent 'patron of the arts'.

Jean and Lancey had their first dinner date in a private
room in a club in London. She could not help noticing the
bedroom adjoining the salon through an open door. He tried
to kiss her.

She said, 'Do you think I was born yesterday?'

Her imitation of the chorus girl was word perfect. The
next day he sent her twenty-five pounds to buy some stockings, and a bunch of violets. She started thinking about clothes
and appearances. The trick, which she never quite pulled off
(she was far too drawn to the void it was designed to hide),
was to present herself as an enigma. It was a complicated
business. The allure of a woman like the twenty-year-old
Jean for a middle-aged man like Lancelot is that she never
quite managed to appear sophisticated. Her naivety was
charming.

You needed money to achieve this masquerade and Jean
was scarcely earning. She was relying on Lancey; this was

the way it was meant to be, according to all the books she had read. She was staying, until Lancey moved her at some point in January 1911, in a very lowly boarding-house. She was behind with the rent. She and Maudie had parted company, possibly because of Maudie's dire warnings regarding Lancelot. She was back in gloomy Bloomsbury without a job but with a lover. With the twenty-five pounds he gave her in her purse she could finally pull rank on the landlady. She told the woman to lay a fire in her room. Whilst the woman was still muttering her complaints, she hailed a taxi. She was going to her favourite shop on Shaftesbury Avenue. It was the shop that the leading ladies of musical comedy patronised. It was warm and softly lit and smelt of freshly brushed animal pelts. She tried on a dark blue dress that was so long and tight she could see the sinews of her thighs as she walked. With a matching coat it cost eight guineas. A dark blue and white velvet cap cost two guineas. When she went outside everything seemed different. But she knew that, like a reflection in a looking glass, it wasn't real.

When she got back to her room, her landlady asked her to leave as she did not want 'tarts' in the house. All this is recorded – every slight and insult from every landlady – in *Voyage in the Dark*, and some of her other novels and many of her stories. With this latest affront, Jean was plunged back to the times at home when she had a fever and could not move from her bed. She was ill, her temperature was high. She wrote a letter to Lancelot and he arrived bearing parcels. He told her not to worry about the landlady, that he would speak to her, and that he would send her his doctor.

The next time they met, they made love. At his house on Charles Street, near Berkeley Square, he led her up the stairs. He knew she was a virgin but she said, 'All that's made up.' It did not matter, she just wanted to be with him. She liked it when he called her his darling. It was as if everything in her head just stopped. It hurt but otherwise she didn't feel anything. She kissed his hand afterwards and had a sudden surge of misery and sense of loss. But once they were walking in the cold streets looking for a taxi to take her home she felt at peace again, holding his hand. He said he would write to her the next day. He moved her into a new room in Chalk Farm. It was large and high-ceilinged with a piano and sofa, table and chairs. She sat at the window all day watching the street hustlers singing their songs and selling their wares. She thought about him making love to her and of the quiet click of the street door behind her as she left to go home in a cab. She never felt quite at home in his house. She was not really admitted into its inner sanctuary – the servants' stiff manners made sure of that. And then she always had to leave before sunrise. But she could get used to anything. She could make excuses to keep the fantasy intact.

When he sent her word, she dressed for him. His car came for her. He took her to restaurants or to his house. She enjoyed their walks along Park Lane and to the Ritz, but most of all she enjoyed being made love to in his house. Fires were lit in every room; there was space and comfort in abundance. It felt right that he should be the possessor of these things and that she should not. She was on his side against the upstarts who wanted a share of those luxuries; who tried to exploit his generosity. Like the cabbie who told him she had thrown up in the back of his cab and demanded money for the ensuing repair job. When Lancey asked her to confirm this and she denied it, he knew she was telling the truth. But when the man friend of a girl she knew said that a girl's clothes cost more than the girl inside them, she sensed he was telling a kind of truth, too. The girl added that Jean should make Lancey get her a flat up West somewhere.

He arranged singing lessons for her instead, He was encouraging her to be independent. He thought she should be getting
on in the world; pursuing a career, like 'her predecessor', he
let slip one evening. She had known her way in the world
but he could see that Jean never would. So she told him she
wanted nothing in the world but to be with him and he
told her not to be foolish whilst pouring her another whisky.
She got drunk and told him about Dominica, about the earth
pulsing beneath her feet, and trailing her hand in the water
when Black Pappy the boatman took her and the convent
girls for a moonlit boatride. And the barracudas swimming
along the white roads that the moonlight made in the water.
When they lay in bed she remembered the nun who told
her to practise being dead. She remembered the list of slaves
on the family estate. Then she dressed and got her taxi home.
The streets were so awfully dark.

Lancey took up all of her time. She idealised him, she
gave him all the love she could not give herself. She loved
him because he was the embodiment of those attributes she
wanted for herself – nobility, gentleness, sweetness of temper,
grace and generosity, respectability and savoir faire. Now, in
a roundabout way, she could procure them and thereby satisfy
her desperate longings. And because she idealised him, she
was sad most of the time – waiting for him to get tired.

The only time she felt excited or happy was when she
had had a drink because then anything might happen. That
feeling of insecurity became exciting.

He introduced her to his friends, if not his family. One
day early in the affair they had lunch at the Savoy with a
couple he knew. A discussion was sparked about an actress
who was appearing in an advertisement for Lux shampoo.
They wondered whether she really did wash her hair in Lux
flakes as she said she did. Jean could not imagine why they

should be interested in discussing such a thing, and despite Lancey's efforts, would not join the conversation. She felt mystified by the minutiae and complex dynamics of polite conversation. Lancey sensed Jean's separateness and rather loved her for it, but ultimately he was afraid of it. When he asked what she was doing with herself for the rest of the afternoon she lied. She said she was meeting a friend for tea and a trip to a music hall. She knew that she could not tell him the truth; that she was sad and lonely. That would have been 'bad policy'.

She did not question why she was sad or lonely.

She tried to figure out the difference between her and Nancy Erwin: what did Nancy, who so famously became Lady Dalrymple-Champneys, have that Jean did not? The difference was that Nancy had been determined to resolve life's journey with 'a very elaborate marriage'. Nancy was a subtle flirt, she affected a mood of coquettish disdain and knew how to smooth over awkward silences. Jean could not help revealing what should be concealed, she did not know the rules of the game of sex, and therefore could never come out on top.

But, at the beginning at least, Lancey and Jean's love went beyond games. He listened patiently to her talk about Dominica. He asked her questions about its flora and fauna and wildlife. With him Jean had the time to talk. She did not feel shy or awkward. They would discuss all the things that mattered to her, and he would gently tease her. It was like having a father and a friend rolled up in a lover. He was so patient and kind that she adored him. And he loved her. He sympathised with her diffidence and difference. What she so readily exposed he hid but longed to express. He never did. Late at night, though, he would wake – in a cold sweat, rigid with fear – from some dream that pushed him over the edge of his cultivated exterior into the blankness beneath. The bell next to his bed was expressly for these occasions. When he awoke from dreams into the chaos of dark thoughts and intimations of nothingness, he rang for his butler, Leggatt, who rushed to his side. Leggatt held his master's hand until his grip loosened and he fell asleep.

Lancey's affair with Jean was like a dream because it always happened at night. Once she told him she wanted to be with him for ever – as his slave, his kitten, his mistress, whatever he liked – but he turned his back on her and said, 'You'll soon be bored with me.' He meant, of course, that he would soon be bored with her. And, in a pang of guilt, he would say, 'Kitten, you make my heart ache sometimes' or 'You're much too sweet for this sort of thing'. He knew she was asking him to save her, to raise her, but he could never marry someone like her.

On 20 May 1911 Daly's Theatre in Leicester Square opened with *The Count of Luxembourg*. Lily Elsie was the star. She had softly curling brown hair and big, almond-shaped eyes set wide apart in a perfect oval face. The Rootsie-Pootsie Girls (Jean was one of them) made their entrée in risqué short skirts that hung just below the knee. They wore pagoda hats with tiny bunches of blossoms decorating the brim. Lily 'in her most bewitching mood of tender gaiety', according to *The Illustrated London News*, came on stage carrying Parma violets, singing,

> You love me, I love you;
> that shall be all life through,
> as we go onward hand in hand,
> making the world a fairyland.

Jean and the chorus sang of her as a 'queen of hearts and queen of song'. Mr Bertram Wallis, 'six feet of reposeful and irresistible romance', played the Count who, with his fair lady, waltzes up the broad staircase of the grand reception hall where their fairy wedding takes place. The King and Queen of England were present at the first performance and Jean peeked at them from behind the stage curtain. They looked bored, she thought.

Halfway through the run Lily Elsie married the Honourable Ian Bullough. Daisie Irving replaced her. She was one of the most beautiful girls Jean ever saw. She had thickly waving, dark red hair, blue eyes and golden eyelashes, which she accentuated with a smear of Vaseline on the tips. She was a tad too tall for a musical comedy actress but slim and graceful. But what really fascinated Jean the writer was her character. Despite being a leading lady, Daisie gossiped and bitched like a chorus girl; Jean noted there was an innocent sort of spite in Daisie, that she herself was unaware of. And in a story called 'Before the Deluge' Jean charts the descent into nastiness that Daisie would follow. She would start by calling a rival a 'tart' then build to a crescendo of abuse that impugned the woman's character and her morals. If one of her friends made a successful marriage she would be especially piqued. In private she would embark on a barrage of insults that ended with a pious expression of sympathy for any children the doomed couple might produce. When she saw said friend, she would congratulate her with tears in her eyes and gushing kisses. What was most remarkable was that she was sincere in both her hatred and her love.

Daisie was generous, they became friends; she could be kind, and Jean's passivity ensured that she did not present a threat, whilst her prettiness and demure grace made her an attractive foil. Daisie's ingenuous bitchiness, her guileless hypocrisy, her fake piety, the fact that she was a raving beauty, were all attributes recorded by the nascent writer. This was not a friendship for Jean, it was covert observation.

Jean was in her element. The girls in Lyon's tea rooms

would gaze at her friend in awe when they popped inside for a cup of tea before the show. Like a worshipful page, she walked behind Daisie into smart restaurants, holding the bouquet that had been thrown at her as she took her final curtsey on the stage. Daisie helped Jean with clothes. She even set up an important contact for her. Kitted out in a new costume, Jean went to see George Edwardes, the great Edwardian impresario, the man behind Daly's the Delectable Theatre. This was a real stroke of luck for a chorus girl, especially as Edwardes had a lot on his mind; for one thing, *The Count of Luxembourg*'s disastrously short run of 345 performances. But he helped her. Jean's meeting with him produced a cup of tea and a real lead. He suggested that she should join the chorus of his number one touring company (a step up from Dance's number two) and visit all the big towns (again, an improvement from the Grimbsys and Ramsgates of her first tour). This time it would be Manchester, Dublin, Edinburgh and Liverpool. If he received good reports of her, he would put her in the next show at Daly's. Any other chorus girl would have leapt at the chance he offered, but Jean declined, preferring to float behind Daisie and wait for Lancey's messenger to summon her for sex and dinner.

After a few months of their strange friendship Daisie called Jean to her flat for twelve o'clock sharp. The conversation forms the climax of 'Before the Deluge'. At first, Daisie is coldly polite. Then she launches into her: 'I hear you've been gossiping and telling lies about me all over the place. I think it's rather beastly, after all I've done for you.' Jean describes denying these accusations angrily and her attempts at rationalising with Daisie: 'Who am I supposed to lie and gossip to?' (Besides, gossip did not interest Jean. She could not understand it.) Somewhat nonplussed, Daisie looked at

Jean as though she had been struck and fell into a faint. A man walked into the room to find Jean standing over a prone Daisie. Then Daisie's mother walked in – and she had never liked Jean. So Jean fled the scene.

She heard the man crooning: 'My poor, darling little girl, what have they done to you, my poor little sweetheart?'

She never saw Daisie again. But she always remembered what Daisie had said about Lancey: 'That sort of man thinks women are just put into the world for his amusement. Make him give you money, but don't love him!' It was too late.

Her lack of interest in the show could be said to be, if not sense, then prescience. *The Count of Luxembourg*, with its Viennese waltzes and high-octane romance, fizzled out quickly, spelling the end of the Gaiety Girl. The accelerated, syncopated rhythms of Ragtime crossed the Atlantic in 1912, along with new, indecorous dances like the turkey trot, the bunny hug and the chicken scramble. The songs shopgirls wanted to hear went something like this: 'Florrie was a flapper, she was dainty, she was dapper, And her dancing was the limit, or the lid.' And they were not accompanied by languid sighs and wide-eyed smiles but by a wink and a shrug of the shoulders.

The change of the feminine ideal reflected the changing society of pre-war England. In 1909 H.G. Wells had published *Ann Veronica*. His heroine, clever and defiant, leaves home, becomes a suffragette, falls in love with an older man, seduces him before he has a chance to seduce her, carries him off to Switzerland, becomes pregnant and still lives happily ever after. It was banned by many libraries. One clergyman protested that he would rather infect his daughter with typhoid fever than let her read *Ann Veronica*. But it was not just in books that women were climbing out of crinolines. In 1913 the 'Cat and Mouse' Act would be passed; suffragettes who had become ill from hunger strikes were allowed to return home, only to be re-arrested once they became better. Few re-arrests were ever made. Gaiety Girls, Daly's, and the clergyman were behind the times.

Jean was moving away from the chorus, becoming Lancey's full-time lover. He did allow her to meet one member of his family, his cousin Julian, an effete young man who flirted with Lancey and enjoyed the effects of his charm. Julian was an astute reader of passing trends and fragile personalities. He was Everard's younger brother, handsome and charming, a gilded youth. Jean hated him. He was patronising and snide, whilst retaining a veneer of affectionate concern for her well-being. He despised her – her vulnerability, her mute appeal for tact and sensitivity – and yet was attracted to her, which made him despise her all the more. As far as he was concerned, she was a little tart. But he loved Lancey and Lancey loved Julian who had what Lancey wanted – that effortless belonging, that deep sense of his own superiority. Lancey even took Julian into Rowe & Pitman, making him a partner in 1913.

For now, though, Julian told Lancey, 'That girl is getting too fond of you.'

It was summer, 1912. The air was fetid in London. From her suite of rooms in Chalk Farm, Jean would venture on to the streets for a midday stroll. She was aware of people breathing the same air as herself, their proximity – as though they were all gasping for the same breath. She felt stifled by all these other people. Lancey sent her a card telling her to pack for a few days in the country; Julian was also invited.

The Savernake Forest in Wiltshire is a magical place. At the heart of it stands the Big Belly Oak which was a sapling at the time of King Alfred the Great. The great oaks of this ancient forest are the descendants of the trees that were among the first living things to appear when the last Ice Age receded.

Inevitably, Jean used this sojourn in the country in *Voyage in the Dark*. She took a morbid delight in noticing evidence of brutality, cruelty, and ruthlessness. In concentrating on the stag's heads in the hotel, she gives us an image of creatures being hunted, trapped, shot, and speared, and hung like trophies. But there was no one with whom she could share her trepidations. She had already worked out that the women who survived what she saw as the assaults on their bodies were not sympathetic to their weaker sisters. But she was happy because she was with her Lancelot, and she would not have to sneak away in the night. She was so happy she cried.

The forest, too, was beautiful but, for her, the wildness had gone out of it. Too many stories, too much history for the trees to stand up against. Lancey said he had been wanting to bring her there since he had met her. It is easy to imagine him, from the way she writes it, defiantly addressing an invisible crowd of detractors. She sat watching him from under the big tree. He sat by her side and told her she was lovely from that angle. She wanted to be lovely from every angle. He tried to make love to her. She wanted a perfect romantic union. They wanted such different things. Her over-estimation of Lancey's worthiness and her desire to be in love was unsustainable. Her sense of her own self and her own needs had become more and more unassuming and modest, and Lancey increasingly more sublime. She gave him her entire stock of self-love, sacrificing herself to him. Sexual satisfaction was lost in all this. Sex frightened her. She could not feel anything, only fear. Or, as a girl she knew from the chorus put it: 'Some women don't start liking it till they are getting old.'

She resented Julian calling her 'the child'. She resented the fact that she could not discuss books with him. She never read. She had nothing to say for herself because she spent her days waiting for Lancey to send for her. But if she could not speak it was partly because she was observing the world around her, and knew she must remain silent.

Julian had brought a girl with him, a girl he was going to leave soon. The girl knew it and she was angry, finding fault with everything around her – the hotel, Julian's manner, their companions. She was angry because Julian was going to New York and leaving her behind without any money. When she repeated this complaint, Julian changed the subject. Assuming an air of paternal kindness he talked about Jean's prospects at Daly's and the singing lessons that Lancey was paying for. Julian, Lancey and the girl continued to talk about Jean in the third person; something that often happened. Finally the girl asked her how she had met Lancey. When Jean explained that it was at a supper party at Southsea all three burst out laughing.

'What on earth were you doing in Southsea?' Julian asked Lancey.

The two men started laughing about the girls they were with. In *Voyage in the Dark* Jean writes about jamming a cigarette into Lancey's hand. It is doubtful that she did this in real life. She is making a point, and she makes the other girl say, 'Bravo.'

All four lovers left Savernake Forest early. On the way home, Lancey criticised Julian's girl – 'She's old,' he said. She was Julian's age, Jean noted.

The next time Jean saw Lancey he told her he was going to New York on business for six weeks and that Julian was going with him. As compensation he sent her to the seaside for a holiday. Six weeks later she received a letter from him. He told her his business was taking longer than he had expected.

'It's always like that,' a girl from the chorus told her. 'They always do it that way.'

Chapter 9:

LANCELOT, PART TWO

On 9 November 1912 an advertisement appeared in the *Daily Telegraph* for Madame Faber's massage services, asking for a manicurist. Fashions in theatre had changed and Jean, who was again calling herself Ella Gray, chose not to keep up. She applied for Madame Faber's job, and on being offered it, overcame her initial reservations. The following year, in May, Jean had an abortion, which Lancelot paid for.

The next letter Jean received was from Julian. He wrote about Lancey's sadness, about how he hated to hurt her, and how she was young, and that youth was the greatest gift of all, and that she had her whole life ahead of her. That she must forget him, that she must know how terribly fond of her Lancey was, and that she mustn't hate him.

How she hated him.

Something snapped inside her. 'She came to England as a girl of seventeen, she died at twenty-three,' she wrote in her diary. Her desire for life and for men was shattered by disappointment; the exhausting round of seduction and betrayal that is set in motion by man's restless sexuality, which so many women enjoy, was too much for her.

Jean's affair with Lancelot lasted from 1910 until 1912. It ended with her accepting an allowance from him on the condition that she left him alone. She never recovered from his rejection. The inexorable logic of sexual humiliation that she had learnt in Dominica decreed that she should debase herself. Even during the affair's heyday, when she sat in her room waiting for dusk and the car he sent to bring her to him, it was a melancholy affair. Its end spelt the beginning of her descent down the social ladder.

She lay in bed for a week, getting up only to take baths and bury herself in water. She was aware of her landlady watching her disapprovingly. Jean received another letter from Julian. A sensible girl, having accepted the money and the introduction to a theatre producer, would have moved on to the next man. But the postscript Julian added stuck in her throat; in it he asked for Lancey's letters to be returned.

It is impossible to know what contact she had with her family at this time – there are no surviving letters or diary accounts – but it is certain that she could not turn to them for support. Aunt Clarice and Uncle Neville were not concerned with the plight of stricken chorus girls. In Dominica, Mrs Rees Williams and her youngest child, Brenda, had no money to spare and not much sympathy. In fact, they would have been horrified by Jean's predicament. Lancey's rejection and her estrangement from her family, even if it was self-imposed, left her feeling nullified. As such she began her pursuit of disappointing adventures and loves that replicated this scenario of loss and mortification; or else retreated, disconsolate and speechless, alone with the chaos her feelings brought. She had lost not just her saviour, Lancelot, but herself. All her certainties – that love lasted for ever, that she was beloved – had fallen away. She wrote a poem to express her despair.

> I didn't know
> I didn't know
> I didn't know

★

The fantasy was over. Jean needed the loving kindness a mother would offer, and that she had never had. She needed someone who loved her to assure her she existed; she needed unconditional love. Without it, and on suffering that first romantic disappointment, she fell into a deep depression that rendered her repetitive and monotonous. She was too exhausted to speak. Her sentences stuttered to a standstill. She had nothing to say. When the blanket of aphasia over-whelmed her – or she became steeped in an excess of cognitive chaos – she had to walk.

On 9 November 1912 she left her bed and walked to Tottenham Court Road. She stopped in a café for some lunch. She picked up the *Daily Telegraph* and looked through the Situations Vacant pages. She saw an advertisement in the 'Medical' column for Madame Faber's massage services. Maybe she wanted curing. At any rate, the advertisement read:

'Manicure, Face Massage, Chiropody, Sciatica, Rheumatism, Swedish treatment. Royal and medical references. Mme Faber from Ostende and Nice. Hours ten to eight and Sundays. – 4, Bird-street, Oxford-St., W.'

Madame Faber needed a live-in manicurist. Jean went straight to her flat for an interview. The flat was decorated with a series of prints entitled 'The Cries of London': people of the street selling their wares. This, at least, is what she described when she wrote about the next adventure in her life. Madame Faber told Jean how respectable she was. In *Voyage in the Dark*, the woman emphasises this point. All Jean had to do, said Madame Faber, was provide a manicure and be nice to the gentlemen clients. She took the job. But she was tired all the time, and not very sporting or cheerful. Madame Faber grew sick of her saying she was tired. 'We're all tired,' she retorted.

In early March 1913 Jean bumped into a girl who had been in the chorus with her. She hardly recognised her at first. Shirley had hennaed her hair and was wearing it short with a heavy fringe. It suited her. She was having a fine time; being wined and dined, having sex because she liked it, and being paid for it, too. She tried to help her old mucker out, and gave her some astute financial advice. Shirley banked half of everything she earned even if it meant she had to do without. Sensing Jean's desperation she took her under her wing and to her flat on Langham Street, off Oxford Street. It was a step up from a Bloomsbury boarding house. Shirley lent Jean a dress, and took her out to dinner with some men friends. She knew men of all nationalities and she always got her meals paid for and a taxi home. One of the men Jean met through Shirley was a big American. Despite being married he fell for her. He gave her enough money to live on to stop her seeing other men. He was rough and violent and ugly; this was the debased version of life with Lancelot.

Jean spent some nights at Shirley's, and others at Madame Faber's. She did not much care where she stayed. Madame Faber, however, disliked Jean for going out on the town with Shirley and coming home late at night. She became especially annoyed when Jean told her she had had supper at Romano's with two men: they could have been potential customers. Business was not going well. Jean noted that Madame was talking to herself – muttering 'brutes' and 'idiots' over and over again. At one point she broke down and Jean was presented with a vision of everything that can go wrong for a woman. Madame Faber was approaching middle age, she was alone and had no financial security, no friends and no family. It was a terrifying spectacle of utter destitution.

In *Voyage in the Dark* Jean gave it a hint, too, of moral destitution. It was as though Madame Faber were apart from the rest of society. She had two voices, Jean noted, a harsh, frightened one and a soft pleasing one that she used for business.

But the big American was a comfort. He did not tell her anything about himself except that he was married with a little girl. He continued to give her money and to take her out to dinner. Then he left and she went out with Shirley to pick up more men. And so began Jean's short life as a prostitute. She began to drink a lot and when she was drunk she remembered Dominica. The misty-blue mountains, her French teacher Miss Jackson, who was the colonel's illegitimate daughter. She remembered the rumours that were whispered about Miss Jackson's mother who was a – what? Jean never did find out. But she remembered Miss Jackson's tremulous voice as she asked the children playing in her yard not to frighten her cat.

In May 1913 she wrote to Lancey: she was pregnant and had no one to turn to. He visited her at Shirley's flat near Oxford Street. He insisted he would look after her. Her knight had returned and her relief was so great that she believed what he said. They talked of her going to live in the country and having the baby. She was in a dream-world, she even pretended the baby was his. But then she noticed that every time he looked at her his face seemed sick and strained. She saw that his relief at finding her still alive was so great he would have agreed to anything. She realised she had to have an abortion. Shirley knew a woman, and with Julian's help, Lancey arranged it. He sent her a Persian kitten. On the next day it was a rose plant and then flowers every day for a week.

Life was being sucked out of her. She felt something heaving within her and could not articulate what it was. She remembered being a child and watching the carnival, and Meta coming into the room – her long, red tongue poking out at her from behind a white mask. A familiar face sprouting fangs. She felt as though she were falling. There seemed to be an inevitable cycle of beginnings and endings in which she was fated to take part. When the doctor came she told him she had had a fall; she was a fallen woman. In her first draft of *Voyage in the Dark* she would write about the experience as though it was she herself who had died.

Things were looking up though. She was ill and people were being nice to her. She felt deliciously helpless, thin and weak. Everyone took care of her and Lancey said she was 'the ghost of my kitten'. Julian even took her out to a nightclub. It was like a delicious pause from the sexual merry-go-round. She was out of action, convalescing.

By June 1913 everyone had had enough of the wilting flower. Julian sent her to Ramsgate with Mabel Hampshire, an artist's model Jean knew from Bloomsbury. Mabel pushed her in a bath chair up and down the front. As soon as she could walk they went out to restaurants for supper, and laughed and giggled like kids. Mabel was surprised at Jean's sudden powers of recuperation, as though nothing had happened. But nothing could touch her because there was nothing to touch.

Before she left for Ramsgate Jean had put the kitten Lancey had given her in a home on the Euston Road. When she got back the man who ran the home told her it was dead. She didn't ask any questions, just accepted the news as though it was inevitable – another crushing blow. What else could she expect? All the feelings of grief and loss and guilt for her baby came pouring out now. She cried all the way home because it was a grief she could afford to indulge; it was manageable.

She had a new flat that Lancey was paying for. But the owner of the flat became suspicious of her and accused her of being a tart. Her daily overheard and the next day handed in her notice. She had discussed it with her husband, she told Jean, and they had decided she could not work in such an atmosphere. Jean could not stay in a cold, draughty flat now that winter was approaching. She needed someone to light the fires, get her breakfast, keep the surfaces spotless and make cucumber sandwiches for tea. She moved into a Bloomsbury bedsitting-room – familiar territory. Breakfast would be brought up in the morning. The maid would light a fire in the grate, and Jean would huddle under the blanket until it had heated the room. She knew now how to pour tea, arrange a bath and keep a fire going. But that was all she knew. She could not cope with a flat.

Her routine was dull. Sleeping all morning, walking to Tottenham Court Road for lunch in a cheap vegetarian restaurant. Back to her room for more sleep. One day a letter was waiting for her from Lancey's solicitors, H.E. & W. Graves. The name itself seemed a portent. It was a cheque with a note attached telling her to expect the same sum each month. As an old lady she wrote, 'It seems to me now that the whole business of money and sex is mixed up with something very primitive and deep.' Jean was hurt and angry by Lancey's display of careless wealth and would have torn the cheque in two and sent it back to the lawyer without a word (very dignified!) if the landlord hadn't reminded her, at that exact moment, that the rent was due.

She knew, in her own words, she 'was a useless person and that I could never get a job'. She cashed the cheque and wrote to Lancey asking him not to send her any others. But despite this initial show of independence, it seems, in the face of poverty, that Jean would keep receiving money for some time to come. She went to Blackmore's agency to ask them for work. She must still have had something to offer, at least in terms of her appearance, because they instantly found her a job as a film extra. It was work perfectly suited to limp, lifeless girls who cannot take responsibility for themselves. Being told where to stand and what to wear and how to say nothing of any consequence seemed about right. But winter 1913 was a bitterly cold one. And Alexandra Palace, where the film was being shot, was made of glass and was unheated and she was sitting around doing nothing in a cotton crinoline dress. It was too cold, so she did not go back again and she never answered Blackmore's calls offering her more work.

For a long time she abstracted herself from her body. People would talk to her, and she would see their lips moving but she could not hear a word they were saying. The triteness of small talk had always dismayed her: it seemed to be hiding the truth about love, fear and betrayal. She did not read or seek solace in the poets who had entertained her childhood. She was not in the mood for consolation – she was dazzled by the injustice, disappointments and wretchedness of life. She was a stricken deer that had left the herd.

On Christmas Day 1913, now aged twenty-three, she passed a 'sad Christmas'. She sat in an armchair all morning looking out of the window on to an empty street. How was she going to get through the day? At midday the landlord knocked on the door with a Christmas tree that had just been delivered. In Lancey's handwriting were the words 'Happy Christmas'. He shouldn't have done that. The tree was garlanded with silver stars and fairy lights, bright coloured parcels hung from its branches. She thought of parties, and people laughing. She tried to imagine herself in the midst of these people, talking and laughing with them. But she could not see herself there. She was not made for such scenes. She did not know what she wanted, and if she did, she would not know how to say it. She was so far removed from herself, from her desires, and from her sadness, that she could not find her voice. She could not bear the tree any longer so she bundled it down the stairs and on to the road. She was going to get a taxi and take it to Great Ormond Street Hospital for sick children.

She hailed a taxi and the next thing she knew she was back in her tree-less room with an unopened bottle of gin sitting on the table in front of her. What had happened to the tree? She could not remember if she'd given it to the driver with instructions to take it to the hospital or if she'd taken it there herself. And she could not remember where the gin had come from. She knew she did not like gin and she could not remember buying it but here it was with a packet of cigarettes lying next to it. Only one thing was clear, she did not want to remember, to think or to feel; she wanted oblivion.

'You're always so ladylike,' says Maudie in *Voyage in the Dark*. 'You make love like a rag doll,' her future husband told her. To be ladylike is to be the object of desire, and emphatically not a desiring subject. 'Women are ridiculous when they struggle,' she wrote. Women do not fight to achieve what they want. It is for men to want.

When her fantasy that she was wanted was shattered by Lancelot's rejection she was alone with her empty self. The stuffing had fallen out of her when she was a child. Instead of guts and determination, of self-belief and motivation, she had plenty of nothing: the desolation – the chaos – of a lonely, bewildered infant.

That winter of 1913 she was teetering over the cliff edge. When she walked down the street she was drifting. The approaches of men on the street startled her into contemplations of violence. She was like all the other people she saw there; the ones without money. Not the beautiful ones with pretty clothes; instead, she was mirrored by those people with beastly lives; who swarm like woodlice when you push a stick into their nest. The early incorporation of her mother's critical voice is an insistent murmur in Jean's thoughts and in her prose. In her writing, she despises her fellow man and woman for representing what she has lost. Despite the fact that from 1919 onwards she will always have a man in her life, she returns to that period of extreme isolation again and again, as if loneliness is her true state of being.

The strange, compelling contribution she made to twentieth-century literature draws on this wealth of emptiness. She writes about long periods of nothingness with an insight born of bitter experience. She re-visits the Christmas of 1913 throughout her life, she recalls the rush of relief as she fell over the edge, of dawning unconsciousness, of not having to try any more, to comprehend, react, parry words, enter the incomprehensible world of other people. What do they mean? Are they laughing at her? What do they want? What role does she have to play to fulfil their desires? What mask does she have to wear? She's tired. Leave her alone. Textual elisions punctuate her words, reflecting her blankness.

Jean Rhys wrote of the hallucinations that filled her emptiness. Her sentences use dashes and dots and form streams of words that have lost their bearings. The triumphant poetry of despair.

Meanwhile, in real life, someone always rescued her. The next person to knock on her door on Christmas Day 1913 was Mabel, the friend who, six months earlier, had pushed her in a bath chair around Ramsgate. Mabel had a pair of red Turkish slippers for Jean that she had bought from Caledonian Market. She clocked the gin and asked if Jean was giving a party. Jean laughed too loud (it had been so long since she had laughed). Once she had stopped laughing, she explained that she had been planning to drink the gin and then jump out of the window. Mabel explained that she would need a taller house to do the job properly, and wasn't it lucky she had come along. They had a few drinks and started to giggle about everything. Then Mabel had a bright idea. Jean should come and live in Chelsea.

Later, Jean said that 1913 was 'a lovely year', but in truth she became superstitious about the number. The first novel she wrote, which Ford Madox Ford called *Triple Sec*, does not have a page 13.

Chapter 10:

WORLD'S END

In January 1914, Jean's friend Mabel found her a room in Chelsea. Mabel was an artist's model and introduced Jean to the artists Sir Edward Poynter and William Orpen. In April, Jean, or Ella as she still called herself, started frequenting the Crabtree Club in Soho. George Bernard Shaw's *Pygmalion* premiered in London. In July, King George V staged a conference at Buckingham Palace designed to resolve the crisis surrounding Irish Home Rule. No agreement was reached. Later in the year, he was sidetracked by a bigger crisis, the outbreak of the First World War. Jean's brother Owen left Dominica to join the British Army. Her elder brother William, having graduated from university, joined the Indian Medical Service.

The world was preparing for war, but Jean was too pre-occupied with her own world to notice it. On first entering the room in Chelsea, she took stock. The table was the biggest thing in it and it was bare, making her scant possessions – brush, comb and powder compact – look poor and insignificant. The next thing she did was to go for a walk along King's Road, Chelsea, an area far more recherché than workaday Bloomsbury. She had spaghetti in an Italian café. She passed a stationer's shop and the display of quill pens in the window caught her attention. They were vivid shades of red, green and yellow. It occurred to her that they would look pretty in a glass on her table. To enhance the effect, she bought several stiff-backed notebooks with red spines and shiny black covers.

She took a bus back to her room that said 'World's End'.

Her new notebooks looked bright and purposeful arranged on the table with a fresh bottle of ink and an ink-stand sitting next to them. She sat at the desk by the open window. The view was endless. Rows of small, nondescript houses occupied rows of endless streets in an endless city. Jean's recurring complaint was that all London's streets and houses looked the same, stressing conformity. Like the gardens, any spontaneity was curbed or walled in.

She returned her gaze to her pens and notebooks and then it started. Her palms and fingertips were tingling. She opened an exercise book, and wrote down everything that had happened to her in the last year and a half: 'what he'd said, what I felt'. Essentially, it was the story of what had taken place between an older man and a young woman; the story of a woman unable to construct her own sexual identity because the words she was given were not her own. The feeling was one of torture: knowing the feeling but not the words to describe it.

When Jean was not writing she paced the bare, wooden floorboards of her room in a frenzy of remembering. She cried at the disappointment her affair with Lancey had been. She grieved over the promise of love that she had lost, and she laughed at her own naive hopefulness. Her tears were wracked and despairing. So was her laughter. She broke off to write and wrote into the night and when she woke the next morning she started again.

She barely noticed the landlady's knock at the door or the breakfast that had been arranged on a tray. The landlady found a dishevelled, tear-stained girl carelessly dressed in a loose silk wrap feverishly scribbling in a notebook. This confirmed her worst suspicions. She told Jean that the lodger below had been disturbed by the sound of wild crying and

laughing throughout the night. She threatened Jean saying
she would have to leave if this disruptive behaviour continued.
Jean got up from her desk and gently pushed the landlady
out of the door. She said she would be quite happy to leave
after a week but the landlady really must leave her alone.

She had never seen a woman look so astonished.

And she wrote day and night for the next week, making
an effort to keep the noise down. She took off her shoes
and laughed and cried softly so that the lodger below would
not hear her. 'You needn't leave, dear,' the landlady said.
'Don't call me dear,' Jean said, and she left as soon as she
had finished writing. It took a week. She had finally accessed
some strength within herself through putting pen to paper.
Finishing this first book was like a weight being lifted from
her. But she was left feeling a dull despair that she was
only twenty-three and there were years of living ahead
of her.

In the spirit of defeat, she moved back to Bloomsbury.

It felt right that she should lodge in the boarding-house
quarters of London, and Bloomsbury was the centre of the
lonely hard-up. They are like shadows criss-crossing long
streets; they go to the cinema at midday, nibble at stale sandwiches and nurse warm drinks in snack bars in the afternoon.
She was amongst her own kind in Bloomsbury.

Mabel found her some work sitting for artists. She posed
in the nude for Sir Edward Poynter, the academician. Since
he was old, it did not occur to her to worry about being
naked. Poynter specialised in the idealised female form, and
was known for his sense of propriety in subject-matter:
Andromeda chained to a rock – the figure's dignity in dire
straits. In a letter to *The Times* he drew a firm distinction
between his classical nudes and the disgraceful *baigneuses* of
modern French painters. For the British, these French nudes

were beyond the pale of respectability. Poynter's harking back to Greek and Roman models meant they had no sexual identity; they were safe. But Sir William Orpen, RA, was another matter. He was part of a younger generation of painters who preferred the boudoir nude of Degas, Renoir and Manet. In his basement-cellar room at 21 Fitzroy Street, a house that had formerly been a brothel, he painted 'the English Nude'. Jean posed for him in a slip. The room was dank and dark with an earth floor. The great feature of his room was a large antique four-poster bed, the posts of which seemed to hold up the ceiling. Surely this was what art was about! Nudes on rumpled beds, sizzling with post-coital sexuality. He often made love to his models, but not to Jean. She intrigued him with her coyness and drew on the side of him that was capable of kindness and friendship. He was unlike men she had previously met through the theatre; he was young and neatly turned out. He was fun to be with. He loved to dance. After a while, when she could hold him off no longer, removing her clothes for him made her cry. But Orpen saw her distress and was kind to her and, his best move of all, he was fatherly. So she posed for him regularly. And after the first tearful time, her clothes came off more carelessly. He called her a nymph, and bought her a blue chiffon dress that coursed along the slight contours of her body like a stream. In the middle of painting her he would put on the gramophone and dance a Highland fling. He took her out to dinner. In fact he was rather in love with her, but she was not attracted to him. She just enjoyed him. Years later she wondered at the fact that she did not take advantage of her conquest. But her youth and prettiness did not feel, at the time, like instruments of power. She did not understand that others could be vulnerable to her appeal.

There was one man she met to whom she was attracted

– a bad lot whom she calls Harry Benson in her first novel, which was never published, the one Ford Madox Ford would call *Triple Sec*. Harry had been an officer and a gentleman; he was trim, had a muscular build, an upright bearing and commanding presence and voice. He wore smart clothes, though on closer inspection the cuffs were frayed, the lapels were shiny and you could see that in fact he was rather seedy. She liked him, he was down on his luck, so she could sympathise with him. When he embraced her she felt a wonderful lassitude descend upon her; she could give up her own volition to his strong arms. She was like the heroines of the flimsy novelettes she liked to read.

'How pale you are! Like a lily,' he said as he kissed her. But she woke up on being kissed. Harry was poor and his eyes were wary, searching for what was around the corner. He had no money so it was easy to turn him down. They became friends instead, and decided to capitalise their scant resources and go into business. In *Triple Sec* they discuss opening a gambling club. She can lure the men in, he can rid them of their money. Then, he figured, she'll let him kiss her – when he has some money. But the club founders, Harry fades from view, and in real life, Jean turned to Orpen for assistance. They arranged to meet, he told her she was beautiful, and kissed her with some insistence in the back of a taxi. She made the most of the moment and asked him for money. She was learning, honing her skills, albeit with a lack of adroitness that made men angry with her. Orpen looked relieved when she told him the amount she was asking for. She realised too late that she could have asked for more. He sat back in the taxi and thought about it. Then he took her home, pushed her on to a sofa and tore off her dress. She had made it clear, after all, what she was after. In the midst of his grappling, she stopped him. 'You're making me *hate* you,' she said. The game was up and she had not enjoyed it one bit.

Jean did not have the pragmatism or long-range forecasting facilities that direct women into high-earning marriages. She could not use her power to her best advantage. It depressed her. She must have noticed that at about the same time as she was posing nude for artists, Gertie Millar, the star of *Our Miss Gibbs*, became the Countess of Dudley.

But she continued to attract men and vamp it up in her own shy way. She met Alan Bott, a twenty-one-year-old sub-editor on the *Daily Chronicle*, at her boarding house in Bloomsbury. In April 1914 Bott took her to the opening night of a type of club entirely new to her, the Crabtree Club. Founded by Augustus John, the Crabtree was the first of the great Bohemian nightclubs. It was raffish, scruffy and in Soho. Bott led her up four flights of wooden stairs into a dark room over a shop on Greek Street. Epstein, Gaudier-Brzeska and Compton Mackenzie were members. The other habitués were journalists such as 'Mr Gossip' from the *Sketch*, actresses, Jewish shopkeepers from the East End, and toffs who liked to slum it in the company of dancers, models and students from the Slade. There was a platform at the end of the room dominated by a grand piano. Jean was fascinated by the actress Lilliane Shelley, who would hop up on to the platform, demand an accompanist and launch into singing 'My little popsy-wopsy'. Shelley was very beautiful and wild, with black hair and painted red lips. She liked people to think she was a gypsy. Her bust was sculpted by Epstein.

It was a decadent place full of skinny shop boys drinking absinthe, hoping people would think they were French. The women wore trousers and talked and argued with the men until dawn. One artist paced the room in dancing pumps, fixing people with glittering eyes and offering them a line of cocaine. Later Jean would call the Crabtree 'a bad imitation of Montmartre', but at the time she only knew that she loved it.

Jean practically lived there; arriving every night at midnight, staying till dawn and having sausages for breakfast. She slept all day till it was time to go to the Crabtree. As an elderly woman she talked about it often. It was the highlight of her youthful time in London, somewhere where boredom was relieved by the tense expectation of the unpredictable and where excitement was a relaxing pastime. She had never felt such involvement before. But from amongst all the wild young men she found an older, dull one to fall in love with.

He was like Lancelot. He was ten years older than her and a gentleman. Well-educated, old-fashioned, slightly severe. He asked her to his flat in the Temple and gave her a nursery tea; slabs of toast with jam on the side, and Fuller's walnut cake by the fire. He had lots of books – from Plato and the ancients to what was modern for him: George Bernard Shaw. At five o'clock when she arrived she was dismayed by his dullness but by half-past six she was entranced by the smell of tweed and the intoxicating feeling of being taken care of. He, too, suffered some kind of enchantment because, over tea, he asked her to marry him.

But her disappointment in love, her sullied dreams of romance and subsequent hurt feelings were too deeply engrained for her to take him at face value. She thought it was an attempt to bed her. Plus she was having too much fun at the Crabtree to contemplate marriage. She tried to repel him by telling him the tawdry details of her life. But he refused to be disgusted and pitied her instead. He wanted to rescue her from all that. And when she cried, he was gentle and kind. By the time he escorted her home, they were engaged.

His name was Maxwell Henry Hayes Macartney. He was a journalist with *The Times* and she could not believe her luck. She was so grateful she made a list of resolutions: 'To get up early in the morning – To stop putting black on my eyes – To take only one hour to dress . . . And two more: To be awfully good. To be a wonderful wife.' It was like putting a dress on. She got up in the morning, and went to tea in the Temple every afternoon. She met his female friends who were nice to her. But it was an odd engagement, spiked with arguments. Jean had learnt too much about love and romance by now. She had learnt about fickleness, her own need for insecurity in order to feel alive and the lack of trust one could place in men. Maxwell did not like her cynical, chorus girl's airs, or her frivolous approach to tying the knot. She thought they should do it in secret as it would be more fun and she told him she dreaded the boredom of marriage. Most of all, she dreaded him going off her. And to prove she was attractive she would not stop flirting with other men – testing her power – and as he became more jealous and withdrawn, her flirting became more desperate and indiscreet.

But the Temple, a quintessential English institution, became her retreat. Arthur Henry Fox Strangeways lived in another of its courts. He also worked for *The Times* as a music critic. He was in his mid-fifties, very cultured, erudite and a confirmed bachelor. He was irresistible. His background was impecunious but impressive. He was Rabindranath Tagore's unpaid literary agent in England and had been Secretary of the India Society. He had written a book called *The Music of Hindostan* which was a definitive account. Despite the solid front he presented, he had had two nervous breakdowns. Like Lancey he had the veneer of social status and respectability and the chaos of inner conflict. All his life he had lived in male bastions, and had been a public schoolmaster for twenty-five years. He rarely mixed with young women. And if he was attracted to Jean it must have been because she did not frighten him; she was a nymph, too fey and passive to be a threat. So he took her to concerts and taught her about music. Strangeways may have seemed to Maxwell a safe friend for Jean to have, but because he was old before his time he was actually the biggest threat of all her men friends. She always talked about him in the same reverential tones she used for her father, and her eyes filled with tears whenever she mentioned him. He and her father were linked in her mind.

On 28 June 1914 she came out of Leicester Square tube station with Maxwell and saw a newspaper headline: 'Archduke assassinated at Sarajevo'.

'That means war,' Maxwell said. But Jean felt nothing. Over the next few weeks, there were long queues outside recruiting offices. One night Jean turned up at the Crabtree and found a notice pinned to the door: 'Closed for the Duration'. But Jean was blithely confident that her future was panning out nicely. She could not comprehend how others might feel anxious. She was living in a nice flat in the Temple, after all, and Max did not make too many demands of her.

She even had the energy and resolve to get a job. In July 1914 *Monna Vanna* opened at the Queen's Theatre, starring Constance Collier. It was set in fifteenth-century Pisa using mid-Victorian fashions, and featuring 'Miss Gray' as one of the 'Citizens, Peasants, Ladies-in-Waiting'. The play, by Maeterlinck, essentially rewrote the Godiva story. A conquering General says he will spare the city he has besieged if Monna Vanna will come to his tent naked. It had been banned until now for this very reason. Collier wore a long, voluminous gown and everyone's modesty was preserved. And the General 'loves her honourably' despite her see-through mantle.

Jean was in the crowd scene as a starving peasant. One of the extras was a professional actress who was outraged at the amount of rouge and lipstick the other girls were applying. 'You are supposed to be starving citizens,' she protested. But the girls carried on rouging up.

Jean noticed a procession of young men through the dressing-room window and another girl told her they were German students protesting against the war. 'What war?' she said, still blithely ignorant of world events. Austria had invaded Serbia on 28 July and Germany declared war on France on 3 August. The following day Britain declared war on Germany. The lamps were going out all over Europe and Kitchener's poster was going up all over England. By the end of the year 1.9 million new recruits had signed up for the great adventure they all thought would be over by Christmas. Jean's own brother had signed up for war, but Jean does not seem to have spared a thought for him. She must have heard the news, however, that on 24 August 1914, her twenty-fourth birthday, Julian Martin Smith, Lancey's arrogant, handsome cousin, fought in his first battle at Mons. A piece of shrapnel hit him in the spine. He died as a result.

The man Jean was supposed to be engaged to, Maxwell, thought of nothing but war. He tried to volunteer but was too old. He would not leave it there and arranged to be sent to France for his newspaper. Jean and the engagement were forgotten. She helped him pack, feeling sad but excited. For the next six months she kept sight of her fiancé by reading his despatches from the Western Front. He churned out sentences like 'our intrepid Army in Flanders has added glorious pages to its immortal history' (1 December 1914). She found his reports very dull. She wrote him voluminous letters. His responses were distracted and brief. She felt alone again; all the men she knew had volunteered and the women were busy.

So between 1914 and 1917 she undertook voluntary work in a soldiers' canteen near Euston Station. It was frequented by soldiers on their way to France, and run by a no-nonsense Mrs Colonel Something or Other who was very British. Jean and a raft of six other girls started on the same day. After delivering a perfunctory thanks to her volunteers, Mrs Colonel issued the rules. Jean, naturally, found them very irksome. They seemed so unfriendly and impracticable. She reproduces the rules in *Smile Please*:

1. None of the men must be allowed into the kitchen.
2. When you bring in the trays you must smile and say good afternoon or good morning as the case might be. But you must not engage in conversation with any of the soldiers.
3. You must not on any account wash the frying-pan. It ruins a frying-pan, to wash it.

Mrs Colonel also warned the girls that the soldiers would claim poverty when it came to paying their bills and that they were to have nothing on account. Jean found that this never happened. Though once a soldier did come into the kitchen and ask her, with a wink, to adjust his belt strap. She did, he smiled, and walked out. She realised later that he had probably done it for a bet. She prayed for him every night but because she was irreligious she doubted that it did any good.

She was aware by now that men were being slaughtered.

However the newspapers did not report it like that: 'Enemies' Front Line Stormed' and 'Our Casualties Not Heavy' was how they described the graveyard of the Somme. Every street in England had families mourning dead brothers, husbands and fathers. As the appeal of Kitchener's poster began to pall, conscription was brought in and the canteen was packed with more cannon-fodder despite the burnt bacon and eggs caused by the filthy frying pan. The only thing that stopped her hating Mrs Colonel was that she subsidised the canteen with her own money. Otherwise Jean resented her officiousness. She worked from nine till five, conscious of the weary older men and the febrile youngsters that came through the doors, and returned to her room exhausted. One day in 1917 Mrs Colonel announced that her canteen had been amalgamated with another in St Pancras so her volunteers were no longer needed.

Max broke off the engagement with a letter. He cited Jean's 'numerous men friends' and his objection to her 'bringing them up to the flat late at night as you apparently do – though I oughtn't perhaps to be surprised'. She could have killed him for saying that. Instead she went cold and empty. She picked up the first volume of Galsworthy's *The Forsyte Saga*, and could not stop reading. It contained ideas that confirmed her feelings: 'words have as little relation to fact as coin to the bread it buys . . .' She watched pigeons through Maxwell's window and bumped into an old acquaintance, a French doctor who persuaded her that she was beautiful and so had power over men, and that she must 'use it'. He told her of the Frenchman's love for La Femme, which filled her with a desire for excitement. She returned to the old routine of dinner with men who picked her up, but this time she did not sleep with them. She entered a new troupe of dancers, working under Madame Zara, and trained so hard for her that Madame gave her a contract. She stopped drinking and started eating more, and moved into a boarding house on Torrington Square. She was back in Bloomsbury.

Here, she drifted into a 'semi-demi love affair' with the young artist Adrian Allinson. He was her age and, with his stooping shoulders and 'chronic gastric weakness', unfit for military service. He was a pacifist anyway, and was prepared to accept the 'social ostracism' that was his punishment for not fighting.

Allinson had always felt like a misfit. His mother was German Jewish and his father a vegetarian teetotaller. But he was clever and talented. They had first met at the Crabtree Club, but it was at a studio party in Chelsea that he was struck by 'Ella'. He described her in his unpublished auto-biography, 'a fair young Englishwoman born in the West Indies'. He describes her 'tender loveliness' and her 'remark-able resemblance to the famous Renaissance beauty' whom Botticelli painted as *Primavera*. Allinson decided to paint Jean as a modern embodiment of Spring, a symbol of hope, 'among the blossoming but soot-laden trees of Manchester Square'.

Through Allinson she came to write one of her most important short stories, 'Till September, Petronella'. It was based on the following course of events. She was staying in a cottage in the countryside with two men and another woman. One of the men was infatuated with her but she was mesmerised by his friend, who was involved with the other woman. Adrian, who had invited her, wanted to turn her into Botticelli's Spring but he had chosen the wrong season. It was autumn and conflict had blossomed into war. This was not a dance of life but a *danse macabre* and Jean's characters quickly took up their positions.

Chapter 11:

PRIMAVERA

In February 1915 Germany began a blockade of England. In April, the British ocean liner RMS *Lusitania* was sunk by a German submarine. In June, the first Zeppelin air raid took place over England. In August, Peter Warlock invited Adrian Allinson to a cottage on Crickley Hill, near Cheltenham. Adrian asked Jean to be his guest.

Peter Warlock was a composer and music critic whose real name was Philip Heseltine. He had changed his name because he had alienated the musical community that had initially greeted him as a prodigy. He liked the name 'Warlock' for its occult associations. Warlock was born in the Savoy Hotel, London, in 1894. His father died when he was two. His mother quickly sent him to boarding school. He was a musical boy, and became obsessed with the composer Delius. In 1911, he met Delius at one of his concerts. The two became close, with Delius acting as mentor to the young man's burgeoning talent.

Peter tried university and he tried to follow his dead father's footsteps into a career in finance, but he was unhappy – first at the University of Oxford, then at the University of London. In February 1915 he landed a job as music critic on the *Daily Mail*. He found the work frustrating and only lasted four months. Unemployed, he spent his days at the British Museum reading manuscripts of early music.

Warlock met many of the most important artists of his

day. He was friends with D.H. Lawrence and the two of them set up a publishing firm to publish the novelist's books. However, since both men were volatile, the friendship and the firm foundered. Before he fell out with Lawrence entirely, Peter married an artist's model he had met at the Café Royal called Minnie Channing. He called her 'Puma' because she had a ferocious temper.

She was a beautiful, lithe woman, and before long Peter had tired of her. The day Jean arrived at the cottage, the first thing Puma said to her was that she would have to attend to household tasks the following day. Puma was asserting her authority. Immediately, Jean was placed in a role she did not see as hers. She resented this. Adrian showed her her bedroom in which he had placed a jug of honeysuckle. He told her he had walked miles to find it. That night, he obeyed silently when she told him to go to his own bed.

In her short story, 'Till September, Petronella', Jean describes Petronella deflecting her admirer's advances by claiming tiredness or depression. Adrian also wrote about their relationship. In his account he writes about an intriguing young woman – languid and lovely – who frustrated him. He describes her combing her long, fair hair for hours on end in her bedroom. She spent most of the day sitting at her dressing table playing with a make-up box packed with lotions and lipsticks. She applied her make-up as though in a trance. When he persuaded her to leave her bedroom for a walk in the gently rolling fields he describes her as teetering painfully on long, slim legs, like a new-born colt in a diaphanous gown. His proposals of tough rambles among the hills, or a bathe in the nearby stream or riding pillion on his motorcycle filled her with horror.

By the second day, the atmosphere, which had been tense from the start, had soured. Adrian was angry with Jean for not allowing him to sleep with her. Peter and Puma, who every night made noisy, sado-masochistic love, were nursing their own quarrel. Jean was in no mood to be obliging, or make compromises. They were pacifists, which might explain why she became aggressively pro-war. On the third night, they refused to eat in the same room as her.

Peter liked to shock people. Adrian told a story about him spotting a Salvation Army officer walking up the street with a begging cup. She was knocking on his neighbours' doors. He swiftly undressed and answered her knock at the door naked. He was holding a chamber pot with the same supplicatory gesture. He enlivened his guests' stay in the countryside by taking a motorbike ride at great speed around the village in the middle of the night, naked. All four wondered why the villagers wouldn't talk to them.

In Jean's story, she describes a young woman falling in love with this beautiful man with classic, straight-boned features and the kind of scathing humour that hypnotises its victims. He was passionately fond of cats. So was Jean.

In *Women in Love* D.H. Lawrence described Warlock as a 'heavy, broken beauty'. He described Puma's eyes as containing 'a look of knowledge of evil, dark and indomitable'. As well as appearing as Halliday in *Women in Love* and in Jean's short story, Peter would feature in other friends' novels. He is Coleman in Aldous Huxley's *Antic Hay*, and Giles Revelstoke in Robertson Davies' *A Mixture of Frailties*. Osbert Sitwell gave him a walk-on part in one of his novels.

On the fourth night, she heard Peter whistling the love duet from Wagner's *Tristan und Isolde* to Puma. This was the moment she fell in love with him. She was so enraptured she even let Adrian kiss her.

Peter did not really like women. His mother had absented herself from his life. The sexual hold that women had over him was something he resented. His need to reject what he desired was overwhelming. The only way he could convey his feelings was by provoking similar feelings of frustration and resentment in others. In this way the little cottage was soon rocking with anger. Puma was angry because Peter consistently frustrated her need for love while at the same time seducing her with exquisite love songs. He only really responded to her when she needled him. He positively liked it when she attacked him with her penknife.

During this brief holiday one thing drew them together and that was their anger with Jean: she would not respond to their friend's advances and they could see that he was suffering. Jean meanwhile drifted around the house, withdrawn and submissive.

'Don't look as if you'd lost a shilling and found a sixpence,' Adrian commented. He also told her to develop a thicker skin and sharper claws. But all she could think about was Peter's resemblance to a plaster cast of a Greek statue – the head of a beautiful man – she had seen in Poynter's studio months ago. When Poynter left the studio for a moment she writes about dropping her pose, crossing the room and kissing the statue on the lips. She recoiled in fright at how cold the statue was and how desperate she was. Peter was as immovable as that statue. On the fifth night of their holiday, Jean was reduced to writing she loved him on a piece of paper over and over again. She told him in writing that she had kissed him once although he would never know it. It is no surprise after her self-abasing idolatry of Lancey that she should turn Peter Warlock into a Greek god.

Her hosts were rapidly tiring of her and dropping many hints that it was time for her to leave. She refused to heed them. But she heard them mock her voice: Adrian said that this strange girl from the Caribbean had a voice that 'offended our musical ears beyond endurance'. It was 'of a most unfortunate timbre, something between a high-pitched pipe and a nasal whine peculiar to certain transatlantic regions'. She was so mortified by their distaste for her accent that she started to whisper. She would speak in a whisper for the rest of her life.

In her old age, she would make a friend called Alexis Lykiard. He wrote a memoir of their friendship. He describes her relationship with Peter Warlock and her courage in writing a short story about him some twenty years later.

'For such a fascinating and gifted reprobate to assume Jean was just another flighty piece was a cruel wound. That such a genuinely musical talent, perhaps even a potential new love, should dismiss her very voice, was equivalent to writing her off altogether, whether as woman or artist. It says much for Jean that she could tell the story so soberly and sombrely, frank without glib hindsight, and facing up as she always did to her deepest insecurities and disappointments. Unmusical, unsociable, unattractive; the forty-four-year-old Jean stared hard at the worst image of a bygone self.'

In this short story, she says something, too, about war. It is not spoken, but the sense of impending doom – of a summer's holiday, a fool's paradise, about to be exploded by larger events– is written into the dynamics that spark and fizz between the characters.

She left the Cheltenham cottage to the relief of everyone and went back to Bloomsbury. Her boarding-house in Torrington Square was so seedy it rented rooms by the hour. She was the only 'pseudo-English' person there. But the other lodgers were warm and inviting, and in their foreignness, fun. There were three Greek men involved in the tobacco trade, an Italian woman who was called 'Signorina' to her face and 'Macaroni' behind her back, a South

American couple who were dancers and a family of Belgian refugees.

As usual Jean did not get on with the landlady, who made her dislike of Jean quite clear by being sarcastic about the quantity of hot baths Jean took. But the flighty young woman ignored her. This only made her more irritated. Tempers were reaching a pitch. Jean, like Warlock, was learning to thrive on conflict. At last, one morning, the Belgian husband told the landlady to leave the girl alone. Smiling at Jean, he pointed to an empty chair beside him. His wife spoke no English but looked on cheerfully as he told Jean their story. Camille was a university man, researching Japanese No theatre, and had been given a temporary job at the Belgian-Congo bank in London. He and his family befriended Jean, and every Saturday she was invited to their room for coffee and great slabs of bread and butter. In their congenial company and shabby room she would meet other Belgians and, once, an Icelandic poet. There were lots of Belgians in London at this time. By the end of the war there would be 240,000 throughout the country.

In the late autumn of 1917 Jean noticed a young man sitting in the corner of Camille's room staring at her. Her friend introduced him as Jean Lenglet. They talked a little and he invited her to lunch the following day.

They sat in a Soho restaurant, the girl from Dominica and the quiet young Walloon. Most women know what to do in these situations; they have conversational gambits. Jean tried one: she looked round the room to pick out a middle-aged woman to laugh at. The idea being that the man would be made aware of the attractions of his companion in comparison to the woman being mocked. Jean thought it an unpleasant habit but gave it a go anyway. Lenglet asked her why she was laughing at the woman. 'She's an ordinary woman, just like anyone else.'

Refreshed by his honesty, Jean admitted there was nothing
to laugh at. They proceeded to discuss the much more
important matter of passports. Passports, which had just
been introduced, were of critical importance to Lenglet at
this time. Since the war broke out a number of states had
started issuing passports as a means of distinguishing their
citizens from those they considered to be foreign nationals;
there was no free movement between countries without
this document.

Lenglet told her he was in London on a 'diplomatic'
passport, and that he was half-French, half-Dutch and lived
in Paris. He was on his way to Holland, on some kind of
business. He kept it vague and she was too vague to pick
him up on it. After lunch, they went to Bichara, an exclusive
Bond Street parfumier. She was impressed. He bought her
one hundred cigarettes and a bottle of scent. He told her
there was another branch of Bichara in Paris, in the Chaussée
d'Antain. Perhaps he sensed that talk of Paris would seduce
her. While he talked she was examining a bottle of dense,
black kohl powder. He asked if she would like that, too.
She would. He bought it for her. As they stood outside
the shop and he hailed a taxi she supposed it was payback
time. He would want to kiss her. But he didn't. Instead,
he shook hands and thanked her for coming to lunch. He
sent her in a taxi to Madame Zara's where she told him
she was preparing for a new stage act. His parting shot was
intriguing.

'It is not a good life for you . . . You will never be a great
artiste and otherwise it is not worth it.'

He took her to the Café Royal every night and Camille
joined them. Over dinner, they argued about London.
Suddenly, because the two Belgians disparaged it, she found
herself defending it passionately. In the face of their resistance

she loved the fog and darkness. Like Warlock, she communicated through discord.

Lenglet quoted Verlaine's 'Il pleut dans mon Coeur'.

> The worst pain of all
> Is not to know why,
> Without love and without hate,
> My heart aches so much.

That's me, she thought. She liked this man.

Jean Lenglet was born in Holland on 7 June 1889. His
mother was Dutch and his father was a French-speaking
Belgian, though Lenglet always said he was French. The
Lenglets were 'good people', respectable burghers who owned
a few wool factories. He was educated by the Jesuits and
after the death of his father ran away to Paris. Here he earned
a meagre living as a freelance journalist by day and *chansonnier*
at night, performing in Montmartre at the Chat Noir and
Lapin Agile. He had a yen for adventure. Before he met
Jean, he had been married, had joined the French Foreign
Legion and fought in Africa. He rose to the rank of second
lieutenant and was gassed on the Western Front. This was
the official version that he told everybody. The truth was
that one month after joining the Legion he was declared
unfit for army life. He had never been close to the Western
Front. But his knowledge of languages, especially German,
ensured that he had some use for the French government.
He served with the Deuxième Bureau, the French intelligence
service, and was sent on secret missions inside Germany. He
was a spy.

He was sure of himself, and sceptical of others, and Jean
liked this about him. He commented, usually adversely, on
her clothes, and this enchanted her. He told her she looked

like a Slav and that if she were happy and had someone to look after her she would be charming. She knew this, and she knew how unjust it was that she had no one to take care of her. Lenglet talked about all the things she wanted to hear about and he seemed to be talking from experience.

The landlady threw a fancy dress party for Christmas 1917, so she can't have been that bad. What we do know is that Jean wore her pierrette costume. It was just like Gertie Millar's in *Our Miss Gibbs*. Lenglet took her into the cobblestone courtyard and, under a huge moon, asked her to marry him. She was surprised but at the same time accepted his proposal as inevitable. She was numb and ripe for romance. It didn't really matter where it came from. When he told her they would have to live in Paris, she said yes, she would marry him. He kissed her, 'carefully', she said.

And then he left London. But at least they were engaged. She knew that there was something disreputable about him. But this made her like him even more. He was not a hypo-critical or complacent English bourgeois. He was an outsider, like her, and if he had to scrabble in the gutter to make a living, then he was her *confrère*. Besides, it was more exciting to be with a man who lived on the edges of respectability. Most important of all, he offered the chance of escape. Escape to Paris.

She did not star in Madame Zara's troupe at Christmas because she did not need the theatre any more. While she waited to join John, as she called him, Camille suggested she get a job at the Ministry of Pensions. Along with her other friends and acquaintances Camille was not overjoyed at the news of her engagement. In fact, everyone greeted the news with disbelief and predictions of disaster. Jean insisted that a bright future was waiting for her in Paris, so bright she was prepared to get an ordinary job while she waited for the war to end. The thought of an ordinary job had never before occurred to her, but labour was short and she found it 'surprisingly easy' to get one.

She worked in the Ministry of Pensions for an entire year. She sorted through piles of papers that she learnt to call 'dossiers' and filled in forms, some of them marked 'urgent' in a red pencil, others marked 'most urgent'. She did not pay much attention to what was written in these documents but they seem to have been applications for pensions. She sat in a long, brown room with twenty other girls each at their own table. She did not talk to them much as she had her fantasy of life in Paris to sustain her. When she was not at work, she enjoyed the Gotha bombing raids on London. When she was at work, she enjoyed reading sad stories from applicants. A Welshman wrote 'Out of the depths I call', others wrote of blindness, a weak heart, and a tapeworm contracted in the services of the Empire. The girls were supposed to get through each application quickly but Jean dawdled. She read the sad stories, imagining the lives, picturing a bleak future for her correspondents. She was nearly sacked for it.

She did not care. Life was exciting again, full of risks but underwritten with certainty: she was going to be married. Women were wearing shorter skirts and smoking in public. They had more freedom. Too late for Jean, she was leaving England. The week before she sailed to Holland she wrote to Lancey and told him his cheque was no longer required. The vindication implicit in these words was delightful. The following day she received a note from him. He asked her to join him for lunch at the Piccadilly Grill. Lancey was having a good war, conducting delicate negotiations for the Board of Trade with neutral countries, persuading them to give free passage to British goods and not to trade with

Germany. He was close to the Prime Minister and had been awarded the CBE. He had access to foreign intelligence which was why he wanted to speak to Jean about her fiancé.

Lenglet was not a suitable person, he told her, and he could support this assertion. When John travelled in Holland he was being watched, he associated with questionable types. Some of his friends had been arrested. He was suspected of being a spy.

'If you marry him you'll be taking a very big risk.' But he knew she liked taking risks, and added, 'If anything goes wrong, will you write to me?'

Once he'd put her into a taxi she began to cry.

She set off for Hoek van Holland with just one dress and the coat she was wearing. She had failed to pay her dressmaker for a new outfit. As a penalty, the woman had kept the trunk of Jean's clothes that she was storing for her. She did not care. She was wildly happy, even though Camille, who saw her off, was in tears. On landing in Holland she knelt on the ground and thanked God for taking her away from a world of lawyers' cheques, grey streets and disapproval. She vowed she would never go back.

Chapter 12:

PARIS

On 30 April 1919 Ella Gwendoline Rees Williams married Willem Jean Marie Lenglet in The Hague. She signed herself as being 'without profession'; he said he was a journalist. She gave her age as twenty-four. She was twenty-eight. No photographs exist to tell us what she was wearing, nor does she write about the event in her existing notebooks. Something that is known is that the groom was in fact already married. Furthermore, because he had served in the French Foreign Legion, he had forfeited his right to Dutch citizenship. He was officially a stateless person.

Lenglet was known to the police of three countries, and when he was not living off his wits he used his charm. He was a slim man with lively brown eyes, and he knew how to look at pretty women. In the 1920s Jean wrote a story about her husband, 'The Chevalier of the Place Blanche'. This was a different kind of knight in shining armour. Not a Lancey at all. In this story, Jean describes a man who prides himself on knowing how to please women and how to get money out of them. It was this that had drawn her to him. His life hitherto had been a more successful, though equally reckless, version of hers. Jean enjoyed being close to a man who used deception as a means of survival. It felt like an honour to be present at the moments when he set aside deception. She was proud to be chosen for such rare intimacy, and it gave her a sense of belonging. This belonging was posited on a sense of alienation from the society that had rejected her. The respectable world represented by Lancey, and the artistic world, represented by Peter Warlock, could go to hell.

The witnesses at the wedding were Jacques Proot, a chemist, and Ennemond Bousquet, a singer. It took five glasses of port for Jean to enjoy the reception. The newly married couple stayed in The Hague for a month or so. Jean did not like it. Its rainy skies and grey, damp streets were too close to London but lacked the intensity, variety and bustle. The newlyweds' domestic arrangements were uncomfortable. They slept on a mattress in a flat above Jacques' chemist's shop. Soon Jean was pregnant. They moved to Amsterdam, then Belgium, Lenglet trying to raise money all the way. Finally they were on a train to Calais with just one passport, Jean's, between them. She could not stop crying. Here she was, with no money, pregnant by a man whom she had known only for a few weeks before waiting a year to marry. He was secretive and surly and he had no documents to show the frontier guards. Lenglet asked her to stop crying, so she sat in the lavatory, quietly despairing. At Calais they spoke to a waiter who sold Lenglet a forged passport. They were on the up again. Jean sat in the bar drinking absinthe as the business was conducted. She caught sight of herself in the mirror. She was thin and haggard. Fancy going to Paris looking like that.

As soon as they arrived, in the autumn of 1919, she fell in love. It was a beautiful morning when they reached Paris, the air was clean and bright. They sat at a pavement café and Lenglet left her for a few hours while he arranged their accommodation. She had never been so happy, sitting in the sun eating ravioli and drinking wine. The light, so unlike London's, seemed tinged with pink. It was the city that her father had spoken lovingly of, that was celebrated by the

poets that Mother Mount Calvary had introduced her to –
a city more knowing than London. The language that she
was hearing was the original of Francine's lilting patois. She
was sitting in a café in the capital city of the country that
had seduced Dominica and been defeated by the English,
whose religiosity was more romantic, whose sense of style
was innate: it was her déjà-vu world. She had always known
it would be like this. She would always be faithful to Paris.
When Lenglet returned she saw by the look on his face that
he had got money.

He found them a hotel in Rue Lamartine, near Gare du
Nord, in Montmartre. He seemed to have changed; just being
in Paris had wrought this change – optimism, generosity
came back to him and a lightness of heart. He told her that
he was owed money for a song he had written. It was called
'La Charme de La Femme':

> C'est un rien
> Plus leger que le vent
> Ce charme

The end of the War to End All Wars brought many writers
and artists to Paris in anticipation of a mysterious, new,
modern era. Official taste in the city was still dominated by
the past: Anatole France, Impressionism, Symbolism, and
Nationalism. But on the streets, the poet Pierre Mac Orlan
called the spectacle before him *le fantastique social*. He was
writing about the exploits of the new freebooters, pirates,
and gentlemen of fortune. Paris was host to Balkan refugees,
white Russians, people without a country. Those without
money became waiters, taxi-cab drivers, drug dealers, or
vagrants. Those who had managed to salvage their valuables
made a run from reality into nightclubs and artificial stimulants.

What they all had in common was what they lacked: a sense of belonging and of the security of living in a world with a future.

Jean's husband had a dubious past as a singer at the Lapin Agile, a famous bar in the notorious Quartier Latin where Francis Carco, Max Jacob, and Poulbot, the creator of the Montmartre ragamuffin, had gathered to eat and drink. Lenglet would tell her about the cabaret bars where street singers and gangsters drank on house credit. He was sucked into the way of life of those who sit around talking and waiting for some miraculous good fortune, or big deal. No one liked working hard. Those nights when he had some ready *sous* for food and drink were occasions for grandiose dreams. Hangovers brought him back to earth again – sullen and bleak.

But Jean was happy, and everything was going to be all right. Even when, on that very first night, she and Lenglet had woken to find the walls of their room crawling with bugs. Lenglet became angry, but she did not care. She wrapped herself in the pink eiderdown and went back to sleep. The room was perfect – it had running water and there were pictures – Gaby Deslys, a dancing girl who introduced striptease to Paris, and Huguette Duflos, an actress with the Comedie Française – hanging on the walls. She could imagine she was in the Lapin Agile. If Lenglet would not take her there, at least he told her about the little room with a low ceiling and battered sculptures and drawings damaged by the damp. She heard about Frédé the barman, and Pierre Mac Orlan, about adventures and Cubism. She was here in this exciting city. The bugs only appeared at night.

They had a *flamme bleue* to keep them warm and to cook with, and a wrought-iron balcony on which they sat to drink white wine and watch the street. Women sat under parasols

Jean in Paris c. 1920

mending their stockings and peeling potatoes. She delighted in their vigour and the city's verve; its logic and perfume, the sense of line and of colour. When she drank wine with Lenglet on the balcony and looked up at the lights of Paris she believed in the value of illusions. She believed in all sorts of things.

Money was scarce. Lenglet was working at something but his hours were irregular and he evaded her half-hearted questions. Every morning Jean went to La Rotonde on the Boulevard du Montparnasse, and sat for hours over a single cup of coffee. She was poor but no one minded. She leafed through *Le Figaro* looking for a job, watching the shop girls who passed her on the streets in their silk stockings and sleek skirts. Smart young Parisiennes sprayed themselves with

Ambre perfume and Fleur de Peche. They wore skin cream made of crushed almonds. Paul Poiret – the designer-king of lushly feminine fashions – said in an interview with *Le Figaro*, 'women were beautiful and architectural, like the prow of a ship. Now they all resemble undernourished telephone operators.'

Finally, she found an advertisement asking for a young woman to speak English to children. She went to the address – rue Rabelais, near the Champs-Elysées – and found a large *hotel particulier*. It stood back from the street in a courtyard on its own, as though it were hiding. A man with a striped apron opened the door and ushered her into an ante-chamber. When Germaine Richelot, the children's aunt, walked into the room Jean realised that here was someone shyer than herself. Germaine did not wear make-up, dressed simply, and had a gentle face and nervous manner. Germaine took one look at Jean's shabby dress and protruding stomach and offered her the job. Her sister, Madame Bragadier, although more businesslike in her appraisal, agreed with Germaine. The pregnant young Englishwoman started straight away. The children were brought in to meet her, the adults left the room, and not knowing what else to do, Jean told them the story of Joan of Arc. She was the woman, she said, 'who chased the English out of France'. The children, though polite, were sceptical. It could be very hard getting people to believe you.

The house was beautiful. Its occupants, Professor and Madame Richelot, their three grown-up daughters and four grandchildren were without affectations or prejudice and eminently sophisticated and artistic. Jean had never met a family like them. She lunched with them every day and listened, amazed and delighted, as they spoke in English and German on her favourite subjects: books, words, and grammar. They were passionately involved in their discussion but never descended into strife. Germaine's father wore the rosette of the Légion d'Honneur in his buttonhole, collected madonnas and tapestries, china, books and pottery horses. One of the madonnas smiled so tenderly that Jean thought she was smiling for her. Germaine told her that it was a thirteenth-century icon and that madonnas were always depicted smiling.

Each room spoke of wealth and discernment. Madame Bragadier was one of the best amateur pianists in Paris and the sound of Bach wafted through the apartments. After lunch, Germaine would make sure that Jean rested on a chaise longue. She placed a rug over her and enjoined her to sleep. She brought her a novel by Dickens. In the blue twilight of that quiet house Jean did not need to read or sleep. She lay awake watching the trees and the sky and the day slowly extinguishing itself through the window. Far away she heard the piano being played and the voice of a governess gently instructing children.

It was October 1919 and she was six months pregnant. The next three months were to be among the happiest of her life. Every morning she woke at 7.30 a.m. Lenglet made them both a cup of hot chocolate on the *flamme bleue*. She took the tram to the church of St Augustin and men stood up for her – '*Passe, femme sacrée*'. She allowed the four polite, perfect children to guide her around the Champs-Elysées. They talked to her all the while in exquisite English until they insisted that she sit and rest on her favourite bench. ('Now sit here, Mrs Ella.') She loved their afternoon strolls. She watched the comings and goings of Paris. And after those long, luxurious lunches during which books and words and grammar were discussed with ingenuous erudition she would be treated to delicious creamy coffee from the most delicate bone china cups. Jean tried all her life to find cups as delicate as those. She never succeeded.

She came to love the Richelots – for a while. But most of all she loved Germaine. Her first and last real friend, she always said, Germaine was thin, sallow and anxious to do the best for everyone. She helped those in need. She was rich and gave her money away. She gave impoverished young women jobs that did not need doing. She used the bus instead of the Daimler. She never married because she was too shy and yet she longed to ride a motorcycle. Although she was shy, she was elegant and never gauche. Despite the fact that her gloves were cotton and her dresses plain she knew all the people of fashion and what they were wearing. She just did not care enough to be like them. She was kind and good and lived in the house that came to represent Parisian refinement for Jean. She felt safe there, knowing that in Germaine 'the pure spring of goodness untainted' resided.

The last time she went to the Richelots she had her first experience of pure happiness in adulthood. The children led her to her bench, she sat down and someone smiled at her. She smiled back and felt it then. All the happiness of the past three months sat deep within her. She was radiant. It was all the more strange and wonderful because she had nothing to be happy about: no money and no idea what to do with the baby. Later she wondered if, just as your hair becomes more lustrous, your eyes brighter and your skin clearer, this was another trick Nature played on a pregnant woman.

Each evening she returned to a more sinuous Paris. Back to the precipitous, fifth-floor balcony where Lenglet's friends – women with subtly made-up faces and delightfully dangerous men – gathered over carafes of iced wine. She was safe at the Richelots – they were rich and kind and able to protect and educate her – but she was not free there. At home she was free but she was not safe.

On 29 December 1919 William Owen Lenglet was born. Three weeks later he died of pneumonia.

Jean writes of the turmoil of childbirth in a short story called 'Learning to be a Mother'. As she herself admitted, she was lucky; she had the money to pay for a room of her own. She could moan in private. At some point during the delivery she asked the *sage-femme* to turn the light out – it was hurting her eyes – but could not remember the word for light. She cried with exhaustion. She remembered the word for anaesthetic, but the *sage-femme* said 'la la la' before turning away. The desperate wordlessness of this experience, the brute force of her body doing its work inspired her, perversely, to write. When the *sage-femme* held up her son for the first time all she could think about was the tremendous thirst she felt. She had nothing to offer him.

In 'Learning to be a Mother' Jean describes one of her husband's friends visiting her. Colette had all the qualities Jean admired: she was smart, beautiful and read Tolstoy. If she only read Tolstoy for his soporific qualities, no matter, at least she read him. She was a true *Montmartroise* – stylish and a good sport. She cooed at the baby as form dictated, and Jean accounted for her own lack of enthusiasm by saying she had wanted a girl. Not 'another *pauvre miserable*', said Colette. Unwanted girls, not wanted by their mothers because what is the point of bringing yet another suffering being into the world of scrutinising light and fingers cold as steel? Besides, a girl is someone who will supplant you in youth and beauty. But a boy can bring you power.

In her story she describes the naming ceremony as being a matter of finding the right name that would admit her son to society and its games. Father, husband, brother were honoured; authority and paternity affirmed. He had been given his place in the world. She did not like her baby son;

he had hurt her too much. Luckily he slept most of the time so he did not intrude on her misery any further. When she was not sleeping herself, she read about the demi-monde of Montmartre, the world she admired and feared, not the hospital ward and the rigours of maternity. The *sage-femme* recognised her lack of enthusiasm for the 'little animal' in his cot and told her in time she would learn to love him. Meanwhile another woman was screaming in another room. 'The less they pay the more they scream,' said the *sage-femme*. Jean could only think of the lies people tell about motherhood. Meanwhile the *femme sacrée* in the next room was helpless with pain. It was a horrible world.

She slept well, but once in the night she heard a little wail. She picked the baby up and held him in her arms. She rocked him, which stopped the mournful sound. Far away she heard the noises of the city and felt warm and happy. She looked down at William Owen and saw that his eyes were open. They were the same almond shape as hers, and sad like hers, too. Perhaps he was sad because his mother had never kissed him, she writes in her story. The nurse had wrapped him in a tight papoose so that only his head peeked out. She decided she would dress him differently when she took him home.

At home, Lenglet had prepared a cradle by the door that led on to the balcony. They laid William Owen in it and Lenglet spent hours watching him, smoking his pipe. It was January but they kept him warm enough and he hardly ever cried. He was a pretty baby and solemn. Eventually Jean became concerned at his quietness. Then he stopped eating. She took him to a doctor and explained she had no money. He directed her to the Hospice des Enfants Assistés. She left William Owen there. She started worrying. Her anxiety centred on the baby's need for baptism. She describes herself as being unable to bear the thought of him being crushed by the world as remorselessly as it was crushing her. Lenglet, by now, must have tired of her anxieties. He was an atheist, and impatient with her sudden need to get the child baptised. But it seemed the most important thing on earth to her. It is as though knowing that she could not give him a good start in life, she wanted him to have the best start for death. On her return from the Hospice, frantic as she was with worry, Lenglet rushed out to buy two bottles of champagne. It was the only thing that would placate her. They sat on the balcony with the two bottles; a girlfriend came round. Soon Jean was laughing. The next morning the new parents received a telegram informing them that the baby had died at half past seven the previous evening, exactly the time they had been drinking champagne and laughing.

He was buried in a cemetery at Bagneux, south of Paris. The burial cost 130 francs, sixty centimes for a carriage, coffin and cross. And the nuns at the hospice had baptised him before he died. The god of the Anglo-Saxon bourgeoisie has little in common with the all-forgiving Bon Dieu of the French. The nuns were kind to Jean, who needed absolution from a creeping sense of guilt. She did not want him to die but she had not really wanted this baby. She kept the receipt for his burial for the rest of her life. She would never forget his almond eyes looking at her.

With the baby gone, life was at least less difficult. The Richelots, on hearing her news and guessing at Lenglet's precarious financial state, procured a job for him. The Inter-allied Commission was overseeing the disarmament process in the former Austro-Hungarian empire. They needed staff and Lenglet was a linguist. Germaine used her contacts to get him a temporary passport and smoothed his way into the post of secretary-interpreter for Lieutenant Colonel Miyake,

a Japanese member of the Commission. It is not known if
Lenglet spoke Japanese, but French, German, Dutch and
English were certainly at his command. He left immediately,
leaving Jean alone in Paris for a few weeks. She was adrift
with grief, numb with it. Germaine saw her every day, lending
her money to buy dresses. She took her to the cinema, warning her about the perils of alcohol but indulging her by
drinking champagne with her.

Germaine and Madame Bragadier had tears in their eyes
as they saw Jean board the *Orient Express*. But she was excited
and happy. She had forgotten everything. She was on a journey. The sulphuric smell of smoke from the engine, the
powerful, swinging gait of its procession across Europe. The
smooth, panelled corridors, millionaires slumbering behind
lacquered doors; the *wagon-lit* swaying and rattling, the tables
in the dining car laid with monogrammed china. A cut-glass
decanter. Linen napkins. Silver cutlery. Faultless service. She
was going to Vienna.

London, Paris, Vienna, the closer she got to these cities
the less real they were.

Chapter 13:

VIENNA

In spring 1920 the Interallied Commission was overseeing the disarmament process in the former Austro-Hungarian Empire. Jean's husband was employed as an interpreter for the Japanese delegation, though he spoke no Japanese. In April 1920 Jean, or Ella Lenglet as she was known, joined him in Vienna. The rest of her family were similarly dispersed. Her older sister Minna was living in England. Her mother, sister Brenda and Auntie B would soon be leaving Dominica to join Minna. The four women would set up home together in Ealing, west London. Jean's brother Owen was living in Australia, and her oldest brother, Edward, was pursuing a military career in India.

Jean arrived in Vienna at the end of its heyday. The Austro-Hungarian Empire was finished. Aristocrats sat in their empty mansions; their women – the ugly ones, that is, took in washing. The pretty ones tried their luck as *mundane Tanzerinnen*. There was not much to eat in this defeated city. The streets smelt, she said 'of lilacs, of drains and of the past'. Vienna's grand boulevards embodied the rigid grace of a city planned by the bourgeoisie. Characteristically, in 'Vienne', a short story, Jean writes about its outsiders: the Japanese commissioners with their rigid ideologies, the dancers, giddy with the charm of being in on the end of an era, and the black marketeers, who had picked up on the sense of abandonment, and were squirrelling away small fortunes. A chancer like Lenglet was in his element. He kept himself busy, juggling

identities as he tried his arm at trading in currencies, taking
dinner at the Sacher, and entertaining Japanese delegates at
nightclubs and music halls. Jean watched, from a position of
security for once, pretty girls and boys offering themselves
for money. Vienna was the most entertained she had ever
been. She was intrigued, the girls, girls, girls – they were so
lovely – and the men – with their graceful manners – who
preyed on them.

The commission found them a large, luxurious flat on the
top floor of a house in the Favoritenstrasse, in the Fourth
District. The sitting room was rather dour, with pictures of
Emperor Franz Joseph and the house's owners, the von
Heuskes, brooding over the heavy dark furniture, but the
bedroom was light and pretty with a piano, Bohemian glass
and low tables for coffee. It had the feel of a boudoir. Jean
was finally given the chance to be the elegant woman Lenglet
had promised she'd be before they had married. A woman
who had time to be charming because she was being looked
after. She wore her hair shiny and dark, in a waved bob.
Her eyebrows sloped in a crescent, following the line of her
almond eyes. Her face was slim and finely boned now that
she had lost the puppy fat that had made her a delectable
Gaiety Girl. She wore dramatic, large stones on her slim
fingers and soft fabrics clung to her body.

The von Heuskes were, like their living room and the
bedroom, sometimes gloomy and disapproving, at other times
elegant and gracious. She found it difficult to reconcile the
two sides to them; either they were nice or they weren't. If
they disapproved of her, as they did when she brought a
nightclub dancer to the flat, they could not also be nice.
Madame Heuske complained that the girl had bumped into
her daughter on the stairs. Jean apologised to Madame but
the hypocrisy of bourgeois morality did not drive her to

distraction as it had before and would again later. Right now she could play the game because she could afford to. She felt secure.

The Lenglets shared the flat with another secretary, André. He was a Parisian and obsessed with women – the dancer was his conquest. Jean was enjoying his company. They dined out every night, and went to louche nightclubs. She put André in 'Vienne'. He would live and die for women, she said, as his father had. She was enthralled by his compulsion towards love and death, sex and gambling. It was so interesting to observe it from a distance. His hair was carefully waved once a week and he wore his suits cut high in the waist to disguise his shortness. She called him a satyr. But he was without pretence or shame, so she liked him. And he often got snubbed. When she saw him being manipulated by a beautiful, self-assured woman she welcomed him, her *confrère*, her 'brother doormat', in a world of boots.

One night they were at a club called the Parisien when she saw a girl with long, slim legs who danced with such grace and spirit and whose elfin face was so exquisite that it broke her heart to think that this fairy could grow old and die. All the men were enchanted, though André fretted that she would cost too much. The next time Jean went there she found out that the girl, despite her popularity, had left without notice. She was next heard of in Budapest where she'd married a barber. Some of these girls' enthusiasm for life was beautiful. Because they were young and lovely life was good to them. It was a joy to watch them revel in their power to love and inspire love in return.

There were so many pretty women in Vienna. The Japanese called them 'war material'; spoils to be enjoyed. These men were interesting to Jean for their contempt for the Europeans. They dismissed the whole continent, except the Germans, whose army they respected and whose custom of keeping women in the home they approved. She was fascinated and horrified by their attitudes towards women: the disdain one felt towards his faithful girlfriend – for being faithful; she would not sleep with his visitor from Japan, who was a prince. And yet, another gave a huge sum of money to his dancing girl when she was diagnosed with consumption. So you could never tell.

Madame Ella Lenglet was the wife of a mercurial conman who, in the aftermath of war, had chanced upon a respectable occupation. It would not last. For her thirtieth birthday the Japanese delegation gave Jean a lavish supper party. Soup and hors d'oeuvres, veal and pheasant, ices, cheese, coffee, liqueurs. Everyone signed Jean's menu, which she kept for the rest of her life. At the top are the names Ella and Lenglet, with dozens of elegant raffish scrawls then three neat and proud signatures: Lieutenant Colonel Miyake; Lieutenant Colonel Oyaizu; Capitaine Oshima, who became Japanese Ambassador to Germany during the Second World War. After it, he was sentenced to life imprisonment as a war criminal.

In the spring of 1921 Lenglet was throwing his weight around. He had money, they were acquiring staff and deferential hangers-on. They had a car, a chauffeur, a maid. Jean had flowers, dresses and rings. She had entered what she calls in her memoir the 'spending phase'. Lenglet was making money 'on the "change"': selling currencies in an over-inflated market was highly profitable. Just one more deal, he kept saying, and they would be quite, quite rich. Jean was thrilled and her relationship to money altered; it became an obsession. When you have been poor for so long and all you want is the accoutrements of wealth, the dresses in the shop windows, the hats, the cars, the comforts, the compliments, the attentions of your inferiors, dinners at the Sacher, and you suddenly have them, you just want more and more. The envious regard of other women, the open admiration of men, went to her head. She was bursting with joy. She made her face up to look like a doll; she put drops in her eyes to dilate the pupils. She wore dresses as light as a feather and fresh as daisies. And she had the 'luxury of a soul': she could afford to think and consider the needs of others. To be magnanimous and dispassionate, not to have to care so deeply about herself that she could not care for other people: this was luxury.

One thing she knew: she could never be poor again with courage or dignity. If she had to deal with poverty again, it would destroy her. She would spend her last francs, yen, lire, krönen, sterling, whatever Lenglet could find for her, on a good meal in a smart restaurant and then shoot herself. She would not allow hope to cheat her into thinking that there was one last person to clutch on to, who would help her. A few years later she would be writing about this period of life as though it were her happiest. But whenever she was happy, thoughts of death and suicide intruded. It is as though a morbid stasis set in when life got too comfortable. She only felt alive when she was anxious.

She sought reassurance, but Lenglet did not like to be questioned. It spoilt his luck. And when she felt fearful her rage returned; rage against women, who competed so viciously with each other, whose smiles were false and whose jealousies were humiliating, and rage against men; the stupid, smiling men you spent hours dressing up for, the prize that all the other women wanted – their attention – to be rendered worthless by their stupidity, their brutishness. It was all empty.

In the summer of 1921 the Commission moved to Budapest. Jean was feeling so flush she made a brief visit to London, where she stayed at the Berkeley Hotel and had lunch with Lancey. She also visited her mother, her sisters Brenda and Minna, and Auntie B. Their move from a crumbling estate in Dominica to a red-brick semi in Ealing does not merit any mention in her writings. Neither does she write of the welcome she received from her family or of their circumstances. Jean would always feel disapproval from the women in her family. She rarely mentions her mother except when her mother was on her deathbed. But now she could at least tell her family, and Lancey too, that her husband was rich and she was pregnant. The big risk she had taken with this marriage had paid off. She was vindicated. It was the only time she enjoyed London.

She enjoyed Budapest even more than Vienna. Jean and Lenglet dined in the countryside outside Buda, then returned to the heart of the city for nightclubs and dance halls. They listened to tzigane orchestras; the girls were even lovelier, the gypsy rhythms they danced to wilder, more vicious and heart-rending than Viennese waltzes. In the midst of this scheming, charming city, tzigane music played endless variations on a plaintive theme – a nomadic culture that crossed borders – a close-knit people with an adventurous spirit for tasting the unfamiliar and getting the most out of life. London, Paris, Vienna, Budapest – one city led to another in a voyage into form and style. She experienced them from the distance of the foreigner – never belonging, always observing. What she found universally was the indifference of urban society towards the individual.

But when she was alone she sat on a silk striped sofa in rooms paid for by the Commission. She was replete with money – proof of her husband's effectiveness – and pregnant – proof of his affections. Long afternoons passed as she wallowed in placid maternity. She felt as though everything she had ever wanted in life was being drawn irresistibly to her. She was ready to receive it. All she had to do was lie there.

One day Lenglet told her that if anyone called from the Verkehrsbank she was to say he was not in. A very insistent man did call from the bank but she told him Monsieur was not there.

Ten days later, in October 1921, on that same striped sofa, Lenglet was sitting with a gun in his hand. Four years later she wrote in 'Vienne' that she cried out, 'How horribly unkind you are to frighten me!' He told her, as shamefaced as a naughty schoolboy, that he had lost money, 'other people's money', and, worse, 'the Commission's money'.

He talked about killing himself, and that he would leave her 4,000 francs and her jewellery. She told him to fight like a man. If he killed himself – she looked him straight in the eye – he knew what would happen to her. He looked away. He must rouse himself. They must escape. As Jean grew more convinced that this was their only option – to run away and leave this horrible mess behind them – his resolve returned. A grim determination to cut his losses. She was right; they had to flee. He was in charge again. They had a brisk supper – roast duck and two bottles of Pomeroy – in their room. By the second bottle he was absurdly cheerful. She loved him for these changes of mood; mercurial, un-predictable, un-English. They hatched a plan, speaking in whispers all the while, creeping round the flat like children preparing for a midnight feast. They packed their bags, and at half past six in the morning tiptoed down the stairs, woke the chauffeur and ordered him to drive them out of Budapest. They were going to Czechoslovakia.

The morning was clear and blue. The car was speeding towards a new future, full of risk and uncertainty, and Jean fantasised about her return to Budapest. She describes this fantasy in 'Vienne'. She gathers Lenglet's debtors around a long, boardroom table. She hands them envelopes of cash and gives each one a receipt to sign. She is the hard-nosed businesswoman, stern and efficient, settling her accounts. She is not a chancer on the run. But at four o'clock in the morning, she woke up crying. Nothing Lenglet could do would comfort her. Not even the pearl necklace he suddenly procured from nowhere. She knew that they were travelling further and further without advancing.

On 22 May 1922 Jean gave birth to her second baby in a small town near Brussels. But, although it was a little girl, motherhood was not different this time round: all she could think about was money. When Maryvonne was two weeks old she left her in the clinic and went to London to borrow money. Lancey, as usual, obliged. She rejoined Lenglet – they sent money to the clinic – and went to Paris.

The Viennese phase of her life – the money, the nightclubs, the successful husband – was over.

Chapter 14:

THE MANNEQUIN

In February 1922, James Joyce's *Ulysses* was published in Paris. In August, Jean and Lenglet returned to their hotel on rue Lamartine. On 17 October, the French civil courts sent a process-server to the hotel, summoning Lenglet to 'réintegrer le domicile conjugal'. He declined and divorce proceedings from his French wife began.

In *Paris by Night* the photographer Brassai counted sixty different expressions for prostitution, thirty for pimp, twenty for brothel, a dozen for madam, forty for male homosexual and six for lesbian. Words for brothels included *maison close, maison de tolérance, maison publique, maison dilutions*, or just *maison*. Slang terms included *bordel, boxon, bobinard, magasin de fesses*. And the girls inside them were classified according to type: going down the scale, *nanas* were fat girls, *punaises* were bedbugs, *morues* were codfish. The girls outside them were *fille galante* — streetwalker, *cocotte* — a step above, and *fille en cheveux* — a woman of the pavement of the lowest kind.

Jean was entering a phase in her life when such categorisations mattered acutely. She and Lenglet had the same room in the same hotel on the grey and dusty busy thoroughfare, rue Lamartine. They had ended up where they had begun. Only this time they had left a baby behind them, and Lenglet had the Commission and a team of French solicitors on his trail. The horror of being caught in the due processes of law caused him to flee Paris. Almost as soon as they arrived there, Jean was the one left behind.

At first, Germaine Richelot came to the rescue. She gave Jean money, bought her clothes, fed her and kept her company. Her generosity and compassion knew no bounds. This made Jean suspicious. She must want something. The second friend to come to the rescue was Mrs H. Pearl Adam, a journalist Jean had met at a tea party in London years before. Mrs Adam had been a hard-working professional since the age of seventeen. She was eight years older than Jean and married to George Adam, the *Times* correspondent in Paris. She invited Jean to stay with them in their flat on rue Taitbout. It felt nice to be sitting on a comfortable sofa again, sipping tea. What was more, Mrs Adam cultivated an atmosphere of literary industry. She was aware of current trends in journalism and the more recherché developments in prose. Jean was well situated for an aspiring writer – not that she would have considered herself to be one. But the lifeline Mrs Adam was about to throw would help Jean start her career.

First things first, though: in November, she felt strong enough to attend to her daughter. She fetched Maryvonne from the clinic in Brussels. Everyone, the Richelots, Lenglet, Mrs Adam, urged her to give the baby up for adoption. She refused. She knew it made sense to give the child up – the father was facing a prison sentence and had absconded, and she was temperamentally unsuited to commitment of any kind. But Jean did not want to give her child up to strangers. She wanted to care for her, even though she knew she could not. Mrs Adam had mother and baby to stay in her flat for a while but eventually Jean had to put Maryvonne in a clinic. Germaine paid for it. Before the child was taken away, someone, either Germaine or Mrs Adam, took a photo of Jean and her baby. Jean held Maryvonne wrapped in a blanket on the balcony of the Adams' flat.

Now she had to earn a living. She tried to teach English but could not think of anything to say. She tried to be a companion to children but kept getting lost and making them cry. The only thing she could do was be still and silent. She became an artist's model again. This time the artist was an English sculptress called Violet Dreschfeld, a classic British gentlewoman, competent and stoical. Violet was tall and gaunt and, because of this, unloved. She took Jean out to the bars of Montparnasse where they met with other English gentlewomen of Violet's acquaintance. Jean could not help noticing Violet's close scrutiny of the painted and perfumed 'femme' she could never be. Not everyone could meet such high standards as the 'femme', but Miss Dreschfeld exercised tolerance towards the aspirant 'petites femmes'. They were less self-assured in their efforts to please, and so easier for men to pick off as they sat, with darkened eyelids, in the café-bar. In short, since she could not stir his desire, Miss Dreschfeld identified with the predatory male.

Jean did not impress her – she was too washed up and desperate. In turn, Jean pitied Violet. She intuited that Violet knew in her heart that she was just another mediocre painter feeding off the Parisian demi-monde. She did not mind too much being the object of Violet's disapproval. She was used to it. Her family made it forcibly felt, largely because, one suspects, Jean was so obviously vulnerable. Implicitly, she asked to be rescued; at the very least she wanted special treat-ment. What she took for disapproval may well have been impatience.

Whereas strength of character puzzled and confused Jean, she could relate to vulnerability. Violet was a woman who was deeply insecure about her appearance and her vocation. So what Jean responded to was a defenceless woman. But Violet had Englishness and financial security on her side, and very few want to be reminded of their fragility. Jean, who could not hide what she believed, alienated this kind and sensible woman. She lost yet another opportunity of gaining a friend. But she wrote a very moving short story using her knowledge of Violet Dreschfeld to examine the difficulties of being an unattractive woman.

At the age of thirty-two, Jean knew she could not pull off the *jeune fille* act for much longer. She had reached an age where she was able to remove herself from the complex emotions that swirled around her conceptions of male and female. It would be this detachment that created a space in which she could write. Because Jean did not take her beauty for granted she was able to empathise with her less fortunate sisters. Her own beauty was unconventional and affected by her emotional state, so she could not depend on it entirely. Throughout her life she would veer between states of thinness when she was drinking, and plumpness when she was eating. But though she did not always realise it, she was always attractive. Her watchful, slanting eyes and stealthy poise ensured that she stood out. Having just returned to Paris penniless and disgraced, one can imagine that she took to drink. She was thin and she was alone in Paris. When she walked the streets or sat in bars, her head was turned by male attention. It excited and distracted her from the routine insecurity of life with Lenglet. It offered up vistas of how life could be, depending on what each man saw in her. She decided to put her looks to good use. She became a mannequin in a fashion home near place Vendome – a parody of the silent, passive woman.

For a short while at least, it was fun being a mannequin. Couturiers in Paris were aristocrats and they inhabited grand mansions on triumphant boulevards. The house Jean worked in was not one of the great names of fashion but it was still haute couture. She got the job on the strength of her legs, which were shapely and well proportioned. Later, Jean wrote about the fashion house, revelling in the vocabulary of beauty: the specifications, delineations and grades: the *gamine*, the *garçonne*, the *femme fatale*, the *jolie laide*, and her own type, the *jeune fille* – young and vulnerable. On her first day she was assessed by an elderly female dresser as to her grade of attractiveness. She describes the 'professional motherliness' of this woman, preparing the girls for display. The dresser took her through the moves that would best demonstrate the spring-like air of the dresses she would model. Jean scrutinised the girls as closely as Violet the artist had scrutinised her. She listed the colours the girls wore on their lips: Rouge Fascination, Rouge Mandarine, Rouge Andalouse. But the drama of these colours faded in the face of her anxiety. She described herself as being desperate to please. She talked about the needles she felt when the cold eyes of customers turned upon her. When a gentleman buyer smiled at her she was pathetically grateful.

As with the chorus girls, the slang her colleagues spoke was incomprehensible. She longed for someone to show and explain and dictate. She could never keep up with such a fast-moving world. There was too much to take in, and in order to feel safe she needed to understand every element of it. She describes in 'Mannequin' the seamstresses stitching and hemming gowns they would never wear as 'heroically gay'. Like Baudelaire's 'singing slaves', these girls plied their needles behind the scenes creating concoctions for the strut-ting mannequins. She did not last very long at the fashion house. The desire to disappear was too great, the fear of rejection too strong.

Lenglet finally returned to Paris after working as a journalist somewhere in central France. His general uncom-municativeness served to force her further into herself. When he returned to Paris he was still on the run from the police but in an act of foolhardiness took a job at Exprinter, a travel agency. He was trying to keep a low profile, so when he did take Jean out with him it was to some badly lit café where he conducted shady deals with other enigmatic characters. She did not bother listening to their mutterings about documents, artworks, and proofs of authenticity. She preferred not to know when valuable antiques turned up in their hotel room and swiftly disappeared again.

She sat in the cafés of the grand boulevards and watched the people pass by. 'The *grues* are the sellers of illusion of Paris,' she wrote. The *grues* were 'little tarts'. The women Jean would come to write about lived their lives in the margins of respectability, and there were so many of them that their individual fates were lost in the throng.

During his stint as a journalist, Lenglet had been producing articles and stories. Jean chose three to show to Mrs Adam in the hope that she could sell them to a newspaper. One had the couplet, 'If you'd be happy all your lives / See that you take to yourselves no wives' as its punchline. Mrs Adam told her that none of Lenglet's stories was marketable. Then something inspired her to leave her diary with Mrs Adam. If Lenglet's style was stale and contrived, perhaps the rawness and bitter concision of her diary would suffice. She had been writing it since she came back to Paris. It chronicled everything that had happened in London, Paris, Vienna and Budapest. Mrs Adam liked it. It was in the modernist vein. It was formless, wild, had no punctuation but was possessed of a compelling clarity. It described her husband's life in a way he could not conjure. Jean was well versed in Parisian lowlife, which, as Mrs Adam knew, was a hot topic at the time. Street thugs called 'apaches' were filling the papers with lurid stories. Their name derived from the 'Casque

d'Or' affair of 1902. Two gangs led by rival pimps fought
over a whore called 'Casque d'Or' on account of her flaming
red hair. A reporter named one of the gangs the apaches.
For the next thirty years every lowlife criminal in Paris was
an 'apache'. Jean wrote about such men and a bewildered,
complicit young woman of uncertain ethnic origins. And
while Jean herself might appear oblivious to world events
because she lived on a knife-edge of economic stability, she
chronicled the socio-economic trends of war-torn Europe.
It was this authenticity that gave her writing its strength.

Mrs Adam was excited. She divided Jean's diary into
chapters, each headed with a man's name, and called the
whole thing *Suzy Tells*. Pernod Suzy Fine was the name of
a drink the English expats had invented: imitation absinthe,
gentian, and brandy. It was very strong. Mrs Adam decided
that the tone of this new novel was bold and yet its style
was 'naïve', and that Ford Madox Ford would like it, too.

The writer Ford Madox Ford was publishing all the great
names of modernism in the *transatlantic review*: Joyce, Pound,
Hemingway, Gertrude Stein, Djuna Barnes, Valéry, Philippe
Soupault, as well as dozens of other unknown, up-to-the-
minute writers. He was a generous impresario as well as being
a highly regarded novelist and critic himself. He produced
over eighty novels, which even he acknowledged was too
many. He wrote one novel considered to be great, *The Good
Soldier*, about a *ménage à trois*.

The poet Ezra Pound convinced Ford to hire Ernest
Hemingway as an editorial assistant. Ford had by then
published scores of novels, Hemingway was a cub reporter.
Ford, a generous patron of the international modernist movement who had once shared a byline with Joseph Conrad,
took the young man on, expecting him to be respectful of
his rank and accomplishments. His new editorial assistant

called him the 'golden walrus' and reported to his friends that his breath stank like the grave. Ford was sentimental, fat and anxious, and not a hero in the Hemingway mould. He presided over chaos in the office, often creating it, and would then collapse, weeping on his secretary's shoulder.

Although Ford was pouring his considerable energies into the *transatlantic review*, it was going under. He would have to begin another novel to pay the rent. His common-law wife and the mother of his child, Stella Bowen, pointed out in her memoir, *Drawn from Life*, that Ford needed new blood to revitalise himself and his writing. When he met Jean in the autumn of 1924, she was thirty-four, talented, lovely and helpless. A couple of months after meeting her, he began writing the second volume of his tetralogy, *Parade's End*.

He was just the sort of man she liked: fatherly. He was not handsome, he was a middle-aged, stout English gentle-man with piercing eyes and bad breath. But she thought – and he agreed with her – that he really was a gentleman. Hemingway writes, in his memoir of Paris, that over a Chambéry vermouth and cassis (which is what Paris shop girls drank) at the Closerie des Lilas, one of the best cafés in Paris, Ford instructed Hemingway (who was drinking brandy) in the differences between a cad, a gentleman and a bounder. A gentleman would always cut a cad but it would be impossible for a gentleman even to know a bounder. And an American, such as Ezra Pound, could not be a gentleman. However Hemingway might possibly be considered one in Italy. Henry James was very nearly a gentleman. Ford went on to say that Christopher Marlowe was definitely not a gentleman. Neither was Trollope, nor John Donne, who was a parson. Fielding, a judge, technically could be considered a gentleman. Ford himself, he explained, was a gentleman, as he had once held His Majesty's commission. Hemingway found it all mildly interesting. Ultimately, though, he found Ford an unpalatable 'heavy, wheezing, ignoble' presence. But he did notice that Ford had a way with women, as Ford's friend James Joyce noted: 'O Father O'Ford you've a masterful way with you, / Maid, wife and widow are wild to make hay with you . . .'

Ford was sensitive and understanding. Possibly as a result of his peripatetic background, German roots and deep insecurity, he clung to his belief of the virtues of the English gentleman. One of these virtues was gallantly, heroically and magnificently to come to the rescue of a fallen woman. Both Ford and Jean always fell in love with the same type of person. But Ford's real passion was for writing. He gave her the confidence to make it hers. He made her write short stories, and when she gave them melodramatic endings he cut them out and told her to stick to what she knew. He made her read Anatole France and Colette and translate her own writing into French if she wasn't sure a passage was working. If she told him she couldn't think of what to write about, he told her to translate something of his and to show it to him the next morning. He was encouraging and supportive, and above all, he understood her. Whatever else happened between Ford, Jean and Stella, he believed in her writing.

So she read France and Colette and Alfred de Musset and Paul Morand. She was struck by Morand's statement that English novelists always preface their books with quotations. 'The text before the sermon.'

She found that witty.

She read Maupassant and turned one of his stories, 'Mademoiselle Fifi', on its head.

Maupassant's 'Fifi' is a Prussian officer who gets his throat cut by a French Jewish tart. Jean's 'Fifi' is a fat, French tart who, trapped in her own romantic fantasy, allows her younger lover to abuse her and finally murder her in the same blood-thirsty manner.

When Jean and Ford met in 1924, he had been with Stella Bowen for six years, which was a long time for him. Stella was twenty-nine to Ford's fifty; she was strong, dependable and practical, which he found quite boring, albeit necessary. Stella held a tea party every Thursday afternoon at the offices of the *transatlantic review* on the Quai d'Anjou. Jean started attending them in the autumn of 1924. And every Friday, regardless of her reluctance, Ford invited her to the 'amusing' *bal musette* he hosted at Bal du Printemps.

The *bal musette* originated in the public dance halls on the outskirts of Paris. Workers went to dance to the nasal sound of a wind instrument related to the Breton pipes or Scottish bagpipe, called the *musette*. As Paris expanded outside its fortifications and absorbed the surrounding villages, these rural dances became part of urban life. The *musette* gave way to the accordion. Each dance hall had its own clientele. Le Chemise Sale for the gangs, the Bal de la Montagne Sainte-Geneviève for homosexuals, Le Progrès on Rue Fagon for Arab pimps and the Tête du Cochon on Quai de Grenelle for sailors and servant girls. The girls wore kiss-curls, tight skirts and satin blouses. Each bar had its 'one and only' singer who crooned tangos, waltzes and java – a provocative strain of *chanson*. The customers sipped at violently coloured drinks – green, red, violet and orange – through straws.

Jean saw Ford's effort at a *bal musette* as a bourgeois imitation of the real thing. Some artists need to delve down to the source, or the limits of their own endurance, or they simply need to feel the heat of the action. Ford did not have the guts to go all the way. Hemingway agreed with Jean's assessment. His dismissal of Ford's authenticity was partly based on the fact that before the war Hemingway himself had lived in a room above the Bal du Printemps. The distinction of having lived in Paris before and after the First World War was important. Hemingway felt himself to be more of a Parisian than Ford.

And also like Jean, Hemingway was contemptuous of Ford's *bals musettes*, but he came along anyway in case there were interesting or important people to meet. The owner had been tipped to reserve the rough wooden tables for the friends of Monsieur Ford. Ford wanted his 'painfully shy' writers to be drawn from their shells. At most *bals musettes*, there would be no need for this. The accordionist would be employed to whip dancers into a frenzy. Jean, however, shrunk from the festivities. She met Gertrude Stein and Alice B. Toklas, as well as the painter Nina Hamnett, but barely spoke to them. Hamnett summarised her thus: 'Ford's girl. Good-looking girl. She didn't speak much.'

She was always wordless when it mattered. She met Hemingway and liked him very much only if only because, at the end of the night, he helped her into her coat before they left. His wolfish solicitude no doubt charmed her. She was not particularly struck by his writing. One man she did make friends with was the journalist Ivan Bede. Everyone who knew Ford and who had met his latest protégée could sense what was coming. Ivan tried to waylay Jean. He seemed quite in love with her, and, more importantly, prepared to come to her aid. But he was young, so, in her eyes, as weak and ineffectual as herself. In 'Tout Montparnasse and a Lady' Jean described a woman – an American fashion artist – who has read the apache novels of Francis Carco and who yearns to meet someone dangerous. Yet this same woman gets angry with an artist absorbed in a rapturous vision: 'one must know where to draw the line'. The *bals musettes* became known as Ford's Nights. He hoped they would generate publicity for the *transatlantic review*, and invited writers, painters and composers. But usually it was bankers, publishers and journalists who turned up. Jean noted that the proprietor watered down the *fine*. This was not the real Left Bank. But for Stella Bowen it would do very well. Once in the midst of a party at the *transatlantic*'s offices she was heard to shout, 'The miserable man! He's threatening to ruin my party with his suicide.'

Stella and Ford were conventional at heart but dearly wanted to be part of the demi-monde. Bohemians were all very well, even picturesque and intriguing at times, but they must not be allowed to spoil the party.

After a while, Ford's Friday night approximation of the demi-monde came to an end. According to Nina Hamnett, 'it ended in a disturbance between the intellectuals who wanted to talk and the dancers who wanted to dance and drink.' Jean sensed that Ford and Stella were feeding off the reputation of Parisian lowlife rather than accepting it. They liked the appearance of wildness, but not the reality.

Stella would never have countenanced people from the real Quarter, actual lowlifes: the apaches, racketeers, and washed-up artists. Neither would Ford – at least not for very long. But Jean found her voice with them. Jean's shy withdrawn manner, her whispering voice and exotic good looks made her an object of curiosity, too. She could sit in a café and engage with the *grues* and their guys. She could feel what they were feeling. Her heart belonged to them. Her researches paid off.

Somewhat in the manner of a journalist researching a hot topic, lucid, investigative and to the point, she proceeded to write short stories based on her observations of interwar Bohemian Paris. This voice appears un-named, always appraising her subject, her reader and herself, in the clear, calm tones of a cool-headed observer, laying bare what she has found. There was some part of Jean that nothing could touch despite the depths to which she sank. This unfeeling part of her acted as a storehouse for her writing.

Just as she had once wandered around Bloomsbury after Lancey deserted her, Jean now wandered around the sordid streets of Paris despite the protestations of her husband. She was drawn to the outer boulevards bordering the fortifications of the old city that were in the process of being demolished. Here dens of apaches could be found. They had their own cafés, their own bars, their own dance halls. Songs were sung about them, books were written, photographs taken on the night-blackened streets where they prowled. Their misty origins lay in the legend of the Lapin Agile: the strange little bar where Lenglet used to sing and that seems to be carved into the side of the hill of Montmartre. In her first short story collection, *The Left Bank*, she writes about a gay bar where the *patron* wore rouge and lipstick. She writes about a bar in the fifth arrondissement, the Harlem of Paris, where Senegalese, Antillean, Guinean and Sudanese gathered. At the Bal Nègre in the Rue Blomet she found real blacks, not white Creoles like her. In a story called 'Trio', she writes about a beautiful, vicious, cunning, supple, slender, half-naked, mixed-race girl. She is about fifteen years old. She is with an older, blacker woman who is vulgar and fat. A coal-black man in a sharp suit is kissing the girl. The older woman quietens the girl who is singing. They were Jean's compatriots and they made her think of home.

Time disappeared for her when she walked. From every street and every house came the shades of men and women who had walked the streets of Paris before her, who were walking them now, and who would follow after her.

These *margineaux* inhabit the stories of *The Left Bank*. Her stories are particularly concerned with young women vulnerable to exploitation and old women whose bodies and spirits bear the scars of exploitation. Like Baudelaire, she was touched by the spectacle of elderly women; she knew what they had been and what they had come to. Baudelaire would trail his little old women for hours, until 'the sky was as scarlet as a wound'.

And when Ford told her to introduce more detail into her stories, more geographical context, more physical lushness, she went back to her text and cut every detail and all descriptions. She was writing constantly now, while Lenglet was scratching a living at the travel agency. When Ford started making declarations of love she was alarmed, then bemused and ironical. He was quite elderly, really: quite harmless and rather daft.

Ford was obsessed. Several nights a week he took the woman he loved and the woman he lived with to dinner at the Nègre de Toulouse. Jean drank Cahors wine made in the Latin quarter. Ford was sure to fill her glass when it was empty. She found his stolid attentiveness reassuring. 'Stella hates you,' Ivan Bede told her. She'd be a very unnatural woman if she didn't, Jean thought.

They drank in the Café du Dome (opposite La Rotonde and filled with Germans and Americans). It was the sort of place that had the authority of age. She took up as little space as possible on the dark leather bench which she saw as a symbol of an unchanging, unquestionable order. The waiters – old and dignified – upheld that law. 'In a Café' dissects the experience of sitting and watching. In the Café du Dome, she was lodged between Ford and Stella. She drank kummel in the Dome, and listened to the chansonnier's song, and watched the reactions of the audience. The *grues* again: the sad story of a little tart who gives her heart to a thankless man who then marries another woman. Finally he passes his old love on the street reduced to the utmost misery. The women rouged their lips as they listened, the men drank heartily; the applause was rapturous.

In December 1924 the twelfth and last issue of *transatlantic review* included six pages of 'Vienne' from a novel called *Triple Sec* by Jean Rhys. Ford had changed her name, deciding that 'Jean Rhys' was more modern than Ella Lenglet. He had also changed the name Mrs Adams had given her novel, *Suzy Tells*. *Triple Sec* is another reference to absinthe. The other contributors in the review were Tristan Tzara, Havelock Ellis, Ford, Hemingway, Gertrude Stein, Nathan Asch, Robert McAlmon and Ivan Bede.

On 28 December Lenglet was arrested at their hotel on 20 rue de l'Arrivée. His newly re-named wife, Jean Rhys, was out at the time of his arrest. Caught as he was in the arms of the law, she lost sight of him for several days. She went to the Palais de Justice every day but they could give her no information. As usual she had no money and no idea what to do.

Chapter 15:

LA GRUE

On 10 February 1925, Lenglet was sentenced to eight months in prison at Fresnes, outside Paris. His employers, Exprinter, had accused him of stealing 23,421 francs. He claimed he had been given the money by his employers to conduct a transaction on their behalf. But the French court dismissed his defence, and found him guilty of an 'abus de confiance', a premeditated fraud. In London, Jean's mother was slowly dying.

Shortly after her husband's imprisonment, Jean moved in with Ford and Stella. They lived in a studio on l'Avenue de l'Observatoire – a road that is long, straight and exact as an arrow – leading out of the muddle of Montparnasse. She was so helpless, so destitute and panic-stricken, and they were so kind and generous, that there was no other option. She kept to her bedroom at first. They left her alone to while away the days in mute depression. Then Stella asked her to pose as a model for her. She gave Jean some clothes and talked to her at great length on her favourite subjects: love, childbirth, emotional and sexual entanglements, prostitution, and being sensitive, which according to Stella was a waste of time. It was the kind of voice that Jean found monotonous and grating. In order not to hear it she daydreamed. In Jean, Stella found a woman who did not want to hear what she had to say about life, art and men. In Ford, Jean found a man who, like her, felt caught in a trap that he could not release himself from. He understood her, and this recognition of themselves as fellow captives was their bond. The strength of their relationship communicated itself through books: writing was the only way out of their dilemma, and this was what Ford was trying to tell her: that loneliness was conducive to being a writer. Ford wanted to share his experience, to make it easier for her, to show her she was not alone. He was encouraging her to form bonds with writers because only people in the same position as herself could rescue her from the loneliness that comes with creativity. It was a relationship between two minds, but in life, the story her elderly abuser Mr Howard had told her of female submission before the dominant male became the subtext of Ford and Jean's relationship. Economics played a major part in it. She was valued, then devalued, according to supply and demand.

Like a drain, the prison that held Lenglet was tucked out of sight. She visited him a few times, but not many. It was too awful to see him there, pale, furtive and unshaven. He trembled when the warden barked at him. Both Jean and Lenglet would write about Lenglet's imprisonment and the subsequent events: Jean in *Quartet*, and Lenglet in *Sous les Verrous*, which Jean would eventually translate into English as *Barred*. Meanwhile, Ford would write *When the Wicked Man*, about his hapless hero's relationship with a hysterical, alcoholic Creole journalist called Lola Porter. Stella would air her views on the relationship in her memoir.

With her husband behind bars, Jean started going out every evening with Ford and Stella, to the great bars of the boulevards: the Nègre, the Closerie, the Dôme. She was so busy she only had time to write to Lenglet on the cheap, lined paper she found in the 'petits bars de Montparnasse'. She told him about her walks around Paris. One of her favourite streets was the rue St Jacques – she called it 'the street of homeless cats'. They prowled and were thin and scraggy, but they were proud creatures and sympathetic after all, she told him. Then she gushed about how nice Ford and Stella were to her. He could only smile bitterly. Ford was in love with Jean's lovely fragility, her mournful and puzzled expression (what lay behind it? what was its cause?), her soft voice and the look of agony in her eyes whenever she was startled, which was often. She was passive and that was fascinating. Ford wanted her so much he almost had to tell Stella about it. Lenglet, in his prison cell, knew what was happening, and that Stella would collude with her husband's restlessness in order to keep him. And with her husband in prison, Jean had no choice. But that was how she liked it. She felt at peace with Ford because he understood her, and wanted her above all others. He read Jean's stories aloud and made Stella listen. He took her to parties and made Stella chaperone them. Jean did not have to try any more.

Lenglet, in his prison cell, was fuming. Jean did not visit him and when she did, she flaunted her connection to the great man who had saved her. He wrote her long, passionate letters to which she responded briefly and sharply. If he could not look after her, if he could not be successful, he did not deserve her love. Above all else, she needed men to be strong. If he was going to be a criminal he should at least be a good one. He knew that he had lost his 'prestige' with her; that she would never forget how he had shivered when the warder had spoken so roughly.

She was in love with Ford. Stella knew she had almost arranged the whole thing but her attempts to control her husband's roving sexuality backfired. In *Drawn from Life*, she wrote: 'I have often had occasion to envy women with a fragile and helpless appearance, and the support that it invariably evokes!' She could not control Jean so she envied her – so much so that she could not bear to name her in her account of the *ménage à trois*. Yet the two women had something in common. Bowen also felt degraded by the act of childbirth. 'There seems to be a conspiracy of silence about the horrors of childbearing and a pretty legend that the mother forgets all about it as soon as it is over. The hell she does! Nor does she forget the feeling of quivering helplessness both before and afterwards, and the indignity of having been reduced, even for a day, to the status of a squealing and abject animal.' Like Rhys, she deplored the biological functions of her body. As a frustrated artist, she resented Rhys for continuing to work, even though she was in love with a man. 'I was still very much enslaved by the terms of my relationship with Ford, for he was a great user-up of other people's nervous energy,' she wrote.

Men are the bigger project, for women like Bowen. 'Millions of women know what that is like.' It was natural to Stella that women should sacrifice themselves to the relationship: 'In order to keep his machinery running, he requires to exercise his sentimental talents from time to time upon a new object,' she writes. 'It keeps him young. It refreshes his ego. It restores his belief in his powers. And who shall say that this type of lubrication is too expensive for so fine a machine? Goodness knows, female devotion is always a drug on the market!'

It was like being in a harem, waiting in a restaurant with Stella to meet Ford for dinner. It was almost comic, definitely degrading. But, as Lois (based on Stella) says to Marya (based on Jean) in *Quartet*, it was better than being a *femme nue* in a music hall.

'They don't get paid anything at all, poor dears.'

The relationship with Ford was central to Jean's development as a writer, but her relationship with his wife was just as crucial in terms of the material it gave her. It would have been interesting to see what Colette would have made of this obsessive attachment between two women. She might have intuited that underneath the hostility there was a mutual attraction. It was as though the man in between them was just a means for them to touch each other. Admittedly, this touching was more like jealous prodding. But Stella's pre-occupation with Jean's appearance is indicative of some kind of longing to delve into the mystery of this seemingly fragile woman. Both women were artists, after all, and inquisitive about the human lot. But cultural taboos were so great they both set Ford up as the focus of their interests. Stella revered him so much she acted as his procuror. First she dressed Jean in her cast-off clothes, then she gave her up for sex. Jean, too, with her craving for maternal warmth, possibly vented some of her frustrations on Stella.

In any case, their intense attachment was transmuted into bitter rivalry. Sympathy gone wrong breeds the fiercest hate, and antipathy, for Jean at least, was easier to express. Stella's hatred for Jean was such that she attacked *Triple Sec* as 'unpublishably sordid'. She really was appalled at how low this woman had sunk. But, despite Jean being 'violent and demoralised' and a drag on her resources, she resolved to set her on her feet.

'Ford gave her invaluable help with her writing, and I tried to help her with her clothes,' she writes. The tone is patronising. The praise she does bestow on Jean is backhanded. 'She took the lid off the world that she knew, and showed us an underworld of darkness and disorder, where officialdom, the bourgeoisie and the police were the eternal enemies and the fugitive the only hero. All the virtues, in her view, were summed up in "being a sport", which meant being willing to take risks and show gallantry, and share one's last crust; more attractive qualities, no doubt, than patience or honesty or fortitude. She regarded the law as the instrument of the "haves" against the "have nots" and was well acquainted with every rung of that long and dismal ladder by which the respectable citizen descends towards degradation.'

As she was for Nina Hamnett, Jean was for Stella no more than 'Ford's girl'. Her work, like that of Céline and Henry Miller, 'stood often for a rather feeble and egotistical kind of anarchism without any of the genuine revolutionary spirit which would seem to be the logical outcome of reflective destitution'.

Jean brought an Antillean flavour into Ford and Stella's life as well as stories of apaches and petty criminality. The assumptions Stella and Ford made about Jean's descents into depression are underpinned with attitudes towards success and failure that make crude dualities of everything: civilisation and barbarism, order and chaos, male and female. Jean, with her white Creole mutability, did not fit into their moral universe.

Jean alludes to the double-edged sword of Stella's kindness in her prefatory quote to *Quartet*:

> . . . Beware
> Of good Samaritans – walk to the right
> Or hide thee by the roadside out of sight
> Or greet them with the smile that villains wear.

This was the text before her sermon.

What Stella could not bring herself to appreciate was that Jean's crisis was real. Her husband was in jail, her daughter was in care and her baby son was dead. She had no home. Her nerves had been shattered by illegal jaunts around Europe and the imprisonment of her husband on embezzlement charges. This chronic insecurity had reawakened old traumas to which she was never able to resign herself – the loss of love, the neglect of a beloved parent. Any further loss entailed the loss of her being.

Meanwhile, Lenglet wore a piece of sacking on his head when Jean went to visit him. He gripped the bars between them like a monkey in the zoo. But, now, when she visited him she felt compassion for him and all the other prisoners, their wives, their girlfriends and their *grues* – the struggling street prostitutes, the strung-out housewives, the banged-to-rights underdogs. When she was in this world her love for men like Ford faded into resentment for those who condemned outcasts. She loved them and anyone who was not Ford or Stella and who did not preside over *bals musettes*.

On 18 June 1925, Lenglet was released from Fresnes. When Ford and Stella asked to meet him, she suspected it was because Stella was curious to meet a real lowlife. He looked a regular Montparno – bearded, bedraggled and thin. He trembled when he touched her, as though uncertain of his right to such intimate contact. When she introduced him to the Fords she felt they were peering nosily at an ex-convict. Their dismissal of him made her passionately defensive of him.

Jean went back to him briefly, which spelt the end of her relationship with Ford. He was prepared to ask her to share him with Stella but he would not share a woman with another man. On the one night she spent with Lenglet she treated him as a loving mother would tend a sick child. She stroked his hair and cried for him. She had two love bites on her arm. He spoke excitedly of his friends – gaolbirds and their *grues* – who had plans, schemes, ways of escaping the mess of their lives. Before he had a chance to execute them he was expelled to Holland.

Lenglet spent the next two years tramping around Europe. He became a sandwich man in Lucerne, sold newspapers in Berlin, was a publisher's courier in Frankfurt, and when all else failed, he scraped a living as a street musician. Jean was never very forthcoming about this period in Lenglet's life because she wanted to protect their daughter from the criminality and vagrancy that he drifted into. As a result, it is hard to piece his life together. Similarly, Jean could draw a veil over parts of her own life when she felt it would help no one to know how low she had sunk.

Shortly after Lenglet left Paris for Holland, Ford sent Jean in the opposite direction, to the south of France. He did not want her, but neither did he want her to join her husband. He found a place for her with a rich American woman who believed in reincarnation. Jean went along with it quite willingly. It was a lovely house, the chance to earn some easy money, her depression would not be disturbed.

She had been rejected by her knight in shining armour. But this was no chorus girl green with expectations. This time she found her cure for disillusionment in writing.

Chapter 16:

JUAN-LES-PINS

In July 1925, Ford and Stella found Jean a job in the south of France. It is not certain where Jean and Lenglet's three-year-old daughter was at this point though it is likely that Jean's friend, Germaine Richelot, was paying for Maryvonne's upkeep.

An American lady was scouring the bars of Montparnasse looking for a cheap writer to help her friend write a book. Ford and Stella did everything in their power to get Jean the job. Ford wrote an article in her name on eighteenth-century English furniture as well as a folk story from Serbia. He showed them both to the lady, pointing out the flair for detail and the narrative power the pieces displayed. There was the writer's versatility to be considered, too. Stella waxed eloquent on how agreeable Jean was, how sympathetic and easy-going, and how the friend of the American lady was bound to like her. Part of the reason they were so keen for her to get this job was that the friend lived in Juan-les-Pins. This was in the south of France, a long way from Paris. When they finally did get her the job Jean was equally relieved to be going.

In July 1925 Jean arrived in Juan-les-Pins. Until the twentieth century, it had been nothing more than a pine grove on the western neck of Cap d'Antibes. A casino was built in 1908, and by the 1920s, Juan-les-Pins had taken off as the original summer resort of the Côte d'Azur. Everyone in Montparnasse mocked the glitzy atmosphere generated by rich people amusing themselves in casinos and pink villas. But Jean did not find it in the least ridiculous. She felt quite at home in the easy glamour of casinos and the luxury of villas. As luck would have it, she was staying in the glitziest villa on the coast, Château Juan-les-Pins. It had been built by a fabulously wealthy Russian on the eve of the Revolution. Montparnassians were particularly scathing of this villa's excessive opulence but Jean liked it immediately. Anything that added to her comfort, or provided a surface feeling of well-being was good news for her. The villa's current occupants, and her employers, were Mr and Mr Hudnut, owners of an American cosmetics firm. They were millionaires and their daughter was married to Rudolf Valentino. They were glamorous rather than vulgar. Their handsome English butler wore elegant livery and had the most marvellously supple bow that he delivered from the waist. Their five Pekinese dogs distributed themselves gracefully around the white sofas. Their paws were never muddy, their coats were always combed. Mrs Hudnut wore velvet gowns with drooping satin sleeves and Mr Hudnut wore purple smoking suits. Music from the casino came wafting in through the French windows every evening, carried on a wave of bougainvillaea scent.

Jean felt as though she were walking on to a film set. On arrival at the Gloria-Swansonesque villa, she was led to an ivory-tower bedroom at the top of a marble staircase. The virgin-white bathroom with its view of a sea the colour of cornflowers was all hers. It was like a dream.

She swam in the sea's coddling waters every morning, washing away the stains of having been touched by so many men. This is what it felt like. This is how purifying she found luxury. The more men she slept with, and the less money they had, the more she devalued herself. Each sexual act was a desecration. The cleansing, calming Mediterranean helped her renew herself.

Once her morning ablutions had been completed, work commenced. Mrs Hudnut could not write and Jean could not take shorthand, but they were full of enthusiasm for the project. Jean sat at a desk and took dictation from Mrs Hudnut who was trying to develop her theory of reincarnation and interior design: her theory was that if you decorated your home in the style in which you had once lived you would be happy. For example, when she wanted Jean to describe a piano it had to have an 'Egyptian feel'. Jean tried her hardest to understand, and convey what Mrs H could possibly mean.

Mrs Hudnut could be great fun, mixing gossip with theorising. The voice they heard singing in the casino, she told Jean, belonged to a Russian prince who worked as a gardener in the villa next to theirs. He was not paid much, so he sang for his supper every night. The Riviera was full of grand dukes and princes working for rich Americans. She then extemporised on the Russian character (they were always trying to borrow money), her husband's eighteenth-century bed, and the vacuity of her life before she became a spiritualist. She believed ardently in the new trend of automatic writing, and she liked long words.

Jean was happy paddling in the shallow waters of this life; there was none of the insecurity of Paris, the ostracism of Stella's friends on Boulevard Montparnasse, the shadows chasing her and her chasing them. She was patient with Mrs Hudnut's rambling narrative, writing it all down clearly and concisely. There was even promise of more work as some of Mrs Hudnut's friends wanted help in writing books. The only hint of a problem was Mrs Hudnut's complaint about the brevity of Jean's style. She wanted longer words and fancier phrases. What she did not understand was that Jean got rid of words in order not to become congealed in them. But Jean obliged her employer – and worked 'chiaroscuro' and 'translucent' into the fairy tale set in a Persian garden that Mrs H had ordered. She knew instinctively that the polysyllabic word has too much to say to tell the truth. But the sumptuous setting, the extreme comfort, made up for the Hudnuts' grandiloquence. She could live very well as a ghost writer, she reckoned, flitting amongst the rich and fatuous, transcribing their silly stories. She could even find a flat and send for Maryvonne – at last, she would be able to take on the responsibility of providing a home for her daughter. She would not be obliged to Germaine or any other charitable friend. It was a dream that helped her endure the self-indulgence of her employers.

She was having fun, too. Every Sunday Mr H took her to the Casino at Monte Carlo. She was a pretty woman and he paid for her to play at baccarat and she let him kiss her in the car. She did not mind. He was so old, he was out of commission. But the chauffeur was watching all the while.

She was happy. Ford was writing her long letters telling her he loved her, and she was being paid enough to save a little money. She wrote to Ford and Stella telling them how happy she was. Then one hot day in August she really was happy. She was walking the long, dusty road between Théoule and Cannes. She had missed the afternoon bus at Théoule where she had lunched with a bottle of wine. She stopped by a wood at La Napoule. Her eye fixed on a tree, she could hear the sea lapping on the shore beyond and feel the sun's warmth on her skin. Whereas in Paris or London she would have attributed to the tree her anxiety or her unhappiness, here its sighs and undulations became her happiness, and soon she was the tree. For once in her life she left herself behind and was intensely happy. Sometimes, but not very often, she had a similar feeling through books. 'It's this feeling of being one with human beings.' But ordinarily she could only access this feeling when she was in conversation with other writers through their books.

Of course, it all went wrong. One morning Mrs H swept into her room, and waved a letter in Jean's sleeping face. It was from Ford. He said she was paying Jean 'less than a housemaid in New York'. He accused her of exploiting Jean, making her write two books – one on fairy tales, one on reincarnation – when the original deal had been for one. Mrs H accused Jean of complaining to Ford. Jean's protestations did nothing to soothe her hurt feelings. Despite what followed, Jean retained her sense of humour when, in *Quartet*, she describes Mrs H storming out of the room trailed by five indignant Pekinese.

Jean's happiness was pulled away from her like a rug from under her feet. Ford, on his high horse, felt he had to defend a writer's rights, and perhaps he felt uncomfortable with Jean's happiness. Maybe he wanted her back where she belonged – on tap in a hotel room in Paris.

The Hudnuts wanted Jean to leave straight away but she could not bear to give up on her happiness so quickly. So, rather in the way she had lingered at Crickley Hill as Adrian's unwanted guest and the butt of Warlock's anger, she lingered on at the villa. It was unbearable for everyone. She was snubbed by the servants, who had heard all about her excursions to Monte Carlo and took pleasure over a favourite's fall, and was derided by Mr Hudnut himself. His wife had come to hear of his stolen kisses. To Mrs H's credit, she saw through the gambits of Mr H and Ford and understood just how distressed Jean was. She accompanied her to Paris and settled her into the hotel that Ford had found her. But when they met Ford on the platform at Gare Montparnasse Mrs Hudnut cut him dead.

Chapter 17:

PARIS AGAIN

By the end of 1925 Ford had moved Jean into a hotel near
Gare Montparnasse. He also sent some of her short stories
to Edward Garnett, a publisher's reader in London. Jean
was writing almost continually, not much caring where she
lived or whether she ate. Maryvonne was living in Versailles
with a *nourrice* paid for by Germaine. Lenglet was flitting
in and out of their lives. In England, Jean's female relations
moved to a larger house in a suburb further west of London.

It was winter 1925, and Jean was back in a Paris as cold and
grey as London after love has left you. The room Ford had
found for her overlooked the Gare Montparnasse. All day
she watched the dingy trains trailing smoke up and down
the tracks as they journeyed to the west of France and beyond.
There were posters outside her hotel window – of smarmy,
smiling children advertising baby food. When she looked at
her bed she could not help thinking of all the other women
(there must have been so many of them) who had lain there,
like her, with men like Ford.

She was so close to the station she could smell the lovers
leaving. Ford was going through the motions of having an
affair. Although she had been happy in the south of France,
now that she was back in Paris she fell painfully and slavishly
in thrall to him again. The script demanded that they make
love in her hotel room when he could find the time. She
was expected to take tea with Stella and to attend social

functions in order to make it appear as though nothing un-
toward was happening. She frequented the shabby bars of Montparnasse, never staying too long in any single one, getting drunker
and drunker before moving to the next and finally going
back to her room when she felt sufficiently numb. After a
while she had to avoid these bars, because the waiters disapproved of lone, drunken women, and because the more
adventurous of Stella's friends drank there and snubbed her.

The more distant Ford became, the more desperate she
became to please him; she promised to show him sexual tricks
she had learnt in the tropics and screamed abuse when he
turned down her offers. His distaste for her becomes apparent
in *When the Wicked Man*. All the prejudice of the coloniser
for the savage turns into an attack on his rejected lover. He
talks about her 'appetites', especially in moments of abandon,
usually alcoholic. She has a 'taste only for toughs and low
life', and a penchant for telling 'fantastic and horrible details
of *obi* and the voodoo practices of the coloured people of her
childhood's home'. He talks about the 'smut', the 'mournful
sewer[s]' of abuse, and 'dancing half nude with a very formidable
racketeer in a regular *tohuwabohu* of negroes, mulatresses and
gangsters'. The *Oxford English Dictionary* defines *tohuwabohu*
as 'That which is empty and formless; chaos; utter confusion'.
It is a Hebrew word translated as 'without form and void' in
the King James translation of the Bible:

In the beginning God created the heaven and the earth.
    And the earth was without form and void; and darkness
was upon the face of the deep.

Jean was chaos. She was a nightmare. He had got himself in
too deep.

Ford busied himself in an attempt to launch her career.

He sent some of her stories to Edward Garnett, a publisher's reader. Jean herself went to London over Christmas to find a publisher. At this point, she may have visited her mother who was still slowly dying, with her youngest daughter Brenda as her carer. Then again, Jean may not have visited her. What is certain is that she was writing. Most of what she was writing would be turned into *Quartet*, the novel that explores her relationships with Ford, Stella and Lenglet.

One night, a few months after her return to Paris, she stood outside Ford's studio on rue Notre Dame des Champs. She listened to the noise made by his party-goers and to the gramophone playing the latest records, 'If you knew Suzie like I knew Suzie'. She imagined Stella mouthing complacencies, being rueful and mildly amusing. She imagined smashing a bottle of wine into Stella's face. She stood there, without her husband, her lover, her daughter, her family, and screamed at her lover and his wife and their guests. She went back to her dingy hotel room and savoured the sweet bitterness of having been abandoned by so many loved ones.

Well into the summer of 1926 Jean was writing in her miserable little room overlooking the station, or maybe Ford had found her another one. It doesn't really matter; one room was much like another. Jean was absorbed in her writing. Every Sunday, she would visit her four-year-old daughter in Versailles. Germaine was paying for the child to stay there until she found a boarding school for her. Jean wrote about a character called Susan (*Susan and Suzanne*, unpublished) who visits her daughter every Sunday only to find that the little girl will not respond to her embraces. The *nourrice* looks on disapprovingly, deploring the mother's lack of maternal devotion.

In August, Lenglet returned illegally to France. Jean visited him in the suburb of Clamart where he had found a dodgy friend to put him up. He was arrested shortly afterwards for

breaking his expulsion order. Six more days in the Santé
prison and then he was expelled again. Lenglet's return – so
obviously ill-fated – had not been the restorative either of
them needed. They were both out of luck and seedy with
it. They would have seen it in the other's eyes, and that
recognition would have been unbearable. Best to stay apart.
Besides, Jean could think of no one but Ford. She was stuck
with her longing for the unattainable; to be in a state of
unquenchable thirst was an agony that had come to suit her.

Ford felt guilty – so it worked! – and paid for her to go
to the Hotel des Oliviers in Crus de Cagnes. She met some
friends of Stella's there, whom she writes about in *The Left
Bank* and *Quartet* as being patronising, suspicious and voyeuris-
tic. Middle-class women who buy into the Establishment and
will not tolerate those who expose its faults. She was back
in the south of France but she was not feeling optimistic
about her prospects. By now not even the waters of the
Mediterranean could soothe her. She drank in her room all
day and took the sleeping draught Veronal at night.

Ford grew tired of her desolation and stopped sending her
money. Germaine had also been assisting her financially. But
Germaine was irritating her with her kindly meant interventions
and plans for Maryvonne. Jean wanted to be left alone in her
misery, not to be shaken out of it. She certainly did not want
to be reminded of her inability to look after her child. When
she ran out of money, she took herself to a back-street hotel
and slept fifteen hours a day. She had no money whatsoever
for food. She ate sometimes at a convent for destitute girls,
which became her only contact with the world. Of course,
she wrote about it, too. She wrote about everything. This
period of starvation turned into a short story called 'Hunger',
which was published three months later. She fed on her own
experience and regurgitated it back again. One thing she wrote

in this story strikes the reader as particularly self-loathing: 'Women are always ridiculous when they struggle.' Women were supposed to be elegant and graceful, not to have to strive for their rewards, but to be given them by gracious gentlemen. When a woman works hard she is ugly.

She stopped starving herself when her husband sent her a letter and a ticket to Holland. 'I have never gone without food for longer than five days, so I cannot amuse you any longer,' was her pay-off line to the reader. John had recovered his luck and could give her and Maryvonne a home again. Their marriage was over but he was still her comrade-in-arms. In mid-December she joined him in Holland.

It did not last. One night in February 1927 she was back in Paris and she saw Ford Madox Ford in a bar near Gare Montparnasse. She walked in, slapped him in the face with her empty glove, and promptly left. She had barely made contact with his face. The onlookers shrugged at this pathetic woman in her shabby coat making a scene.

Ford felt it incumbent upon him to meet her for lunch. He impressed upon her the importance of keeping up appearances. As he lectured her on propriety over lunch in Montparnasse, he reminded her of Queen Victoria. Montparnasse was where Max Jacob had come to 'sin disgracefully'. He seemed quite absurd to her at these moments. As ever, she was lost for words. Did Jean ever really love Ford? Perhaps it was the idea of being loved and in love that she clung to. In any case, Ford felt an obligation to her, like Lancey before him. He supplied an allowance for Jean through his lawyer. More practically he passed on a commission for a translation. The book was *Perversité* by Francis Carco, a true Parisian bohemian, a friend of Apollinaire and Colette. Ford chose well, because Carco wrote mostly about the apaches who prowled the alleyways of

Montmartre. He knew that his ex-lover felt at home in this world. Jean got the job done quickly because she understood the subject-matter so intimately. *Perversité* is the study of a man who is passive, shy and scared of the world. Carco builds up quite quickly to the violence unleashed in him when he is subjected to cruelty. He wrote it mostly in Parisian argot, so Lenglet had to help her with some of the more obscure terms. Ford got her some money for the translation.

In March 1927 *The Left Bank* was published by Jonathan Cape with an introduction by Ford. It was well received but had little impact on the life of its author.

Lancey wrote to her: 'My dear kitten – I was very glad to get your letter & I shall be intensely interested to read your book – I have been often anxious about you as I've not heard a word from you – I was in Paris for a day at Easter & could so easily have come to see you. Is all well. Write & tell me. Lancey.'

She was still in Paris, still writing *Quartet*, living in a 'depressing hotel' in rue Vavin, near the Luxembourg Gardens. Germaine Richelot had not given up on her. She was still helping her with money and kindness. But by summer Jean had turned against Germaine. Her kindness seemed too much like pity. Jean could not believe that Germaine could feel anything but contempt for her. Also, Germaine was rich and comfortable enough to think of Maryvonne's needs. Jean resented this. When you are so desperately unhappy, and there seems to be no way out of it, it is hard to attend to the needs of others. It may have seemed as though Jean was crying out for help, but really she was crying out for the pain to end.

In October 1927 Jean took her daughter to rejoin Lenglet in Holland. The three of them lived in a dismal street in The Hague till early 1928. Maryvonne was five and a half. This was the only time she would live with both her parents.

Jean felt pity for Lenglet rather than love, and that pity

was unbearable to him. Their relationship had never been a particularly sexual one, more a meeting of attitudes: a pair of outcasts who formed a union against the world. By now, her apathy was pervasive, and though he loved her beauty, her sadness and her loyalty, he found sexual solace elsewhere. She stayed at home, vaguely anxious, vaguely jealous.

At the end of 1927, Ford had left Stella for another woman.

Jean was still working on *Quartet* when she heard from London that her mother was close to death.

Minna Sophia, Mother, Brenda and Auntie B were all living at 28 Woodgrange Avenue, in leafy, suburban Acton. This in itself was enough to make Jean feel excluded. Miss Woolgar was Mother's nurse, close to Brenda, not lesbian close, not quite. Gwennie, now Jean, almost missed her mother's funeral service at Golders Green Crematorium. To make up for it, she had a screaming fit at her youngest sister. Her family was appalled by her histrionics and by the state of her. Gwennie, as they still called her, was a drunk, a down-and-out, and an unfit mother. That she had also published a volume of short stories as well as a French translation and was working on her first novel meant nothing to her exasperated family. Jean writes about her mother's funeral in *After Leaving Mr Mackenzie*, a book that came after *Quartet*. The anxiety she felt at being confronted by her relatives, massed seemingly against her, took time to be filtered through her writing. What comes across is her heightened sense of alienation in the face of this cabal of women grouped together in seemingly perfect harmony.

While in London she saw Lancey for one last time. This was also the last time he would lend her money. He was grand now and entertained the young princesses at Mount Clare, and the Queen – my cousin, the Queen – as he called her – at his country estate. This connection to expensive royals made him feel 'a comparatively poor man'. He was not very nice to poor people any more; he, like so many others, was tired of Jean's suffering.

She went back to Holland but that was over, too. She and Lenglet sent Maryvonne to live with friends and Jean set about selling *Quartet*. She sent it to Jonathan Cape, who had published *The Left Bank*. Cape shied away from *Quartet*, fearing it was libellous of Ford. Besides this concern, Jean's writing in *Quartet* forced English readers to look at their attitudes to sex and money in an unflattering light.

Edward Garnett, the former associate of Ford's, sent the manuscript to Chatto and Windus. Garnett had recommended *The Left Bank* to Cape and was equally impressed with *Quartet*. He also sent it to Leslie Tilden Smith, an agent who had previously expressed an interest in *The Left Bank*. Leslie lived with his daughter Anne in Boyne Terrace Mews, Holland Park. He got in touch with Jean. Since she was an intriguing and gifted writer, destitute in London, compelling and fragile, exotic and shy, he invited her to stay in his home (five rooms, a shared bathroom and a kitchen over a stable). The kindness of strangers is easier to accept than that of friends, especially those who have seen it all before.

It was May 1928 and Leslie was the latest in a long line of rescuers, and she turned to him with eager gratitude. He was another perfect English gentleman, ex-public school and Oxford. He was divorced and lonely, and needed someone to look after. She could feel safe with him. She lay in bed all morning, and got up when she felt like it. She was gracious and petted. She and Lenglet made their separation official on 19 June. Maryvonne returned to live with her father.

Jean was back in London.

'Writing took me over,' she said of the next ten years of her life. 'It was all I thought of. Nothing and nobody else mattered much to me.'

Chapter 18:

LONDON AGAIN

In September 1928 Jean Rhys's first novel, *Quartet*, was published in England as *Postures*. She was living with Leslie Tilden Smith in Holland Park, London, and writing her second novel, *After Leaving Mr Mackenzie*. In the same year, the Equal Franchise Act was passed giving women equal voting rights with men, and the novelist Radclyffe Hall published *The Well of Loneliness*, about a lesbian relationship, only to have it withdrawn from sale on grounds of obscenity within weeks. Jean's estranged husband, Lenglet, was living in Amsterdam, working as a private tutor in French and English. Their daughter Maryvonne was living with him.

Jean's publishers insisted on a change of title; they considered *Quartet* to be too vague. They were wrong and she knew it but she complied, bitterly regretting it ever after. The reviewers recognised the power of her style but sneered at the characters and events it described. The *New Statesman*: 'On an extended canvas one becomes more than ever conscious of the unsatisfactoriness of getting drunk as a remedy for every trial and trouble.' The *Manchester Guardian* agreed: 'The limitations are the limitations of the subject, of the characters . . . Miss Rhys is an artist . . . but a great deal depends on what she does next.' They did not want to read about low lifes. She was still an outcast, and although she had found a nice, safe man and a life that she could devote to writing, she still felt the slights and snubs of alienation.

Lenglet's new career as a tutor was not successful. He had suffered a reversal of fortunes and was destitute again, so Jean decided to bring Maryvonne to London. The experiment in motherhood lasted six months. 'My mother tries to be an artist and is always crying,' wrote the six-year-old. Jean was writing her next novel; a demanding, noisy child disturbed her concentration. She asked Leslie's nineteen-year-old daughter to take the child out for the day. When they came home at four o'clock, she shouted, 'You are much too early!' She hadn't finished writing and drinking.

Jean never gave up her fantasy of motherhood. But she did give up her child. Maryvonne went back to Holland to live with her father, or his friends when he was incapable of looking after her. For the next ten years Jean would plan trips to London for Maryvonne, wanting to be a good mother, but when the child arrived, the reality of looking after another person got in the way of her intentions.

In 1928 she persuaded Leslie to pay for her to stay alone in Paris. She booked herself into the Hotel Henri IV, behind the Quai des Grands Augustins. She wrote about Julia, her new heroine, staying in the same hotel. Julia read most of the time. Jean wrote. They were the same haunted woman. She was convinced that Ford had betrayed her over the publication of *Perversity*. His name had appeared on the title page instead of hers. It was not his fault but she was not to know that. The publishers, in fact, got it wrong. Despite Ford's requests they would not put it right, preferring his well-known name to hers. Jean worked this betrayal into *After Leaving Mr Mackenzie*. She wrote about Julia walking into a bar and slapping her faithless lover, faintly, about the face. She wrote about Julia turning up late to her mother's funeral, about the rest of the family ganging up on her. The lesbian nurse and the dowdy sister who devoted her prime to caring for Mother, were in there too. As was their contempt and horror at Julia's louche life and constant applications of lipstick. Maybe their jealousy, too. The two frustrated, still young women waiting for an older woman to die before they could live.

Meanwhile, Ford had read *Postures* and began writing *When the Wicked Man*, published in 1932. In it, he called her a 'blackamoor'. She would not find out till much later but it turned out that she was right: he did betray her. What she could not know was that he, too, was hurt by her perceived betrayal. But his feelings did not count because he was not a defenceless woman.

Early in 1929, *Postures* was published in America. Critics claimed it sordid but powerful, so, in fact, she was not as defenceless as she thought she was.

At the end of her life, Jean described her relationship with Leslie Tilden Smith as a 'fifty-fifty affair'. His daughter described Jean as moving into her home and staying there 'for ever'. Leslie was in love with Jean. When they met she was thirty-seven, claimed to be thirty-three, and was still very beautiful with a pretty figure, alluring eyes, a carefully made-up mouth and a lilting, whispering voice. Her past was tantalising, and she knew how to be charming. But she could not keep it up for long.

He must have seen something of her dark side, too, and that could have been an attraction. Maybe she expressed something he did not dare give voice to. He was certainly devoted, giving up everything to help her write. He had never been a particularly successful literary agent, so perhaps her demands on his time prevented him having to acknowledge that. It was around the time of the publication of *Quartet* that Jean became a prolific letter-writer. Her letters to admirers of her work, some of whom became friends for life, reveal a kind and thoughtful woman. She needed distance to be a good friend and writing gave her that distance. And in her letters she makes light of her situation. Her letters to Maryvonne are imbued with a rueful tenderness, especially as the girl grew older, that cannot fail to touch the heart. There must have been moments when she expressed these moods in life. Her 'fifty-fifty' relationship with Leslie perhaps gave her a sense of security that allowed her the chance to exercise her wit and charm. Perhaps the fact that the relationship *was* 'fifty-fifty', and so did not absorb her totally, meant she could explore other relationships and feelings that were not so intense. In turn, she must have brought some excitement and colour into Leslie's life. If she did, she captivated him with them.

Maryvonne

In the little mews house in Holland Park, they worked every day on her book. He proofread her latest pages, did the housework, and gave her space. On Maryvonne's visits to London, he looked after her. Maryvonne preferred him to her mother, which caused some resentment with Jean. But he let Jean hit him and scratch him when she was drunk and in pain. He did not mind when she threw the typewriter out of the window. His niceness annoyed her. It could not possibly be real. Human beings are not nice and kind to each other. He must be a fake, and she was determined to prove it.

After Leaving Mr Mackenzie was published in February 1931. The reviews were ubiquitous and uniformly excellent – everyone admired her prose though no one liked the content. The reaction of Rebecca West (the mistress of H.G. Wells, and the creator of heroines as strong and mildly unconventional as West herself) was typical:

> It is doubtful if one ought to open this volume unless one is happily married, immensely rich, and in robust health; for if one is not entirely free from misery when one opens the book one will be at the suicide point long before one closes it. Miss Jean Rhys has already, in *The Left Bank* and *Postures*, quietly proved herself to be one of the finest writers of fiction under middle age, but she has also proved herself to be enamoured of gloom to an incredible degree.

Jean felt the ignominy of being – or having been – desperate, poor and alone all over again. Even if she was not, now, desperate, poor or alone, she felt these states acutely and this was what she wanted to write about. But reviewers were telling her that writers who dwelt on these matters were unwelcome. They liked her style, just as men liked her appearance, but they did not like the pain underneath it.

She had, however, some staunch admirers in the literary world. Peggy Kirkaldy wrote to her; Peggy was known for her soirées and was well connected in the literary world. She offered to introduce Jean to Dorothy Richardson, Elizabeth Bowen and Osbert Sitwell. Jean met her alone for cocktails, argued with her shortly afterwards, but Peggy persisted, and they became friends for life. Jean would write to her when she was in extremis and when she was happy, because Peggy understood.

Lenglet understood, too. What is remarkable about Jean's relationship with Lenglet is how it developed into such a strong friendship. Now they were divorced, they tried to help each other. He wrote her comforting letters about Maryvonne. The child did love her, he assured her. No, she doesn't, wailed Jean. In January 1932 she visited them in Amsterdam and read Lenglet's fictionalised version of her love affair with Ford, *Sous les Verrous*. It was another betrayal but she did not see it like that. Her heart was his. Her love for him was a rare, precious kind of love that was more pity and pain – a beautiful, piercing pity that did not degrade him but raised him into purity. He was a victim, like her, and his suffering made him beautiful.

In a magnificent act of generosity, she translated *Sous les Verrous* into English, called it *Barred*, and did for Lenglet what she would never do for herself. She sent it to Rebecca West and other luminaries as well as the publisher Desmond Harmsworth who published it that April. It was reviewed, like *Mackenzie*, in the *Times Literary Supplement* and other prestigious publications. It made Lenglet a success. He quickly wrote another novel to capitalise on it. His long-forgotten career as a journalist was resuscitated, and it was all because of Jean.

In September 1933 her divorce from Lenglet came through. This was her first experience of legal injustice. Despite the many sexual betrayals on her husband's part, she was named by him as the guilty party. He cited her relationship with Ford. This rankled. For someone like Jean who mentally interrogated and judged herself in her head all the time, the process of prosecution was intensely uncomfortable. Now here was a man in the robes of state voicing her self-hatred and accusations against herself in a court of law. It was official: she was guilty. But it was unfair.

She married Leslie on 19 February 1934. She was not the whispering, shy creature with an interesting past with whom he had fallen in love. But he had committed himself by now and stuck with her. It seems she got the men she needed when she needed them. At this point, after the bewilderment of Lenglet's mercurial qualities and the confusion of Ford's predatory paternalism, she needed someone steady and compassionate, and here he was. Leslie could not be described as practical because no one practical would put up with a woman like Jean Rhys. But he had her best interests at heart. She could not have been easy to live with as she was drinking two bottles of wine every day. The alcoholic blur this induced was a release from the voices in her head that were torturing her. These voices had now been joined by real voices in literary journals and in a court of law. In desperation, Leslie scraped some money together to send her to the seaside for a month in order to dry out. She did as she was told, but in a letter to Evelyn Scott, another admirer, she confessed: 'I'm relying on the kick I'll get out of my first drink.'

It was the promise of that kick that kept her going throughout a month of abstinence by the sea. In itself, a month off from drinking was easy. She could take things slowly: eat three meals a day, be an invalid, pace herself.

When faced with real life she needed her kicks, and her release into numbness.

When her wedding day came, she said she was thirty-eight but in fact she was forty-three. She was not alone in her equivocation. Leslie's father was a clergyman still living in the shade of Queen Victoria's reign. Leslie felt his father would not appreciate his marriage to an alcoholic lady novelist whose books dealt with the sordid realities of the demi-monde. When it came to his own and his father's expectations, Jean was not Leslie's only problem. His literary agency had foundered by the time they were married. Underneath his façade as the English gentleman publisher he could not manage a business nor handle money. He was at a loss when it came to financial matters. His solution was to borrow half his inher-itance from his father and to become a freelance publisher's reader. It was an insecure occupation that would be his only source of income for the rest of his life.

This was a marriage of two middle-aged people who were rapidly crumbling under the pressures of daily life and social pressures. Yet Jean married Leslie in the hope that everything, including herself, would change.

A few years later, she scribbled down her thoughts concern-ing her wedding day. It was a note to Leslie that he never received. It said,

> Coming forth from my [?]
> loveless frowning bridal day
> I saw a [?]
> Behind me frowns and scowls
> Before me what?

Her manuscripts are often like this: decorated with illegible scrawls, a mark that does not want to be transformed into a word. Why should she make herself clear? Some things cannot be said because people do not want to hear them. The reviewers had told her that.

What her scribbles reveal is that she still felt isolated and unloved. The miracle of 'happy ever after' on which girls are brought up had not happened. It never would; it never does. It is a fantasy. This bitterly disappointed her. It was the greatest betrayal.

I didn't know
I didn't know
I didn't know

No one would ever love her absolutely and truly for her true, unadorned, un-adult self. Getting drunk distracted her from the truth; it kept her in the illusory present; the illusion being her image of herself culled from magazines; or a fleeting vision of a pretty lady in a park. But it did not stop the truth of herself – the bits and pieces that signified how empty and hollow she was. After a day of writing, the drink would kick in. Then she would attack Leslie both verbally and physically.

People were noticing the bruises and cuts on his face. His daughter was convinced by his explanations of falls and foolish clumsiness. Hamish Hamilton, a publisher and man of the world, was not. He recognised the signs, and decided to speak to the culprit. His conversation with Jean is unrecorded although he is reported as saying, 'She didn't seem to resent my interference.'

In fact, she probably felt grateful for it. She was like a child who has to be told how to behave. Unfortunately, Leslie refused to lay down the law. He would not look at her when she was ugly. Within a year of marriage, he had no choice because the ugliness spread, and the drunken, violent tantrums began to repel him. He did not say anything, which would have driven Jean even madder. Instead he withdrew, which drove her insane. Cold, quiet, English disapproval and the tight-lipped restraint from action were what, ultimately, would drive her into an asylum. Though he did not physically leave her, she had brought about her own abandonment – in every sense of the word.

For this first year of their marriage, they were impoverished and constantly on the move, from Holland Park to Bloomsbury, Hampstead, a bungalow on the Thames, and shabby rooms in Paddington and Victoria. Jean could be very funny about her and Leslie's insolvency. Above all, she liked to be entertained. And this was entertaining. On 18 February 1934 she wrote to Evelyn Scott, another impecunious writer and a rare, passionate admirer of Jean and her work.

Here I may say we still are in two Bloomsbury bedsitting rooms. And I don't see us getting away in a hurry either. Never mind [this would come to be her catch phrase]. This morning (it was rather funny) a huge coloured lady presented herself while I was still in bed and demanded her rent. Very chic she was, pearl earrings and everything (and I believe a compatriot). Leslie was in the bathroom.

She wanted to be paid on the nail. 'Can Mr Smith give me a cheque?' she said.

'No,' I said, 'I shouldn't think so.'

'Why not?' she said.

There was no answer to that so I just looked vague.

'Perhaps,' she said, 'Mr Smith could let me have so much.'

'Well,' I said, 'it'll be a bit difficult today.'

'Why?' she said. A forthright creature.

I said, 'Well you see today is Sunday.'

She said, '*Why* should Sunday be different from any other day,' and I looked very shocked. So she retreated.

Isn't it funny me upholding the Sabbath?

This is a rum house. The West Indian lady is the late owner. She's just sold the house to two German Jewish ladies (born in Wales and very sympathique.)

Throughout this tumult, Jean kept writing what would become her favourite novel, *Two Tunes*, later to be called *Voyage in the Dark*. In another letter to Evelyn, she wrote:

Well, Evelyn, I don't know if I've got away with it. I don't know. It's written almost entirely in words of one syllable. Like a kitten mewing perhaps. The big idea – well I'm blowed if I can be sure what it is. Something to do with time being an illusion I think. I mean that the past exists – side by side with the present, not behind it; that what was – is.

I tried to do it by making the past (the West Indies) very vivid – the present dreamlike (downward career of a girl) – starting of course piano and ending fortissimo.

Perhaps I was simply trying to describe a girl going potty.

Voyage in the Dark is the story of her love affair with Lancey, and the beginning of the end of her innocence and youth. The discipline she imposed on her prose was formidable, admirable and inspiring. It is the discipline of the relentlessness of words that are loaded with meaning. This is why she did not need many of them. They carry so much weight – the faith that she withdrew from people she redirected into words. Words like *gamine*, *garçonne*, *femme fatale*, *jolie laide*, *jeune fille*, *belle comme une fleur de verre*. These were the mannequin words, and the words of betrayal. These words were the lyrics to two tunes that she had had to learn.

Loyal Leslie took it to Hamish Hamilton and Jonathan

Cape, both esteemed publishers, who both gave her mono-
syllables a negative response. Hamilton wanted her to cut it
until she felt there would be nothing left. Cape felt it was
too 'grey', greyer even than *Mackenzie*, which had not sold
well. She tried to be indifferent but the truth was they had
rejected her truest self, and she felt it deeply. Leslie did not
give up, and tried the manuscript on Michael Sadleir of
Constable. He liked it, wanted to publish it, but wanted her
to make one change: the ending. This change would be, he
explained, 'Not of course to my own taste, but to please
prospective readers'. It was the only ending, as far as Jean
was concerned. But Sadleir was adamant.

Underneath the story of Anna and her gentleman lover
and the ensuing procession of less and less gentlemenly men
is the story of a child's consuming need for her mother. In
writing Jean nearly recovered her loss.

Of course Jean's real mother is not mentioned. Instead we
get a series of women: women who are needy – chorus girls
– and women who are needed – a stepmother and landladies.
This endless list of women – landladies, dressers, sages-femmes
– who leave a hole, create need, repudiate need, and never
satisfy it.

Michael Sadleir was right: the ending had to change. Jean,
in a fit of self-pity, had ended her novel with Anna dying
after a back-street abortion. She paid two visits to Sadleir's
office to discuss possible endings. The first visit saw her rushing
out of the meeting in tears. The second saw her grimly acqui-
escing and resenting him ever after. But the revised ending
was better. She instilled more bleakness into it by being more
subtle. less adolescent. The doctor, a man whose movements
are like a machine's, she notes, concludes the book with the
words, 'Ready to start all over again in no time.'

In October 1934 *Voyage in the Dark* was published. Even

the reviewer for *The Lady* liked it. She recommended it to 'those well-balanced women of normal resource who "cannot understand" how any girl ever takes to the streets for a living, and also to those who sentimentalise over those who do'. Reviewers everywhere found this book more palatable than her last three. In some ways, this is because it was a familiar story of Edwardian gaiety girls and bounders and the loss of innocence. It is what happens after that loss of innocence that so shocked Jean's readers. But this book was enough of a success for Constable to issue a paperback.

In January 1935 Jean received a letter from yet another influential admirer of her work, the novelist Rosamond Lehmann. She was thirty-four and the author of three novels that had created similar, though more manageable, shock waves. She could respond with sympathy to what Jean was doing. She wrote praising her novel and asking to meet her.

Jean accepted an invitation for tea at Rosamund's house. Rosamund's sister Beatrix, a well-known actress, and Mrs Violet Hammersley, the widow of a rich banker and patron of the arts, joined them. All three women were looking forward to meeting this daring new writer who had clearly drawn on her life for her work. Jean turned up dressed like an Edwardian matron in dusty black. She wore an old-fashioned hat and lacy gloves that she refused to remove. She sipped at her tea primly and spoke little. This was the act she had prepared and she was sticking to it. Mrs Hammersley tried drawing her out with risqué stories of Paris where she had lived. Beatrix winked at her saucily. Rosamund had no choice but to accept her new friend's show of respectability.

Although Jean had not been able to remove her disguise, she had liked Rosamund and wrote to say so. Rosamund wrote back to her, saying, 'I guessed, and now am sure, that you are frightened of people.' This was an invitation to drop the act.

The next time she saw her, Jean had a black eye. The last time she saw her, Jean was too drunk to speak.

Their second appointment to meet was against the backdrop of George V's Silver Jubilee. It was spring 1935, and Jean was disgusted by the celebrations and public displays of national, back-slapping complacency. Faced with a bruised and angry version of the Edwardian lady, Rosamond sympathised, and arranged to meet her again at the Café Royal on 14 June. Jean did not turn up. At four o'clock that morning, she and Leslie had been arrested on Wardour Street, Soho, for being drunk and disorderly – they had had a fight. After a night in the cells, Jean was taken to Bow Street Magistrates' Court where she pleaded not guilty. Leslie, who was more realistic, pleaded guilty. The magistrate dismissed Jean's plea. Husband and wife were fined thirty shillings and sixpence each, plus a doctor's fee. Leslie rushed to the Café Royal and explained away the bruises. He told Rosamond that he and Jean were terribly sorry but they had had a car accident.

A few weeks later, Jean invited Rosamond to tea at her and Leslie's rooms in Bury Street, which was quite a fashionable address. Their neighbours were Quaglino's restaurant and the Marlborough Hotel. Rosamond knocked on the front door of the narrow house, and Leslie opened it. He looked unwell, said his wife was ill. But he invited her to follow him up the dark, narrow staircase. Jean was lying on a sofa, her clothes in disarray, surrounded by wine bottles and manuscripts. She was too drunk to recognise Rosamond or speak to her. She lay on the sofa calling Leslie's name. Rosamond was puzzled as to why Jean was asking him why he looked so sad. She was pushing him, taunting him, over and over again. He said nothing.

Rosamond took one look at the mess on the sofa, registered Leslie's impassive face, and walked out. She never wrote to Jean again.

Chapter 19:

THE NEIGHBOUR FROM HELL

In September 1935 the Reverend Tilden Smith died. He left his son a legacy worth £2,500. Leslie and Jean, who were quite impoverished, spent some of the money on a trip to Dominica.

It had been almost thirty years since Jean had set foot in Dominica, and now she was making the journey back to her childhood. Of course, everything, including herself, had changed. But she had to go back to Dominica to revisit her fantasy of her childhood Eden. In so doing, she came up against the reality of a parochial, backwoods island. She came back to her island a novelist, and a notable personage for such a remote outpost of an old empire. News reached her neighbours that a literary couple were staying at the Hampstead estate. A *faux*-Genever in the south of the island had been loaned to her by a friend of her late mother's. Custom dictated that introductions be made, invitations to lunch issued, acquaintances formed.

The lady in the estate to the right was Elma Napier who, in the 1940s would be elected to the Caribbean legislature. She was everything Jean hated. She had only recently arrived in Dominica and yet was already pontificating on its beauty, and on changes that needed to be made. She busied herself hosting parties and organising people. Jean recognised the fierce energy of the woman who invited her to lunch. After ten minutes of desultory conversation, Elma did a 'war dance' which was directed at Jean, 'tomahawk in hand, smile on face'. Over the first course, she complained about a book she had written that had been offered to Hamish Hamilton and declined. After lunch, she gave Leslie a long novel to report on. Jean could be humorous about her neighbours' war dances and veiled aggression, but only in writing.

The lady in the estate to the left also asked this sought-after literary couple to lunch. Knowing that Jean was a novelist she bored her rigid with lengthy monologues on the prolific, popular gardening writer and novelist Beverley Nichols. She talked about his books till Jean wanted to scream or swear at her. Instead of changing the subject or asking her hostess questions that might guide her into more fruitful territory, her fragility reasserted itself; she lost all sense of who she was, and agreed with everything the stupid, garrulous woman said. This vanishing act cost her. She was miserable for the rest of her stay.

But one visit pleased her. In Roseau, before she left, she met Owen's children, Ena, Mona and Oscar. The rest of her family had spurned them, a form of snobbery she found hard to forgive, and Leslie was suspicious of what he called their 'begging'. But Jean liked them and did not mind when Owen complained about the amount of money Jean had given him. She liked Ena especially and admired her long hair and pretty baby. Ena told her that Jean's father had once asked her why she did not call herself 'Rees Williams' as opposed to 'Williams'. It was her right to, after all, was the implication. It was yet another instance of Dr Rees Williams' decency.

In another bold act of exploration, Jean made an excursion into Carib territory, a reserve on the north-east coast of the island, which the island's administrator and her former dancing partner, Hesketh Bell, had secured in 1903. At that time, there were only a few hundred Caribs left on the island, the rest having been wiped out by Europeans. But the Caribs were the original colonisers of Dominica and their ability to survive in the wild interior made this one of their last outposts. Jean had always been fascinated by the stories of Carib rebellion and daredevilry she had heard from women like Francine and Ann the *obeah* cook. For instance, she would have heard that the Caribs' first act of the day was to bathe in mountain streams. When they did consent to be servants they were dubbed '*indolents et fantastiques*'. They were indifferent to money, scorned trade and notions of profit, and had a total lack of ambition which rendered them perplexing to their fellow islanders. Furthermore, they attached no value to virginity, chastity or marriage. Most intriguing of all, one of their traditions was that of adopting a pseudonym, which they rigorously maintained throughout long journeys, so that their words and actions were considered to have been performed by a stranger. They travelled light, they reinvented themselves. Towards the end of his life, Jean's brother Owen wrote a short story whose heroine, a young girl named Missy, is clearly based on Jean. Written in the melodramatic style favoured by Jean the chorus girl, Owen's story describes Missy's encounter in the heart of a jungle with a half-white, half-Carib boy. Missy's story is strikingly close to that of Antoinette in *Wide Sargasso Sea*. Perhaps it contained a grain of truth. As an elderly woman in her cups, Jean often hinted that she had once kissed a Carib boy in the rainforest. What is certain is that she never forgot their fierce sense of liberty.

When they arrived back in London, Leslie's money had run out. His sister, who had inherited more from their father as a result of having borrowed less, and who was single and self-effacing, was kind. She agreed to pay Leslie's rent and living expenses for as long as he needed. He did not feel the need to inform Jean of his sister's generosity, and she probably did not ask where this fresh injection of cash had come from. All she knew was that Leslie moved them into 22 Paultons House, a top-floor flat in a Chelsea square overlooking a mature garden. This was a far remove from rooms in shop-soiled Bloomsbury. It was a proper home. She bought furniture to complete their domesticity. She loved the dainty side of home-making; the arrangement of flowers and the distribution of artistic touches throughout a room. She put up a wall hanging in the living room and bought plump cushions for the sofa. She hung portraits and sketches of herself by various artists throughout the flat. She had a daily come in to clean. She was happy.

She also had another new friend, the Jamaican novelist Eliot Bliss. Her autobiographical novels, *Saraband* and *Luminous Isle*, were published at roughly the same time as Jean's. Their heroines were young women who were searching for freedom and strength.

Bliss was born in Jamaica in 1903. Her father was an English army officer and she was educated in English convents. She took her name from T.S. Eliot and George Eliot. She had a lot in common with Jean, though not as much as Jean would have liked. Some of the strength that Eliot had, which she possibly inherited from her father, reminded Jean of what she lacked. What was it, Jean wondered, that she had inherited from her father?

Nonetheless there was a lot for them to enjoy in each other and to talk about. Once a fortnight throughout the summer of 1937, Eliot came to the pretty Chelsea flat. Jean cooked West Indian suppers for them, and the two women happily discussed books, each other's books, and their homeland. The woman Eliot engaged with was elegant and slim, with fashionably 'blue'd' white hair. It was hard to tell her age (she was forty-seven). Her capacity for drink was far greater than Eliot's, though Eliot would gamely try to keep up. Leslie would quite often have to carry Eliot, comatose, to the spare bed. Then he would put Jean to bed, too.

Sometimes the evenings would not end so equably. Jean would get into a rage with Eliot, accusing her of being an 'unfeeling aristocrat', of being respectable, of not being, in other words, down and out, or achingly vulnerable. This is something that had alienated many of Jean's friends from her. But Eliot paid no attention to the rages of her friend.

'She wasn't attacking me,' she said. 'She was attacking the world. I'd seen it before, in other artists.'

Eliot left England in September 1937 and it was only this that separated them. She appreciated her friend for the good things she had had to offer: loyalty, wit, camaraderie and kindness, and the capacity to listen without judging. Jean was unshockable. If she had not heard it all before, she had done it herself or had imagined it. She knew the worst of human beings from knowing the worst of herself. No one else's bad behaviour could shock her.

Jean and Leslie had a peaceful summer. They had the means and space to tolerate each other: to be loving and thoughtful. It is easy to forget that Jean could be good company. Leslie does not seem to have ever forgotten that. If everything was going well and there were no money worries and she was writing, then she could live well. In Paulton House, Jean even had a room to write in. But these happy moments did not last. For some unknown reason, Jean could not write in her room. Perhaps everything was a bit too perfect. So in November 1937, Leslie sent her to Paris where the World Exhibition was being held.

For the duration of the Exhibition two hundred fountains, sixty metres high, dotted the banks of the Seine. Light shows took place each night, transforming the city into a kaleidoscope of spotlights. The dancing lights were choreographed in time to scores especially composed by avant-garde musicians such as Milhaud, Auric and Honegger. Paris was making its claim to be the 'City of Lights' under the shadow of European dictatorships.

Jean found the Exhibition cold and sterile. Instead of viewing the spectacle on the grand boulevards, she went to the street fairs of the *banlieues*. She saw naked women, a two-headed man, little girls on merry-go-rounds, the odd and the common-place illuminated by gaudy electric bulbs. The music she listened to was the sound of the hurdy-gurdy and the roar of desperate animals trapped in cages. The booths, the puppet-shows, the roller-coasters were set up in Montmartre, Bastille, Denfert-Rochereau, and the Boulevard de Grenelle.

It was while she was exploring the outer reaches of Paris that she thought about her next novel. It would feature a character called Sasha Jensen, except her real name is not Sasha. Jean refuses to make clear what Sasha's real name is. She is very much like her creator. This book is a daring break with conventional narrative. Sasha makes no connec-tions between past and present, between old lovers and new: they are all the same. Any connections the reader might try to make are impeded by Jean's elliptical prose. What is not conscious or available to Sasha is not available to the reader. We have to read the novel the way that Sasha experiences life: fractured, bewildering, with a hint of menace.

Jean was fascinated by fairgrounds, by the kaleidoscope of the grotesque and the vulgar. Like the Dominican carnival she witnessed as a child, the undercurrent of violence and anger was closer to the surface than in everyday life. She was drawn to fairgrounds by the crowds of working people. There was an edge of wildness to their enjoyment. Like the bars she frequented, she never knew who or what she might encounter. This excited her. She liked to run into strange types. One night she was picked up by a strange man.

His name was Simon Segal. He was a melancholic Russian Jew, eight years younger than Jean, and down on his luck. He had come to France in 1925 to be a painter. His subject matter, like Jean's, was unpopular: he painted poor people and scenes of violence. Like Jean, he was single-minded to the point of obsession in the pursuit of his vision; as though he were chasing it to the very last edges of darkness. He was never likely to sell much. Jean liked him. She bought a painting from him, he stood her up, but he respected her, and they met again. He shook her hand in a farewell gesture and called her 'Amie'. That was enough. The brevity of the friendship was enough. He had said it all. She transcribed every detail of their brief relationship for her next heroine to puzzle over in *Good Morning, Midnight*.

There is another encounter with a stranger in this novel. This one involves a man in a neighbouring room in Sasha's seedy boarding house in a cold and depressing Paris. The man's name is 'Monvoisin', which translates as 'my neighbour'. Jean the novelist knew very well what neighbours meant for her in a way that, unfortunately, Jean the woman did not. They were projections, usually hostile, of her fear and rage. Crowds in the street and *mon voisin*. People frightened her but what frightened her most was the rage within herself. She could not see other people without imagining that they had the same violent urges. *Good Morning, Midnight* illustrates what it is like to conjure up the worst in people: in men, this meant violence and rejection instead of a loving embrace. It could be that she met such a man – a man who hated what he wanted and so took it violently – in Paris in 1937. In this novel, she describes a commercial traveller in the next room to Sasha, who follows her every move with hungry eyes. He makes Sasha feel uncomfortable because she sees herself in him. It is the discomfort of recognition; an expression of her worst, recurring nightmare. Jean wrote *Good Morning, Midnight* knowing full well that plots are not important because it is always the same story. The story behind this novel is very simple, very familiar, and seldom told: Sasha is in her forties, down at heel and has no family. She finds herself living in the inevitable seedy boarding house in a cold and depressing Paris, depressing because she is no longer *une jeune fille* or that other creature with power, *une femme sacrée*. Her livelihood and hence her well-being have hitherto depended on her attractiveness to men. She now confronts the terrifying spectre of ageing female flesh and the diminution of male desire. She faces the distinct possibility of destitution. Wandering around the streets of the city, she stays in bars just long enough to get herself drunk. When she has had enough to drink, she returns to her room, where she doses herself with barbiturates and sleeps. She offers herself to the reader and to passers-by in states of dreaming, drunkenness, or drugged semi-consciousness. These states of being produce startling, hallucinatory and disorienting effects in the novel.

While the World Exhibition was taking place in Paris that November, Jean was making an exhibition of herself in the bars and cafés of her youth. She was drinking heavily and making no attempt to hide the fact. Being looked at meant being judged, like the Judgement of Paris, except no man in Paris was going to judge forty-seven-year-old Jean the fairest. Men would be judging her with hostile eyes, to ascertain what they could get from her.

This particular trip to Paris ended with a stay in a clinic near Versailles. Jean had had some kind of breakdown. 'No artist tolerates reality,' said Nietzsche. Jean had written about that oppression with a stunning clarity of vision, and she paid the price.

She came home to Leslie, and wrote compulsively and desperately, mostly in the mornings. She covered the bed with paper. The rest of the time she drank heavily. She became so frustrated that she tore up her contracts with her publishers and the painting she had bought from Simon Segal. She even tore up the book that she was writing and that Leslie had typed. Never mind. She started again.

Leslie, or his sister, could no longer afford the relative luxury of Paultons House. He and Jean moved to Taplow, near Maidenhead in Berkshire – one of the quietest villages in the Thames Valley. Parts of Taplow dated back to the 1590s. Its red-brick, stolid charms made no impact on her.

'I'm drunk mostly all the time,' she wrote in her notebook. But it was when she was drunk that 'the Man in the Dressing Gown appeared from Heaven knows where to supply the inevitable end:' *Mon Voisin*. She was writing when she was drinking, inviting her nightmares to surface. But she kept on writing. Throughout 1938 and 1939 she did little else. Dark memories were flooding in, which called a halt to her writing, then she would appear to be dreaming. Leslie would cajole her back to her routine.

Good Morning, Midnight was published in April 1939 and received the fewest and worst reviews she had had since *Quartet*. No one wanted to read it, not even the French. Her old confrère, Jean Lenglet, sent her a letter of rejection he had received from a French translator: 'Malgré tous mes efforts, Plon ne veut pas publier GM,M. Comme Stock, il admire les qualités incontestables du livre mais le sujet (en ce moment surtout) effroye tout éditeur.'

Lenglet was right. Jean's dark vision was too much for her contemporaries. This was not the right time for her.

She did not publish another novel for almost thirty years.

Chapter 20:

ENEMY ALIEN

In 1939, while the rest of the world was agog with war, Jean and Leslie were living somewhat obscurely in various cheap lodgings. Jean began writing a first draft of *Wide Sargasso Sea*, as well as short stories and autobiographical pieces. At the same time, her eldest sister, Minna, developed Parkinson's disease. Her youngest sister, Brenda, became a nurse again. In December, Aunt Clarice died, aged ninety-one.

Shortly after *Good Morning, Midnight* was published, Leslie gave Jean a copy of *Jane Eyre*. On reading it, she was struck by what she called 'a marvellous idea'. The story of the mad Creole in the attic was one that needed telling again – this time from the mad Creole's perspective. With the rapidity that only great ideas can engender, this marvellous one became a book that she called *Le Revenant* – 'the ghost', or 'the one who returns'.

By this time she and Leslie had returned from their exile in Taplow and moved back to Chelsea. Back in London she wrapped herself up in bed and wrote the prequel to *Jane Eyre* very quickly. Leslie, as excited as herself by what she was writing, typed it equally quickly. He told her this could be the one; even she felt it was a turning point. But then one night, after an drunken argument, she took the completed typescript and burned it in the grate.

This was the second novel she had destroyed, although she had managed to salvage *Good Morning, Midnight*. The fact that both books speak so honestly of her deepest fears, and her barely acknowledged desires, must be a clue as to how painful it was for her to write them and then unleash them on her readers. How frightened she was by what she was writing is signified by her destruction of her typescripts. It might even have made it worse that Leslie liked them. She would never recover from the feeling that she would never be accepted. If anyone said she could be, she had to prove them wrong.

She started *Le Revenant* one more time, but this time kept it in her head, every word of it. She left it there, fully formed, waiting to be delivered on to the page. This time it was to be called *Wedding in the Carib Quarter*. In her excitement, she jotted down some notes, and composed titles for each part – there were to be three. Then she opened a bottle of wine to celebrate. When she had recovered from her drinking session, the story had gone.

'It went for keeps,' she wrote on the page where she'd scribbled her notes for it. 'Attention Miss! Or madam. No playing around with ME.'

It was at this point that she threw Leslie's typewriter out of the window. They were living on the fifth floor of an apartment block, but she did not stop to think. 'ME' was her unconscious speaking. Memories, or perhaps fantasies from her childhood were brewing inside her. They had something to do with the Carib quarter, as she herself half-revealed in another drunken aside:

This feeling I have about the Caribs & the Carib Quarter is very old very complicated . . . When I try to explain the feeling I find I cannot or do not wish to.

No playing around with ME.

Fantasy can be just as resonant, just as real, as reality. The fantasies of generations of European colonisers involving 'primitive' tribes, cannibalism, incest, mixed-race liaisons, sexual guilt and anxiety, were transmitted down the generations to Ella Gwendoline – Jean Rhys. The fear of what she desired was overwhelming, if only she could remember what it was that she had desired. Incest taboos, seduction theory: it took a lot of alcohol and courage to get her there but she gave voice to the fears and desires that tormented the little girl inside her.

Then the war came. It killed *Good Morning, Midnight*. Jean was ahead of her times in terms of subject matter, and contemporary in the atmosphere of impending catastrophe that she had created. Perversely, she was out of step with her readers and the modern world. It was too much information. Too much reality. She had created a doom-laden urban landscape that was negotiated by a vulnerable woman. Furthermore, this urban setting evoked a city of darkness at a time when citizens of Paris and London were preparing for their own cities' destructions. As Lenglet had said, 'en ce moment surtout', her readers could not cope with such relentless introspection or such a frank exposition of what it really means to be vulnerable. The exploitation, fear and cruelty she described was happening on a massive scale. No wonder people found *Good Morning, Midnight* hard to read.

The disappointment crushed any chance Jean had of creating another modernist masterpiece any time soon. At this point, on the brink of war, she did not see herself as part of a tradition or as speaking for a lost generation. If she could have seen what she had in common with her peers, perhaps she would have felt some comradeship with them. Instead she felt comradeship with outsiders. Artistically, alienation worked well for her. Sasha's acquiescence at the end of *Good Morning, Midnight* is a distortion of Molly Bloom's in James Joyce's version of a modernist masterpiece.

Jean did not parade her literary allusions, acquaintances, or associations. They bled into her writing. This makes her writing all the more subversive – an ironic echo, a passive-aggressive swipe at the masters. Her anger was so much a part of her – of who she was – it coloured everything she wrote. This in turn makes it all the more charged with power.

'I will never succeed in England. Never,' she said.

There was to be no Blitz spirit for Jean. For once, she really was alone.

It is uncertain where she was living when war broke out but it still seems to have been Chelsea. Germany invaded Poland on 1 September 1939. In the same week, the seventeen-year-old convent schoolgirl Marvyonne arrived in London to visit her mother. On 3 September, Britain and France declared war on Germany. A week later, Leslie took his wife and step-daughter boating on the River Thames. They could not help noticing that trenches were being dug in the park. Jean had seen the country preparing for war before. The first time round she had been unconscious of anything apart from her own misery. This time round, she was a mother and a published novelist and had lived through one world war. She knew what was coming.

As a rare gesture of familial solidarity, she took Maryvonne to visit her sisters, Minna and Brenda, in the suburban green lanes of Acton. They negotiated the semi-detached villas and corner shops to find the two ugly sisters to Jean's Cinderella. But they did not seem so dreadful now – they had their own problems, which made her have some sympathy for them. For their part, they could not treat her with contempt – they were too low.

While German armoured columns drove deep, and with awesome speed, into Poland, the Luftwaffe took control of the air above. The speed of Germany's invasion of mainland Europe gave it the name *Blitzkrieg*, or 'lightning war'. The Polish armies were soon encircled and forced to retreat.

Lenglet wrote to Jean insisting that Maryvonne return at once. He was convinced Hitler was about to invade England, but as Jean pointed out: 'He doesn't seem to have realised that he'd invade Holland first.'

Despite this, she let Maryvonne decide where she wanted to spend the coming war. This life-long passivity is probably what influenced her daughter's choice. She chose her father. Maryvonne left her mother to return to a country that was a sitting target. Jean would lose touch with her daughter and ex-husband for the duration of the Second World War. All she would know was that Holland was occupied by the Nazis.

The first months of the war were an anti-climax for most British people. In anticipation of air raids, children were evacuated from expected target areas. A strict night-time blackout was imposed. Heavy curtains hid interiors, street lighting was extinguished and motor vehicles inched along the roads. Gas masks were issued to everyone. When no great onslaught from the air occurred, relief led to a slackening of precautions. These quiet months from September 1939 until May 1940 were known as 'the phoney war'. But Jean's fears were not phoney, they were real. In these first few months the Dutch would bear the brunt of the *Blitzkrieg*. They had no hiding place in the Second World War, geography made sure of that. From September 1939 until May 1940 when Hitler actually invaded, the fascist terror was closing in on Jean's daughter. The fretful mother could not dissipate her anxiety by sharing it with anyone. Her mistrust of others and her inability to stem her rising panic meant that she believed no one else could feel the war as she was feeling it. It was only happening to her, and at a vast, uncross-able stretch, her loved ones overseas. War reinforced her isolation.

On 15 February 1940 Leslie was commissioned as a Pilot Officer, a purely administrative role, in the Royal Air Force. She moved with him to his posting in Bircham Newton, in the north-west corner of Norfolk. It is most likely that around June 1940, a month after Hitler's invasion of Holland, she had a breakdown, or was in some other way an embarrassment to her husband, and had to be removed from his posting. She next turns up in a small village in the north of Norfolk, called West Beckham.

In the nine months from 7 September 1940 to the end of May 1941, most of which time Jean lived alone in this obscure Norfolk village, the Luftwaffe dropped some 46,000 tons of high explosive and 110,000 incendiaries, a total of 54,420 tons of bombs, on English towns and cities. She was terrified. Over 40,000 civilians were dead, 86,000 seriously injured and 150,000 slightly injured. The war was no longer phoney. Two million houses were destroyed or damaged, 60 per cent of them in London. She longed for someone to join her. Leslie's job, or his personal preferences, meant that he could not.

It was very rural and very quiet in West Beckham, far from the bombs of the Luftwaffe. This peaceful village was a few miles from the beaches of Cromer and the picturesque market town of Holt. A lovely old church sat in the middle. It was the hub of the community, with a Sunday School known affectionately as the Panda Club and a thriving choir. The RAF gave her a house to live in – large, square and red brick – on the furthest edge of the village. In a short

story called 'Temps Perdi', the phrase she had used to describe
her father's life, and which means 'a waste of time', she
describes the house in its wartime camouflage.

Everything old and beautiful had been taken out of it and
replaced with utility goods and beige paint. The house was
hiding behind a veneer of neutrality, like a hypocrite who
covers his sneer with a smile. 'Everything wears this neutral
mask,' she wrote, 'the village, the people, the sky, even the
trees have not escaped.'

Jean took her feelings from landscapes, and if the shadows
were large and forbidding so were her feelings. If the light
was dappled green and the foliage was dense, the complexity
and profusion of life overwhelmed her with its fragility.
She could not cherish it enough, or make it safe, so she
would cry.

In 'Paradis artificiels', Baudelaire writes:

'Your eye fixes on a tree . . . What would be, in a poet's
brain, only a very natural comparison will become a reality
in yours. You first attribute to the tree your passions, your
desire, or your melancholy; its moans and oscillations
become your own, and soon you are the tree.'

At times Jean had experienced an intense closeness to nature
that eclipsed any intimacy human beings could offer. But in
the midst of wartime England, even trees had lost their truth.
She tried to lose herself in books, but they, too, seemed
complicit in some kind of campaign against her. There were
voices in her head. But this time she had reason to be wary
of her neighbours.

Xenophobia was growing throughout England. Since the
spring of 1940 the popular press had been pressing for the
internment of 'enemy aliens'. Jean would have had more in

common with the Italians, Austrians, Germans, Reds, Celts
and Conchies than the rural, church-going villagers of West
Beckham, near Holt. During the last week of June and the
first two weeks of July 1940, 23,000 'enemy aliens' were
rounded up to be interned in camps dotted around Britain.
They were imprisoned without trial and without respect for
their human rights.

She could hear people talking about her; she could hear
the men who delivered coal to the house mocking the 'crazy
old foreigner' who was living there, the madwoman cowering
in the attic. The house itself was creaking with hatred. She
filled her notebook with her suspicions, her fears, her obses-
sions: that people thought she was a witch, a spy, an enemy
alien. It was the only thing – writing her fears down – that
kept her from total breakdown. In writing, she could distance
herself from her fears, intellectualise her suspicions. The
mockery she felt that she was subject to was an expression
of the distaste she felt the English had for women. She could
put a name to it if she wrote about it.

Leslie finally joined her in February 1941. Then this
happened:

> Ella Gwendoline Tilden Smith, of Holt, was fined for being
> drunk and disorderly on the highway at Holt.
> 　. . . Police Constable Haverson stated defendant was
> unsteady on her feet, her appearance was dishevelled, and
> her breath smelt strongly of spirits. She broke out into a
> stream of abuse of the English race, declaring, according
> to one witness, 'I am a West Indian, and I hate the English.
> They are a b— mean and dirty lot.' The disorderly conduct
> . . . arose only after one of the witnesses had thrown water
> over her. Mrs Tilden Smith was very distressed because no
> news had been received of her daughter in Holland since
> the invasion of that country.

The newspaper account is telling enough. Another short story, 'I Spy a Stranger', spells out more literally the paranoia, mistrust and ugliness of wartime parochial England, where a woman screaming in the street merits public derision and a bucket of water being thrown at her. Celts, Reds and Conchies were the objects of suspicion and hostility. So, it seems, was Anglo-Caribbean Jean Rhys whose father was Welsh and whose daughter was somewhere in Holland.

The war realised Jean's oldest and deepest fear: that behind everything and everyone something opposite and horrible is hidden. She tried suicide. Another wartime story, 'I Spy a Stranger', describes the relief of sinking into a coma by taking a handful of pills. It, too, focuses on a lone woman of no fixed abode and foreign appearance, and the suspicions she provokes in people who cannot place her. What this story makes clear is that Jean was staying in a large house in a small village surrounded by people she could not trust, relate to, or engage with. This was her closest to madness. She was unspeakably lonely. Even her loneliness frightened her. The story ends with the heroine being taken away to an asylum with high walls and barred windows.

After the incident on the highway of Holt, Jean was sent to an asylum. In the spring of 1941 she was let loose on the city of Norwich. She stayed in grungy digs on a street in a dreary suburb called Chapelfield. For the first time in her life, she was recommended to the care of a psychiatrist, a Dr Rose who had a private practice in Norwich. Perhaps this contact with a professional who could understand her helped her because she did something unusual and that was to contact a friend.

She still had a friend from the days when she had been an exciting, if somewhat disturbing, new voice on the literary scene. Her correspondence with Peggy Kirkaldy had been punctuated by gaps brought about by Jean's irritation at Peggy's penchant for namedropping and literary chitchat. But they had remained friends nevertheless. She decided to visit Peggy who was living in Colchester. This journey – Norfolk to Essex – was a long way for Jean to go on her own. Long past the city limits of male desire; vulnerable in an entirely new way and now with the added pressure of being surrounded by the English bull-dog spirit at its most bullish.

Her visit was characterised by manic behaviour on her part and stunned submission on Peggy's. When Peggy expressed her irritation, Jean exploded. She must have said something very rude to Peggy because Peggy refused to respond to her craven apologies. Jean wrote many, voluminous letters apologising for having talked too much, and for saying whatever it was that she had said. But really all her letters were about herself. She did not address herself to how Peggy might be feeling. It was many years before she got a reply.

On 23 March 1941 another blow came: Lancelot Grey Hugh Smith died. Another friend down. Jean was desperate. She tried one more. She wrote to a Dominican girl called Phyllis Shand Allfrey who was living in England. They had met just before the war, and Jean's beloved childhood friend, Willie, was Phyllis's uncle. Phyllis picked up on her desperation and luckily had a friend who could help: the Reverend Willis Feast who lived in Norfolk.

He came to visit. The fact that he was a man of the cloth must have seemed like a godsend. Like Phyllis, he responded with sensitivity. The Luftwaffe's bombing campaign had reached Norwich. Clearly, the woman was vulnerable. He invited her to come and stay with his family in their country vicarage. She would stay with them in the village of Booton for the entire summer of 1941. It should have been heaven, but it wasn't.

It should have been heaven because the entire household respected her privacy and yet catered to her needs. She did not have to join the family and their other refugee guests for dinner. She was given the best bedroom. The women of the family brought her meals to her room on a tray. Leslie came to visit her once a week. She had her fifty-first birthday in August. Everyone was sympathetic. The Feasts' daughter said she looked like Claudette Colbert. Two men friends of Mr Feast came to visit and she flirted with them.

On her visits into the city of Norwich she would dress very primly and formally, and put a feather in her hat. When the sun was shining she could sit on a rug in their lovely garden and read Ernest Hemingway's *For Whom the Bell Tolls* very slowly. She was not particularly taken with his writing but she did recall that night in Paris in the twenties when he had helped her into her coat.

She could be very sweet when she was feeling safe, 'regal', even, her host described her. She talked about books with him, which he enjoyed very much. She was so open and unaffected in her enthusiasm for books that men like Feast would always be entranced by her. One afternoon she sat reading under the tree, wearing a tight dress with some buttons missing, which attracted a male audience.

Most of the time, though, she could not hide from the fact that the war was on and there could be no communication with her daughter in occupied Holland. Jean hid in her room, under the covers, not wanting to face even nice Mr Feast. She was not writing, and when she did not write her fears and suspicions overwhelmed her. When Mr Feast managed to coax her to the local Lyons' café for lunch she complained incessantly. It was declassé. She was used to much finer dining. Did he think a Lyons' café was all she was worth? Was he, in fact, insulting her? Her suspicions infected every

effort of kindness on anyone else's part. He tried to interest
her in the traditional pursuits of English ladies. He tried
flower-arranging. He even picked some rhododendrons for
her. She never arranged them. Nothing could please her.
She must have been intolerable to someone less patient than
a kindly vicar or a Leslie.

His friend Mr Griffiths, the rector of a neigbouring parish,
certainly grew impatient with her. Jean, as though she had
been poised for an attack, leapt to her own defence by accusing
Mr Griffiths of being 'self-satisfied'. Furthermore, she told
him, his wife and sister wanted to stab her with their knitting
needles. Mr Feast tried to pacify her, she grew more hysterical.
Mrs Feast slapped her to shut her up. And so it went on for
weeks and weeks, until, in September, the bombs stopped
dropping on Norwich. The Feasts were greatly relieved. It
was safe for Jean to move back there. That September she
moved to Thorpe, a suburb of Norwich.

The obvious targets for German bombs were ports, industrial centres and railway depots. Hence the Luftwaffe targeted
areas like Bristol, Southampton, and the Docklands, all of
which got hammered. But Hitler also had a policy of *schreck-
licheit* ('frightfulness'), where nice, quiet places, like Coventry
or Norwich, got flattened for no better reason than to demor-
alise the populace. The Nazis abandoned the policy when
they realised it did not work. The bombing had strengthened
morale, rather than weakening it. But the vilification of enemy
aliens, fifth columnists, and the Germans that was occurring
on a daily basis in the popular press drove Jean mad. Certainly
the Germans waged a dirty war, but war, as she knew, is a
dirty business. No one keeps their hands clean in wartime.
The British were just as wanton in their destruction. In 1943
the Allies destroyed Hamburg and around 40,000 civilians in
just two aerial bombardments. In 1945, British bombers blitzed

Dresden into oblivion, killing around 50,000. The organised disavowal of its own war must have exacerbated her hypersensitivity to British hypocrisy.

In early 1942 she was drinking in a pub in suburban Thorpe with her husband when some locals annoyed her. She shouted, 'Heil Hitler!' to shut them up. The repercussions were severe. The RAF had no time for a hysterical, white Creole driven mad with anxiety for her Anglo-Dutch daughter born in France and missing in action in Holland. As a result of Jean shouting, 'Heil Hitler!' in a pub, Leslie was demoted and quickly moved to Bristol for 'Supernumerary Admin Duties'. Norfolk was clear of enemy aliens.

Jean did not go with Leslie to Bristol. This could have been because of the demands of his job or because they preferred to remain separate. This was not a happy period of their marriage. Jean was too unstable to connect with someone who was supposed to be close to her. She moved to London, to a street that had been bombed to pieces during the Blitz. She probably felt more at home here. Darkness and ruination lay around her. Windows were boarded up, litter was left on the streets, weeds were growing in cracks on the pavements. Rats were having a field day. Houses were not so solid, it seemed.

In August 1942, Jean and Leslie went on holiday in the Gower Peninsula and experienced some respite from war. Wales was the home of Aunt Clarice, with whom she had spent innocent, dreamy weeks in St Asaph writing her first short story. Like most of the Welsh countryside, Gower's beauty seems drenched in ancient folklore; the wilderness untamed by cities or towns, and yet somehow as familiar as a favourite, velvety-green gown. There was the calm, blue sea, too. Its sandy beaches were deserted. Further inland, she walked in fields so full of cowslips their scent beckoned her to join them. This was where her father came from, where once she had taken Maryvonne on holiday. They had actually been happy together here.

One thing she liked about Wales was that the women had an air of independence about them. Their English counterparts appeared insecure or defensive whereas Welshwomen carried themselves with authority. They were not so bothered about being wanted by men. They knew they had power – and that power did not reside in their looks but in their social standing. She fell in love with the Gower Peninsula, and for the next ten years hatched plans to escape there. It was yet another fantasy but it sustained her.

Leslie resigned his commission a few months after their Welsh holiday. He told his wife that he was working at the Air Ministry, but the truth is he had returned to scratching his living as a publisher's reader. The war was still raging but 1943 is a blank. She left no record except a short story called 'The Insect World'. It describes a woman called Audrey who lives alone in wartorn London and reads obsessively. Her friend, Monica, queues for their rations. Audrey does the housework and cooking. They dine out three times a week. She does not seem to be having such a bad time.

As Jean was writing 'The Insect World' the V-1s, or doodle-bugs, were dropping like flies. 'FLY' was the official designation which described the V-1's pilotless process. One hundred to 150 a day were aimed at London. Typical of cockneys to give these devastating weapons a diminutive name like 'doodlebugs'.

'There had been the big blitz, then the uneasy lull, then the little blitz, now the fly bombs,' she wrote in 'The Insect World'. The insects in this story, like the ones that had plagued her childhood, are the like the ones plaguing London and that plagued her mind: nasty, destructive creatures running around in circles, endlessly proliferating, and making a nasty mess. The noise they made was terrifying. A sinister buzz like that of a fly fizzed through the air followed by ominous silence, and then the explosion. What happened was that the missile exploded on the surface. As it did so, it caused a vacuum, which caused a second rush of air as the vacuum was filled. This caused a pushing and pulling effect that radiated outwards.

In London suburbs where terraced houses were packed together, up to twenty houses would collapse from just one bomb. Brick walls were pulverised into small fragments. Further away from the immediate impact, roofs and window frames were ripped out of houses, exposing contents and innards. Further out still, windows were blown out and roofing slates shattered. Every time a flying bomb landed hundreds of houses were damaged. This was a cold, wet summer and repairs took many months. Londoners were homeless in their tens of thousands or shivered in cold, roofless houses.

In 1944, in the midst of this bombardment, she and Leslie moved into a flat on Steeles Road, Hampstead, near Primrose Hill. It was paid for by Leslie's sister. Due to some mis-calculation on the Germans' part – the bombs were intended for Tower Bridge – the V-1s followed her here. All in all, however, Hampstead got off lightly.

Hitler's next trick was a rocket, forty-six feet long and five feet in diameter, which carried about a ton of explosives. The V-2 was launched on the far side of the Rhine in Holland, where Maryvonne had last been heard of living with Jews. Since northern France was in Allied hands and their armies were advancing into Belgium, Holland was the only possible site from which the Germans could attack London. The V-2s, with a range of 225 miles and a speed

of 3,600mph – faster than the speed of sound – were the
only things getting out of Holland.

The suburbs of north-east London took the worst of the
attack. The noise they made could be heard from miles
around; Jean, in north-west London, would have heard the
tremendous roaring sound as the V-2s descended to earth
followed by an ear-splitting thunderclap as they hit their
targets. They were highly succesful: 8,938 Londoners died
and tens of thousands were injured in the period between
June 1944 and May 1945.

This last year of war was when Jean wrote up her wartime
stories. It was a wretched time. The conflict seemed never-
ending. These stories chronicle her isolation, her fear of the
machinery that entraps human beings, her escape into reading,
and the horrors of a mechanistic war. There were to be no
cheery propaganda messages for her.

Even though they were in relatively comfortable surroundings in hilly Hampstead, Leslie refused to allow his daughter
Anne to visit them. He said that Jean was difficult, impossible,
'so please don't come'. He told his daughter he had had to
leave the RAF because of her.

One day, when the bombs were raining heavily on the
other side of London, Leslie and Jean walked from their flat
in Steeles Road through the Victorian terraced streets of
Hampstead. They climbed to the top of Primrose Hill. The
name had been given to this hill in the fifteenth century after
the flowers which grew here in abundance. At 260 feet high
it was the ideal site for a heavy anti-aircraft battery which
now sat useless in the face of the new weapons. To the
south, Jean and Leslie had a view of Regent's Park. To the
north and east of them, London was ablaze with incendiary
devices. Jean and Leslie prayed for her daughter in Holland.

Chapter 21:

THE SOUND OF THE RIVER

From 1938 to 1945 Jean's short stories suggest she managed to find shelter through constantly moving to new abodes. When the war finally ended, the only thing that could end the trauma for Jean happened: she got a letter from Maryvonne.

Jean had already noticed that her daughter had more of her father's resolve than her own passivity. In 1935, when Maryvonne was thirteen, she had written, 'Maryvonne has turned up to visit me. She is so tall and gawky and sweet and sings so loudly all over the place that she's bringing me to life again. She is of a hopeful disposition I notice, spent hours yesterday making a contraption with chalk and cotton wool to clean white shoes with! Hopeful and practical. So unlike me, thank God.'

Ten years later, Maryvonne's actions during war proved the girl's strength of character. On returning to Holland in 1939, she had worked with her father on the Dutch Resistance newspaper *Vrij Nederland*. For two years, they had kept it alive, then Lenglet had been arrested by the Gestapo. He had been helping stranded RAF pilots escape the Germans and return to England. Maryvonne was arrested alongside him, and sent to prison. Her youth and the fact that there was no evidence against her helped effect her release. On being released, she joined the Resistance. Her mother summed up this period of Maryvonne's life as being full of 'incredible adventures'. It is a rather breezy, dismissive summary to describe such fortitude and resourcefulness in the face of such adversity. Perhaps the news of an impending marriage was more to Jean's taste.

Maryvonne told her mother she had met a young man, Job Moerman, whom she was about to marry. Even better, he had aristocratic connections, being, as Jean put it, 'a man on Prince Bernhard's staff'. Jean's daughter was happy, alive and about to be married. Jean was thrilled.

The bad news was that Maryvonne feared her father was dead. He had been tried, along with two other Resistance workers. He had helped thirteen enemy pilots, the court had been told. The two other men were sentenced to death, and shot. Lenglet was declared insane, and sent to an asylum. Either he had pulled a fast one, and pleaded insanity, or the Germans had considered him insane for insisting on being shot to death alongside his comrades. What is most likely is that a Dutch friend with far-reaching contacts managed to have his sentence commuted. It was so like him – exciting, mysterious, and finally elusive. Imprisonment seemed always to be the culmination of his adventures.

But this was no romp through interwar Europe. Lenglet spent the next three years behind bars again, first in an asylum, then a Dutch prison. This was bad enough, but then in September 1944 he was sent to a concentration camp, Sachsenhausen, in Germany. Lenglet was joining Polish and Dutch civilians and Soviet prisoners of war. Most inmates did not last long; they died of typhoid, or died of beatings, hangings, torture or starvation. A gas chamber was in regular use at the camp until the end of the war.

In 1944 and the beginning of 1945, when Lenglet arrived there, due to the Allied advance, the number of prisoners increased dramatically. In April 1945, because of the Soviet

Army advance, 33,000 prisoners were forced to leave the camp on a Death March. The SS intended to load them on ships, and then sink the ships. The ships never set off. During the Death March 9,000 prisoners died of exhaustion or were shot because they were too weak to walk. All that Maryvonne knew of her father was that on his arrival at Sachsenhausen he had immediately asked to plead guilty to the original charges made against him. In effect, what he saw there was so terrible, he was asking to be executed. The Germans sent him back to Holland for a re-trial, and he was duly sentenced to death. But the Allies were breathing down the Nazis' necks. Lenglet was sent back to Sachsenhausen in time for the Death March. This was all that Maryvonne knew of her father, but at least she was safe.

Leslie and Jean were relieved from the immediate horrors of war. But at the ages of sixty and fifty-five respectively, these horrors would linger with them for the rest of their days. They did not have the reflex for recovery that the young possess. Leslie organised a retreat to the English countryside for a holiday. This was Jean's fantasy location for gaining respite from the world.

In the last week of September 1945 she and Leslie went to stay in a rough workman's cottage in remote and rainy Dartmoor. Leslie was drained by his experience of war, Jean was frightened. The only thing she was not frightened of was him. Perhaps this is why for the past ten years they had been arguing so much. She knew she could get away with it. One night, a week or so into their holiday, even though their cottage was isolated, their neighbours could hear them screaming at each other.

The next day, 2 October, Leslie was dead.

Jean wrote a short story about her husband's death called 'The Sound of the River'. In it, a woman wakes up to the first fine day in weeks. She can hear the sound of rushing water from the river at the end of the garden. The sound of water flowing endlessly is the sound of death. She attempts to wake her sleeping husband with the words, 'It's a lovely day.' There is no answer. She touches his hand, and it is cold.

What happened was that Leslie seemed fine on awakening, got out of bed, and went downstairs to make a pot of tea. A few minutes later, he returned empty-handed complaining of a terrible pain in his chest and arm. He got back into bed. Jean got up, made him a hot drink, gave him a hot water bottle and some of her pills. Leslie, who was sure the pain was not angina, nor sciatica as Jean had suggested, knew that their landlord, the nearest neighbour with a telephone, was out all morning. He asked Jean to leave a note for the landlord, requesting a doctor. As she left his bedside, he said, 'Oh Jean, what a terrible strain for you.'

She gave several versions of what happened that morning. Some of these versions were for Leslie's concerned and suspicious relatives, one was entirely fictional. In 'The Sound of the River' she wrote that the woman went to the landlord's house, found the room with the telephone locked, walked up and down for a bit, then broke open the door and used the phone. In another letter to Leslie's daughter, she said that she had left a note for the landlord, as instructed by Leslie, and had gone back to the cottage. She went on to explain, 'I sat on a sofa thing for a moment for I'd had 'flu and felt giddy. I heard a strange groaning nose but it was a few seconds before I connected it with Leslie.' As Leslie lay on his deathbed Jean was probably already composing her story. Writing was the only way she could make sense of her life. She certainly was not engaged with reality. She became 'giddy' if life proved too pressing or stressful. She switched off, and retreated to her own world.

'I was there so far as I could be to the end,' she told
Leslie's daughter. This much is true.

But Anne suspected that Jean had killed Leslie. In Jean's
short story, she transposes this suspicion to the doctor who
arrives rather more promptly than his real-life original. In
her letter to Anne, events gather pace, heading towards a
fine climax. On eventually connecting the 'strange groaning
noise' with her dying husband, she rushed upstairs and found
him unconscious. At this point, she ran to the landlord's
house, broke down the door and phoned a doctor. She then
ran back to Leslie's bedside; 'as I took Leslie's hand in mine
he died'.

Jean told her own relatives another version of the story
of Leslie's death; while her husband was dying upstairs, she
sat downstairs having a drink and a smoke. She told Peggy
Kirkaldy something else, and this rings truest: 'He died really
while I was trying to telephone for help . . . so we didn't
even say goodbye.'

Her panic expressed itself as inaction. She probably did sit
on the sofa instead of rousing herself and being effective. She
was honest enough to admit to her own helplessness, feeble-
ness, call it what you will, but others would not admire her
for this frank admission. Although they too might not have
acted promptly at some stage in their lives, or might have
been held back for reasons to do with strange, subconscious
motivation or selfish reasoning, they would not admire Jean
for admitting to hers. Not that she expected to be admired.
She, too, was shocked at her inability to help Leslie. She
could have done more. She could have been a better wife.
She could have been happier with him, argued with him
less, cared for him more. Surely, at sixty, he was too young
to die? Was it her fault? Had she abused him? Was she a
bad person? She could not sit comfortably with herself, she

was so wracked with fears of her own 'badness'. In her short story, her suspicions and everyone else's were voiced by a doctor – an official personage, an authority figure, a judge. Soon the figure of a judge would lose his symbolic value and become all too real – a clutch of magistrates, a prison governor and a few psychiatrists. But for now, the judge was fictional and, like other people, was judging her culpability in Leslie's death.

On 10 October 1945 Colonel Edward Rees Williams of Knottsfield, Budleigh Salterton, Devonshire, took charge of his sister, Ella Gwendoline Tilden Smith, who was in shock. Edward took Jean and his niece, Maryvonne, to view Leslie's body at the crematorium. 'It was a fine and clear day,' wrote Jean to Leslie's daughter, 'and I had all the time the feeling that Leslie had *escaped* – from me, from everyone, and was free at last.'

Maryvonne returned to Holland to her new husband. Jean was determined not to burden their young lives. But she had no one left to look after her. Luckily, Edward, recently retired from the Indian army, had a strong sense of duty. His wife Gertrude was equally stiff with Victorian starch. They asked Jean to stay with them in their new home in Devonshire. After a few days of dismay and disapproval on their part, Jean realised what she was up against, locked herself in her room and refused to eat. This did not mean she wanted to leave. Far from it. When Edward and Gertrude tried to force her out of her bed, she tied herself to it. She screamed at her brother until he lost his stiff upper lip and screamed back. Gertrude had never seen Edward lose his sang-froid before. She was most discomfited to see brother and sister go at each other like cat and dog.

Jean did not get her way. She would have preferred to stay with them, throwing tantrums, but was sent back to the flat she had shared with Leslie in Steeles Road. In November 1945, she was back in London. All she had for company was

> a novel half finished. I should like to finish it – partly because Leslie liked it, partly because I think it might be the one book I've written that's much use – mostly for Leslie.
>
> But I've a *horror* of London. I will go to pieces there alone.

Enter Max Hamer, Leslie's cousin and the executor of his will. He came to Steeles Road to tell her there was no money. He saw the flat needed re-decorating, so he started painting it. In February 1946, she describes him as 'still hanging around'. By autumn she has changed her name by deed poll to Hamer, and moved with him to 35 Southend Road, Beckenham, Kent. The house was built in 1840 – 'one of my favourite years' – the year of Antoinette's honeymoon with Rochester. The house had an overgrown garden and apple trees. It was like being in the country.

Chapter 22:

SUBURBIA

On 2 October 1947 Jean married Max Hamer, Leslie's cousin, and became Mrs Ella Hamer. She recorded her age as fifty-five (she was fifty-seven). He said he was sixty-three (he was sixty-five). On 25 November Princess Elizabeth, the daughter of George V, married Philip Mountbatten. England was in the grip of rationing, and the ensuing winter was one of the coldest in its history.

Max Hamer worked in a law firm but was restless to try new things. He would soon start dealing on the black market, investing in nightclubs and clapped-out music-hall acts. He would try inventing things that never quite worked. He was naive and excitable.

Max was Jean's third husband. He was impulsive, very unlike the English men she had encountered before, and yet he could act the perfect gentleman in various guises. Jean would have liked this, plus she would have enjoyed the swiftness and decisiveness of his courtship. He was born in 1882, eight years before her. He too had been married and had two children, one of whom died in infancy. He too knew what it was to be poor, ill, fatigued and friendless. When he was seventeen he had joined the Navy. He had served twenty-one years, covering the First World War. In 1920 he was invalided out of the Navy with shellshock. He took up the law. In 1939, on the outbreak of war, he rejoined the Navy. Like Leslie he signed up for 'admin. duties'. He

ended the war a Lieutenant Commander, and joined a firm
of solicitors in Gray's Inn. Sometimes he had the bearing of
a reliable lawyer. At other times his naval background asserted
itself, and he looked like an officer. He had dark blue eyes
and sensitive hands.

The war had left Max a nervous wreck. He wanted a
peaceful, prosperous life back on Civvy Street. He needed
rescuing as much as his cousin's widow. He wanted to start
a new life, to reinvent himself, so he did everything 'properly':
since he was already married and he was living with another
woman the problem of respectability could be solved by
changing Jean's name. Appearances were important, truth
could wait. When the divorce came through he would do
the right thing and marry her. Both Jean and Max wanted
to be respectable. They were like children playing at being
married.

As for Jean, when she moved into his house in Beckenham,
she thought she had finally found her pastoral idyll. When
he gave her his name by deed poll, she knew he really cared
for her. When he divorced his wife of thirty-five years to
marry a penniless widow, she was grateful. The house was
delightful, large and rambling; at last she could relax, stop
worrying about money, and just 'flop'. She wanted to spend
their money – his earnings and her allowance – on 'hairdos
and housecoats'. At the age of fifty-seven, she wanted to
look the part of contented housewife. But Max had plans.
They would renovate the house, live on the ground floor
and rent the two top floors as flats. He called in builders,
but it was one of his black-market deals, and the builders
absconded with his money. It was winter now, and Jean was
in a draughty, damp house that badly needed renovating.
Besides the stark reality of living in a draughty, damp house,
she soon discovered that Beckenham was not really the

countryside, nor was it London. It was a suburb, and it was freezing.

On being defrauded by black-market builders, Max argued with his partners in the law firm at Gray's Inn Road, and promptly resigned. Now they had no guaranteed income. Jean had married another Lenglet, only this one talked a lot. He told her everything, and her shrewdness saw right through him. But she suspended disbelief for his sake. He was rather poetic, after all – and sometimes people could be rather amusing, even when they caused grief to everyone around them. He found a new partner, a man called 'Yale', with whom he was, as Jean put it, 'mad' to make money. Her letters chronicle Max's financial dealings in such a way that suggests she was standing back watching, waiting for the crash to happen. Her tone is detached because Max's schemes are so patently hare-brained, though her sympathies are never in doubt. She loved Max for his hopelessness as well as for his courage. More than that, she wanted his dreams to come true.

Max and Yale invested in spurious night-clubs. They hired 'music-hall acts' who never caught on. They met an inventor who they swore would make their fortune. Max even tried his hand at inventing things himself, like a miniature robotic car driven by a miniature robotic man who opened and shut his mouth in time to a gramophone playing comic songs. 'Valiant' Max, as Jean called him, was irrepressible. A small fortune was always around the corner. While Max remained positive and scheming, she could just about convince herself she was the contented housewife that her hairdos and house-coats signified.

Her preoccupations were almost entirely domestic. The garden was quite wild, and though the apple and pear trees had lots of fruit it was difficult to get at them because of the blackberry bushes. But she soldiered on, exchanging her flowery housecoat for trousers, a thick coat and gloves to pick the fruit and make pies for Max. But trouble was brewing.

In January 1949 Jean sent her daughter belated seasonal greetings:

> As you know I do not feel I have the right to bore you with my troubles. I think very very strongly that your baby and Job [her husband] and life in general – well, that's enough for you to cope with, though you are very brave and very sensible (which I'm not).
>
> In fact the worst part of all this has been the feeling that I've let you down and not helped you enough or been the right sort of person for you. However when I tried to write you a conventional Xmas letter – well I *could not* – and that's that –
>
> The words looked so silly. My dear I hope you'll try to understand this collapse and why I tell you of it.

The troubles concerned a black cat called Mister Wu. She loved this cat so much she had written a song about him.

> My black cat is a gentleman
> A gentleman proud and true
> He has teeth and he has claws
> But he'd never use them on me.

She loved wild creatures who were vicious or deceitful to others, but not to herself. They made her feel proud and safe. They were her protector and her vengeful angel. Apart from this love song to her cat, Jean was not writing. Her writing had fallen away on Leslie's death. It had further stalled due to the excitement of a new love affair. Now the fantasy of that love affair was unravelling. She and Max were in

financial difficulties. Snow was falling heavily and not melting
gracefully. Mud was everywhere. She could not write in
these conditions. Max did not have the wherewithal of an
officer or a gentleman; she had not found her idyll or her
saviour. She wrote many, voluble letters that were in turn
funny, brave and sad. Many, especially those to her daughter,
contained mute appeals. But she rarely saw anyone other
than Max and the people of Beckenham. Her cats became
her only companions.

Like her, cats need to be quiet for long periods of time.
Like her, they seek out both silence and the dark. Cats were
like her writing. She stalked in the darkness for long periods.
She seemed to be doing nothing and then the pages appeared
all of a sudden, self-possessed and complete. Cats are pure
wildness, too, and like Jean they love to sleep.

'Sleep is so *lovely,* better than food or thinking or writing
or anything,' she wrote in a letter to her daughter on 9
March 1949.

She preferred sleeping to thinking because she was haunted,
specifically by the idea for a book that she knew she had to
write. It was like an unfinished piece of homework.

If I could earn some shekels I'd fly from damp and bloody
Beckenham and finish my book. Oh *God* if I could finish
it before I peg out or really turn into some fungus or other!

I think of calling it *The First Mrs Rochester* with profound
apologies to Charlotte Brontë and a deep curtsey too.

But I suppose that won't do (I'm supposing you've
studied *Jane Eyre* like a good girl).

It really haunts me that I can't finish it though.

So she preferred to sleep, to dream about her unfinished
novel.

Writing took even more of a back seat when her neighbours made their presence felt. Mrs Hardiman and her husband Horace at number 37, knew nothing of Jean's preoccupations with writing or with cats. They had a dog. First he killed a cat of Jean's called Gaby. Then the unthinkable happened: he killed her black gentleman, Mr Wu.

On 1 April 1948 a newspaper account appeared.

'I lost my head and threw a brick through the window because her dog, a killer and a fighter, attacked my cat,' said Ella Gwendoline Hamer (56), a writer, of 35, Southend Road, Beckenham, accused at Bromley on Tuesday, of breaking a pane of glass, value £5, belonging to Mrs Rose Hardiman, of 37 Southend Road. Hamer was bound over and ordered to pay £5 to Mrs Hardiman.

The local newspaper, *Bromley and West Kent Mercury*, published a weekly column entitled 'Smiles in Court'. In it, the court reporter delighted in repeating the desperate pleas and excuses made in court by miserable sinners attempting to gain clemency from the judge. Over the next two years, they had plenty of opportunities to laugh at Jean Rhys.

'Yes, I threw the brick through the window and I shall do it again,' Jean told the police when Mrs Hardiman called them. She then went on to plead not guilty to malicious damage. Her reasoning was that Mr Wu was dead. It was Mrs Hardiman who was at fault. Her dog had killed her cat. The broken window was a result of this. So she, Jean, could not be guilty.

Her arguments were quoted in 'Smiles in Court':

Defendant (a woman): Did you warn me about your dog, saying it had better not see my cats, as it would kill them?

Witness (also a woman): No, I said that it would chase them. That is natural.

The Chairman (Mr A. W. Hurst): Yes, it is natural for a dog to chase cats. I know, I keep them.

When the magistrate told her that she would be remanded on bail for thirteen days, she replied to the great amusement of the court reporter:

'Not for thirteen days – that's my unlucky number.'

Jean did not have many illusions but she believed passionately in lucky numbers and the goodness of a cat.

She made good copy for the suburban English who would have had no sympathy for her lack of logic. They would have derided her empathy for cats, her fear of numbers, her rootlessness, and her hostile paranoia born of fear. The suburban English organised their lives efficiently, and were comfortable to the point of complacency. Like a window, complacency was something Jean would always want to smash. The readers of 'Smiles in Court' had no truck with Jean's sort; they harnessed their energy, drove motor cars, went to work and to church and wrote letters to *The Times* when they were angry. If they weren't comfortable, they would go to great lengths to hide the fact. And women like Jean, with their rootlessness and their non-conformity, were unsettling, and so needed to be ground down. 'Women are ridiculous when they struggle,' Jean had written. Women who go public with their rage are cast out.

By October it was becoming very clear to Jean that Max was heading for financial meltdown. She told him she wanted to leave him. She changed her mind when he told her he could not repay the fifty pounds he had borrowed from her account. She was stuck. So she stayed in the house in Beckenham and waited. In November, the rooms upstairs were finally ready for rent, and Mr and Mrs Daniell and Mr and Mrs Bezant moved into the top two floors. This was good because it meant money coming in, but it was bad because it meant there were more neighbours. And this time, they were in the same house as her. Every night, they could hear her fighting with Max. She was drinking and shouting – most unseemly.

After a dreary Christmas, Jean stopped drinking and started sleeping more. When she tried to pick up 'Mrs Rochester', she fell asleep after writing two lines.

One night in April 1949 Jean was trying to read a book. The Bezants were giving a party, thereby making a noise. She went to their flat on the floor directly above hers, and asked them to stop. Mr Bezant insulted her; this woman who, until recently, had been screaming abuse at her husband on a nightly basis was now daring to complain about noise. She slapped his face.

Sidney Bezant told the court that his party was over by eleven o'clock. As his guests descended the staircase, Jean, who was standing in the ground-floor hall, shouted abuse at them. She then came upstairs and said something rude to his wife. He intervened, she punched him. He called the police. A constable arrived and she called him, 'Dirty Gestapo'. Then she hit him in the face. He arrested her, and took hold of her. In so doing, he twisted her arm. Then, and her heroine would later do this to her hero, she bit him.

On 12 April, four years after the end of the Second World War, two years after marrying Max Hamer, and a year or so into drinking and sleeping herself to oblivion, Jean was charged with assaulting two men, Mr Bezant and a policeman. She pleaded not guilty. Her previous offence against a previous neighbour was brought up in court. She was bound over to keep the peace for a year. She was fined four pounds – three pounds for the bitten policeman, one pound for Mr Bezant who had been struck. She was given twenty-eight days to pay her fine. But there was more.

On that same day, she left Bromley Magistrates Court unaccompanied. Max had just started a new job, as a lowly clerk, with Cohen and Cohen, another law firm, so had returned to work. On reaching the house, she could not find her key. She became distressed. A policeman helped her climb through her bedroom window, but she slipped, had a fall, and hurt herself. By now she was in real distress. She finally got into the house only to come face to face with the neighbours. The Bezants and Mrs Daniell were standing in the hall.

The court was later told that she began to use 'foul and violent' language. She told them to 'Get out of this house. This is my property. Get out.'

Jean told the court Mr Bezant had provoked her by saying, 'I see you didn't like what happened in the court today. I have got you where I want you now and I'll get you lower still.' There was more shouting, then Jean said, 'If you think I am going to pay this fine, you have made a mistake. I would sooner go to prison for life.'

Jean told the court that Mr Bezant raised his arm. He told the court it was to protect himself. She said he took a swipe at her arm, which she had placed on the banister. He said she then struck him twice – on the arm and on the face. She said her hand fell on him as she tried to regain her balance. He said, 'Ah, another assault, I've got you. I am going for the police.' She ran down the stairs blocking his way and stood with her arms across the front door.

Mr Bezant called the police. The next day Mrs Bezant and Mrs Daniell claimed that Jean had assaulted them.

On 23 April she was charged with two separate cases of

assault to which she pleaded not guilty. She pointed out that there were no witnesses whereas Bezant had 'his wife and umpteen others'. They were inventing the charges. The magistrate did not believe her, and she was found guilty of assaulting Mr Bezant. The prosecuting counsel withdrew the second charge, saying it had not been made 'in a vindictive spirit', but because 'the lives of my clients are being made intolerable by this woman'. It is hard to understand why the Bezants did not move out of 35 Southend Road.

The magistrate decided that a psychiatric examination of the defendant was in order and adjourned the case for twenty-one days. Jean did not turn up for her next court appearance, on 27 May. A warrant was issued for her arrest. Her tenants made further complaints. She failed to turn up for her next court appearance, on 17 June, or the one after that, on 24 June. There was no sign of the fine being paid either. On the 24th, Max telephoned the court to say his wife was ill.

On Monday 27 June, Jean appeared in court on the charge of assaulting and beating Mr Bezant a month earlier. She had been seen by a psychiatrist who had diagnosed her as a hysteric. Jean told the court that the psychiatrist had been 'very fair', but that it was 'rather odd to say that she was hysterical because she wrote books. It was rather English . . .' but she could not go on. She tried to explain herself but once again the words would not come. She pleaded with the magistrate, telling him she was a writer. She hoped he would see she was respectable, that she was intelligent, that she was a thinker, but she could not find the words to explain herself.

Instead her voice grew loud and shrill. 'Why don't you make a law to stop gossip?' she asked the magistrate. He must have looked stupefied. She went on to tell the court of her fear of the whispering gossips, that if they could be prevented, it 'would stop half the misery in this country'.

She stood in the box and waved her hands in the air and spoke in too loud and unregulated a voice about her awful experiences in Beckenham, about how she had been tortured and persecuted. This was not just about Beckenham, this was about the horrors of war and the pressures of life and the unjust unfairness of it all. She wasn't rich enough to leave this hateful place, she told the magistrate, or to leave England, though she desperately wanted to. No one understood her and no one sympathised.

The magistrate remanded her in custody for a week pending another medical report. Jean was led from the court, 'protesting loudly' that it was not fair.

She wrote a short story about her ensuing stay in Holloway Prison and the events leading up to her sentence.

Chapter 23:

CATS' HOME

On 27 June 1949 Jean, or Ella Hamer, was sentenced to five days' imprisonment in Holloway Prison. She was placed on the hospital wing. On release she wrote to her friend Peggy Kirkaldy saying she hated prison but that she liked the inmates. She did not tell her family she had been imprisoned. Her daughter Maryvonne was living in Java, Indonesia, with her husband Job and their baby daughter. Jean's younger sister, Brenda, was now married to a wealthy man, who at some point over the next few years granted Jean a weekly allowance. Owen was too poor to be able to assist, but Edward contributed to Jean's maintenance. Her older sister Minna died this year.

Of all Jean's lovers, friends and relations, only Lenglet knew what prison was like. He had written to Jean on hearing of Leslie's death. Lenglet was used to dramatic reversals of fortune. He had got a job with the Red Cross, and went to Poland where he published a novel, *Glorieuzen* (*The Glorious Ones*). It was based on his experiences of war. He was taking the terrible hardship and trauma he had experienced and turning it to his advantage. He had not lost his chutzpah, neither had he lost his charm. He met a countess, the former wife of the head of Poland's National Bank. Like his own ex-wife she was alone, helpless and penniless in the aftermath of war. Like Max's, Lenglet's courtship was determined, persuasive and brief. He rescued the countess and her son from the devastation of Poland, and married her.

He took his new family to Amsterdam where he started writing again. Two novels appeared in quick succession – *Poolse Nachten* (*Polish Nights*) and *Bij Ons op den Heuvel* (*On Our Hill*). They were not successful. Lenglet had not responded appropriately to a new, post-war audience. He began to feel alienated by his peers; a forgotten man. Ultimately, he could not sustain the miraculous resurgence he experienced after he left the camp. The 1950s were to be as bleak and lonely for Lenglet as they were for Jean and Max. After all he had been through, there were too many adjustments to be made. Jean was luckier; she had not endured the physical hardships of a concentration camp nor the years spent in an asylum. But she was to get a taste of it.

At Bromley Magistrates' Court she was remanded in custody for a week, and sent to Her Majesty's Prison Holloway, Parkhurst Road, London. A policewoman led Jean out of court, deposited her in a car and she was taken to the place where Oscar Wilde and Mrs Pankhurst had been incarcerated before her. An all-female prison since 1903, it had been built in the gothic style in 1852. It stands on rising ground, its castellated towers looming over the cowering, terraced streets of north London. Made of red brick, and designed to look forbidding, it was the Victorian asylum of popular imagination – or a nightmarish boarding-school, to which unclaimed, unloved and therefore unlovable orphan girls are sent. The foundation stone was inscribed, 'May God preserve the City of London and make this place a terror to evil doers.'

Once inside the gates, she stood in a queue with other women who were waiting to give up their handbags, their dignity and their identities. They handed their possessions to a uniformed woman sitting behind a barred window, rather like a counter in a post office. Jean gave up her purse, her

compact, her comb and a dirty handkerchief. In her short
story, 'Let Them Call It Jazz', she describes her heroine,
Selina, standing at the top of a staircase, looking down into
a grey void. The railing is low enough for her to jump over.

'Oh no you don't,' says a woman in uniform, grabbing
her arm. She had not even been thinking of suicide. The
warder had just assumed it. Before Selina can explain herself
(but then, there is never enough time to be heard), she is
put in another queue and there is a young girl crying in
front of her. Jean says that Selina is all dried up and hard
inside. There were no more tears. The weeping girl was
lucky, she says; she could still feel. All the same, Selina tells
this girl to stop crying, because it's what they want, these
prison people. You could not give them that satisfaction.

Jean was put in the prison's hospital wing. When the
warder banged the door shut on her cell, she felt relief. They
thought they were shutting her in. What they did not realise
was that they were shutting 'all those other dam' devils *out*'.

Jean adapted to prison routine quickly. She got used to
the observation panel in the door, and to being inspected
throughout the night. She got used to the thick, scratchy
nightgown they gave her, and the skinny tree outside her
barred window. Like Lenglet, she was a survivor. The worse
the conditions, the more she could rationalise her feelings,
instead of being swamped by them. The more she lived on
the edge, the less life touched her. She did not get irritated
or alarmed. For example, when a nice male doctor came to
see her, a female warder stood guard throughout his examination. He asked her questions about her mental state, but
she refused to answer him fully because she could see the
twinkle of anticipation in the warder's eyes. This woman
was waiting for lies, and Jean did not want to indulge her.
The less she said, the less she gave in to them. She did not

want to give them the satisfaction of thinking they were right. She was already thinking like a prisoner. She knew this world.

At night, in her cell, she could hear a woman singing from the punishment block. She would never forget this song, the 'Holloway song', she would call it, and put it into her story of prison life. Selina asks another inmate what the words to the song were as she could not catch them. The reply is that the singer was telling 'the girls cheerio and never say die'. It is striking that the songs that really matter to Jean are wordless, rather in the way that childbirth was a wordless experience. It is as though words have lost their relevance. It is the life force that propels them that matters.

She stayed in the hospital wing, and met the governor, the assistant governor, two doctors (one male, one female), female warders – some of whom still had a heart – and a lot of inmates. The governor and the female doctor were smoothly smiling hypocrites. They said what they thought you wanted to hear and moved on. They made promises they did not keep, but maintained the façade that they were doing their job, and all was well with the world. The assistant governor seemed intelligent and sensitive – Jean could spot humanity a mile off. The male doctor seemed pleasant but was probably offloading the dirty work on to his female colleague. She could spot equivocation also.

It was like being back in the chorus line. She met an 'old gypsy' who was tough as boots and whom she admired, and young girls with bad teeth and thin hair whom she pitied. Most of all, she listened to how they talked. They called London 'the Smoke' and cigarettes 'doggins' ; they had the vigour and charm of cockney sparrers. They were fascinating, and she would put them in her story.

On 4 July 1949 she was put on probation for two years

on condition that she attend a clinic for medical and psychiatric treatment.

On 10 July 1949 she wrote from Beckenham, 'I've grown to hate Beckenham. It's not town and it's not country – it's nothing except a lot of housework, which I do badly.'

She was keeping up her correspondence with Peggy and Maryvonne. But she told her daughter nothing of Holloway. To Peggy she was jovial: 'my career has been a *trifle* stormy and it all ended up in Holloway. Yes dearie – am now an old Hollowayian . . .'

In September she was still in Beckenham, thinking about the song they sang in Holloway. Nothing much came of it. Her bravery was enough to keep her going but not enough to make her write. By November, she was hosting her usual winter flu which was a combination of fatigue, disillusionment and alcohol abuse. Max was keeping himself busy. He had made a new friend called Michael Donne.

Jean spotted Donne for a conman straight away. Max, predictably, did not. He set up a business with him in East Ham, far from Beckenham, in Michael's territory. He was spending all his time away from Jean, on the other side of London. He even inveigled Michael into his law firm, Cohen and Cohen. Very soon, he promised Jean on a rare visit home, he and Michael were going to make some money.

Then an extraordinary thing happened – Jean saw an advertisement for herself in the *New Statesman*. It read:

Jean Rhys (Mrs Tilden Smith) author of *Voyage in the Dark*, *After Leaving Mr Mackenzie*, *Good Morning, Midnight*, etc. Will anyone knowing her whereabouts kindly communicate with Dr H.W. Egli, 3 Chesterfield Gardens, NW3.

Jean replied to the advertisement. She was indeed the writer Jean Rhys, last heard of ten years earlier with the publication of *Good Morning, Midnight*. A woman promptly wrote back. She was the actress Selma vaz Dias, married to a Doctor Egli. Selma had appeared in Alfred Hitchcock's 1939 film *The Lady Vanishes*, a title that had some resonance given Jean's current predicament. At about the same time as Selma was searching for the long-forgotten author, a novelist called Julian Maclaren Ross told an editor at Andre Deutsch that Jean Rhys had died in a sanatorium. Her own publisher, Constable, had told Selma that she was dead. It would be many years before the editor at Andre Deutsch, Francis Wyndham, would find her alive and writing.

Selma was in her forties and very dynamic. She had adapted *Good Morning, Midnight* into a dramatic monologue and needed Jean's permission to perform it. The idea was that the BBC would eventually broadcast it on the radio. Jean gave her permission, and tickets were printed for a live performance on 10 November 1949. Selma gave her the script to read, and Jean, who was always generous and encouraging to other authors, found it very 'sensitively' done.

She was excited and pleased about this latest turn of events but the reality of her life was too much for her. Actually turning up at the performance was more than she could do. Her fear of her neighbour Mrs Hardiman had returned and she was incapable of leaving the house. The gossips had recommended hostilities. She wrote to Peggy, 'my bitter enemy next door is now telling everybody very loud and clear that I'm an imposter "impersonating a dead writer called Jean Rhys".'

She sent a telegram to Selma apologising for not attending the performance or telephoning. The phone had been cut off, though she did not tell Selma that.

On 16 November, six days after the performance, Jean was arrested for being drunk and disorderly. Mrs Daniell called the police after an altercation with her. It was a quarter to two in the afternoon and the police found Jean in her nightgown and slippers walking up and down Southend Road, stopping the traffic, and talking to people. She was waving a piece of paper in the air, saying something 'about the BBC'.

In her seventh appearance at Bromley Magistrates' Court the magistrate heard that 'garbage had been emptied over her' (that would have been Mrs Daniell), and that 'all she had had to drink was a little wine to warm herself'. Max was conducting her defence. He told the reporters crouched eagerly over their notebooks that there was 'less than a quarter of a bottle of Algerian wine in the house'. His client could not possibly have got drunk on that. 'Valiant' Max convinced the magistrate that there was not enough evidence to convict, and the charge was dismissed.

On Thursday, 24 November the front-page headline of the *Beckenham and Penge Advertiser* read, 'Mrs Hamer Agitated'. The standfirst read, 'Only Had Algerian Wine'. The story of her public humiliation took up the entire front page. This was the day Selma vas Diaz was coming to visit.

The visit was nevertheless a success. Jean forgot to put coffee in the pot, and poured Selma a cup of hot water, but Selma was too self-absorbed to notice Jean's distraction. In fact, she confessed, she had not expected Jean to be so gentle and quiet. To Jean's relief, she had not seen the front page of the local newspaper. If she was calm and quiet it was because she could only really appear to be functioning when the chips were down.

Selma's visit reinvigorated her. She decided to write a story about Holloway prison called 'Black Castle'. She wondered if Selma could do a monologue of that. She would write it in patois so the story is told by a young black girl recently arrived from the Caribbean in London. In fact she would not write the story for another ten years, when her memories were gradually unfurling on to paper. The snatches of dialogue, the revivification of long-gone companions would fill lonely hours in a comfortless bungalow in Devon. She needed time and distance to make sense of her life.

In the meantime, Selma was giving a talk on BBC's Third Programme about Jean's short stories. Jean promised she would listen. Jean could play alert and competent, but when the moment came to turn on the radio and tune into the right wavelength her resolve failed her. She missed the initial broadcast because, she said, there was an electricity strike. She missed the repeat because 'the Third Programme was unobtainable'. She had too much to worry about to be able to attend to these matters, Max was borrowing money from Michael Donne, and Maryvonne was ill. As a writer, one would assume that a public acknowledgement of her work would be uppermost in her mind, as a mother you could argue that her daughter's illness would take precedence. But what really worried her was the thought of Max with another woman.

In December Max disappeared for five days. Over Christmas she worked herself into a frenzy. Was he being unfaithful? Did he not love her any more? Had she been abandoned again? When he returned she told him their marriage was a failure, and that she wanted to give it up. She packed a bag, and again asked him to repay her the fifty pounds he had borrowed from her. He did not have it. She asked about the inventor he swore would make their fortune. He swore once again that Roberts was a great inventor and would make then rich. She swore at him. Then they started to quarrel.

The really annoying thing was that whenever they quarrelled
it always appeared to be her fault. Max finessed his way out
of it. Jean, on the contrary, was a harridan, a drunkard, or
just mad.

In his old age, Max had become a reckless gambler. He
clutched at any chance of making money. He talked of money
constantly. He was rarely at home. He was desperate, and
so was Jean. She did not trust him. She could not tell if he
loved her enough to stay away from other women, and this
insecurity propelled her into histrionics. Perhaps in his panic,
he did run to the things some men run to when everything
falls away: sex, schemes, anything but intimacy. But whatever
he was doing, he was not creating the conditions for mutual
trust, and Jean was immersed in paranoia. She felt painfully
vulnerable – an unstable woman with limited resources teetering on the brink of old age. How on earth could someone
like her hang on to a man?

The sneer behind the smile; the thought that everyone
was laughing at her – Max and his phantom (or were they?)
women, the lofty, disdainful neighbours, the stern police, the
mocking reporters in the court – her own bewilderment and
humiliation destabilised her to such an extent that she could
not write for years. She lacked trust in herself, in the world,
in language, in writing. Everything and everyone was against
her, but the person who was most against her was herself.

One Saturday night in January 1950 she had her last clash
with the Beckenham neighbours. This time it was Mr Daniell.
This time it was she who pressed charges. He had hit her.
She went, very drunk, to Beckenham Police Station at around
midnight. She had been assaulted, she wanted to say. But
she could not keep her cool, or explain herself calmly. She
feared she would not be believed, she knew she would not
be heard. She panicked and started screaming. She could not

believe in communication and comprehension between two human beings. People did not listen, and they did not understand. She ended up calling Mr Daniell a 'dirty stinking Jew'. She said there was no justice, and that England was run by 'rotten stinking Jews'. These were the same Jews who had sheltered her daughter during the war. But now they weren't the underdog. Now they were the faceless unsympathetic authorities whose spite and might were pitted against her. She was ejected from the police station but stood outside it screaming abuse to the delight of a gathering crowd. She was arrested.

On Monday 16 January 1951 she appeared at Bromley Magistrates' Court. She got there late, blamed the buses, denied the charge, said she usually travelled by taxi and that she was not drunk. She was fined one pound. 'I have such a bad reputation in Beckenham that no one will believe me,' she told whoever would listen.

On Thursday 19 January she quarrelled with Daniell a second time, and then on the Saturday a third time. He charged her with three assaults. She appeared in court a few weeks later and was remanded on bail yet again. But it did not really matter by now. Six days previously, on 13 January, her 'unlucky number day', she heard from the Law Society that Max had been arrested. The charges were serious: larceny and obtaining money by false pretences.

He was so similar to Lenglet. And like Lenglet, he was Jean's pal, her *copain*. Now that he was in trouble, they could be happy again, safe in each other's company because he needed her. Finally, she could trust him.

On 30 March, Bromley Magistrates Court decided enough was enough. Jean was given three weeks to leave Beckenham. She sold her clothes and two Chinese vases brought back from the Boxer Rebellion by Max's uncle. All these stories – how did Max's uncle find these vases, what were they like – stories that others would dwell on – were too insignificant to tell. Jean found a home for her last remaining cat. The woman smiled smugly as she handed her pet over as if to say she had always known that Jean was inadequate. Jean dwelt on this fact.

She moved to London with Max who was currently appearing at the Old Bailey. They found a room in Kensington. When he wasn't in court, they spent their days at the cinema, in pubs, museums and Westminster Abbey. It seems that by 1951 London had softened for her. She especially enjoyed their visit to the Victoria & Albert Museum where she admired the Persian vases, 'such a consoling blue, quite glorious and perfect'. The fifteenth-century portrayals of the Madonna were also consoling.

Whenever she was in crisis, she always found her inner peace – the bottom of the abyss was where she belonged after all; she was safe there, no one could push her down any further – and, best of all, someone always surfaced to rally round. This time it was Max's sister and Lord Listowel, his distant cousin, who topped up the funds provided by Brenda's husband. She thought of suicide often but was really quite upbeat because there was nothing else to be. There was certainly nothing to lose.

She even came to like Michael Donne, and had long conversations at the Old Bailey with the police witness appearing for the Prosecution. She discussed the ins and outs of the case with him. Both she and Detective Inspector Protheroe had a grudging admiration for Michael. Jean thought he was 'chirpy'. Protheroe called him 'The Bright Boy' or 'The Fiddler', and said to him, 'Well Donne, my lad, you say you're a musician, if you fiddle in heaven one half as well as you've fiddled on earth the heavenly choir'll stop to listen.' Jean had to laugh. It stopped her crying.

On 24 May, Max was sentenced to two years' imprisonment
at Maidstone Prison for larceny. Jean followed him to Maidstone, and took cheap rooms on the high street. Her next
surviving letter, written to her daughter, is from an address
in Maidstone. On 29 May 1951 she wrote to tell Maryvonne
about the weather.

> North Snow. East Rain and Snow. West Rain. South
> Rain and Sleet . . . few hailstorms are usually thrown in
> for good measure. Also there is a nice lovely strong wind
> straight from Siberia. This has been going on for seven
> months or so − I simply don't remember what the sun
> looks like.

She had stopped drinking. She went to the cinema, and read.
She found solace in books. Koestler, Sartre, H.E. Bates and
Conan Doyle told her about a world she recognised, a world
in which she felt comfortable. She allowed herself to enjoy
the atmospheres they created. The gas-light, fog, and hansom
cabs of Conan Doyle in particular made her feel at home.
She was nesting within the fantasy England of her childhood.

She visited Max in prison − it was just like the old days
with Lenglet in Fresnes, only this time she did not have to
fear being a woman alone. She had an income from her relatives and Max's. She experienced a kind of independence
she had never known before. She had just enough to live
on modestly, and this suited her. She was now content with
small things. There were no distractions. She could read and
write in peace. In reality, as ever, she was not really alone:
she had Max to visit in prison. And in some ways, a husband
like him was easier to manage when he was behind bars.
She did not have to worry about him getting into trouble;
she did not have to worry about him running off with another

woman. He was not going anywhere, any time soon – certainly not without her knowledge. She was safe.

She sat under trees by the River Medway and watched the birds. She explored Maidstone, her new home in Kent. She walked along the banks of the river as, when a young woman, she had walked along the boulevards of Paris and the streets of Bloomsbury and the West End, for hours on end.

When she tired of Maidstone, she moved northwards to Chatham, which was closer to the Channel and had a more Dickensian charm in its sprawl of smoke-blackened streets surrounding an ancient dockyard. She could see the tide come in and out of the mud flats where the empty keels of warships lay waiting to be constructed. The docks had been here since Henry VIII's reign and were contained by a stern, high wall. Outside that wall were the pubs and houses that had been home and refuge to blockmakers, caulkers, pitch-heaters, blacksmiths, joiners and carpenters, sail-makers, riggers, and ropemakers, as well as bricklayers, labourers and sundry others.

She found her new home in the Ropemakers' Arms.

She was 'the cat with nine lives', she told her daughter in a letter written on 22 October 1951. 'Don't ever worry about me,' she said. She confessed, however, to missing her cat. She still dreamt of him, and she talked to every cat she saw in the street, or on doorsteps or in restaurants.

She was happy living above a pub. The rooms were small, low-ceilinged and dark – 'but not without a certain something attractive – for it's an old house'. And it was cosy to live in an old attic.

In this place where I'm writing now there is a row of black elephants on the mantelpiece, a table with a place to read, apples and some flowers (a present from the landlady

this morning), a lot of books and an electric fire. So you
see what more can I want? She (the landlady) is a real dear
and so is her husband. Jesus Christ was quite right about
publicans (and about sinners too in my opinion). They are
nicer than other people – I sincerely hope that they will
walk first into Heaven leaving the holy righteous and
respectable outside looking very puzzled.

Publicans such as these had seen it all before and remained
cheerfully accepting. Jean did not drink in their bar. She did
not need to. She was self-contained, besides, she knew she
was saving up for a real 'debauch' around Christmas. There
was no point in drinking unless it was to excess.

She longed for company, for people with whom she
could discuss books and ideas and clothes and whether one
should dye one's hair blue. But in the absence of like-
minded people she did what she had done as a child, and
communed with books. Reading was a conversation with
another mind.

She must have been happy otherwise she would not have
been able to write. Her diary took on the form of a trial in
which she was the defendant. The language is modelled on
her own and Max's appearances in court. But here she has
more to defend than drunken brawling. Her whole life comes
under review and she is found wanting.

She had survived two world wars, guilty as charged. She
had behaved badly and been sent to prison. She was guilty.
She had put herself beyond the pale of civilised, lofty neighbours. She was guilty. Her desires made her guilty because
they reeked of oedipal taboos; her rage made her guilty
because it was so violent that she had to be guilty of mass
destruction. She was guilty.

She had to write about the horror of cross-examination,

of hard, unsympathetic questioning, and always being asked the wrong questions. If only they knew.

The question they should have asked was the one that tormented her, and that she asked herself now over and over again. Was she capable of loving another?

The Counsel for the Defence asked leading questions, or at least questions that she knew would present her in a more sympathetic light:

'Did you in your youth have a great love and pity for others? Especially for the poor and unfortunate?'

'Yes,' she replied.

'Were you able to show this?'

'I think I could not always. I was very clumsy. No one told me.'

'Excuse of course!' declared the Counsel for the Prosecution.

She could not go easy on herself for too long, but had to scourge herself of any self-pity or dissimulation. Of course she had felt love and compassion, but she could not see in herself the seeds of goodness.

'It is untrue,' the Defence continued, ' that you are cold and withdrawn?'

'It is not true,' she said. No, not at all true, but:

'Did you make great efforts to, shall we say, establish contacts with other people? I mean friendships, love affairs, so on?'

'Yes. Not friendships very much.' Well, no, she could not sustain friendships. They were too complex, too much give and take, especially with other women. She wanted a mother not a friend.

'Did you succeed?'

'Sometimes. For a time.' True.

'It didn't last?'

'No.'

'Whose fault was that?'

'Mine I suppose.'

'You suppose?'

Silence.

At times, her prosecutor tormented her with legal niceties and pedantries that she had picked up at the Old Bailey and Bromley Magistrates Court. She had internalised their persecutory voices so successfully they flowed from her pen on to the page.

'The phrase is not "I do not know" but "I have nothing to say",' explained the Counsel for the Prosecution.

'The trouble is I have plenty to say. Not only that but I am bound to say it.'

'Bound?'

'I must.'

'Why?'

'I must write. If I stop writing my life will have been an abject failure. It is that already to other people. But it will be an abject failure to myself. I will not have earned my death.'

She had to explain herself. She had to put herself down on paper. The 'good, evil, love, hate, life, death, beauty, ugliness' that was in her and that she could not share with others because she did not know how until she had removed herself from them and put it all down on paper.

'Did you in your youth have a great love and pity for others?'

Oh yes, so much that it hurt. And it still did.

She had failed.

Max was released from Maidstone Prison in May 1952. He was a broken seventy-year-old man. He had been struck off the Solicitors' Roll; the Navy had withdrawn his pension, and he was not eligible for statutory old-age pension either. He had not bothered to pay the stamps when he had been working. For the next eight years, Jean and Max were dreadfully poor and limped from one rented accommodation to another in London, Wales and Cornwall. They lived off the compassion of others. They were old and poor and ill. Sometimes, Jean's brother Edward sent them a food parcel as well as her weekly allowance. Max also had well-meaning relations.

Jean maintained her contact with literary people such as Selma and Peggy and made new friends such as the writers Morchard Bishop and Oliver Stoner. But she kept them at a distance, not trusting herself to be able to meet them and come away with their respect and liking of her intact. Instead she kept up lively correspondences in which she exchanged views on favourite books (like *The Turn of the Screw* with its fog, ruins and sexual hysteria) and chased ideas that came to nothing – like the dramatisation (by Selma) of *Quartet*.

'Don't you like ruins?' she asked Morchard Bishop in a letter dated 11 January 1953 and posted from Norwood, south London. 'There are so many in the West Indies. I grew up with them.' But she was not ready to write about them yet.

Chapter 24:

WIDE SARGASSO SEA

In 1955 Jean, or Mrs Ella Hamer, moved to a large, cold bungalow in Bude, Cornwall. Max came with her though he never recovered from his ordeal in prison. Their relatives – Jean's sister Brenda's husband and her brother Edward as well as various of Max's cousins – gave them an allowance. Jean's brother Owen was living in London. His health was broken and he was financially dependent on his wife until he died in 1958 falling down the stairs of their flat. In the same year, Maryvonne and her family were forced to leave their home in Indonesia due to the unstable political situation. With some reluctance, they returned to Holland.

It had a dream kitchen. That is how mundane her dreams were. Every morning, in her dream of a kitchen, reality hit her. She had to wrestle with the boiler. It drove her to such a state of frustration that she would be screaming and swearing at it. Relief came later in the day when Max lit a fire at tea time in the sitting room. The boiler would be working by now, and Jean could sit down to write letters. Bude was some way off, so shopping was out of the question. She depended on tradesmen calling. She could rely on the baker and milkmen: 'the others – one never knows!'

The path from her bungalow to Widemouth Bay – such a lovely name – was bare and rocky and there were hardly any trees. She missed the trees. The place seemed so bare without them. Trees confer shade and shelter, strength and solidity: without them, this sandy coastline seemed so exposed that when the tide dropped all she could see was sand and strange rock formations. She liked the sand beneath her feet, but the wind whipped around the bungalow mercilessly. She was struck, once again, by the English propensity for misnomers when it came to homes. This was no Belair.

She wrote to her grand-daughter, Ruth Ellen:

My dear little Ruth,
  Thank you for writing. I am in a bungalow in Cornwall near the sea and I wish you were here too.
  This is a rocky coast and up to about fifty years ago it was the wreckers and smugglers coast. I sympathise with the smugglers but the wreckers were bad hombres.

She then tells Ruth how they smashed up ships and stole the cargo.

However they are not so enterprising now. Though different I think from the English.

She did not like Cornwall. Too many bungalows. There was a bus three times a day to the nearest 'metropolis', and the shops were no good. There was no library and the girl at WH Smith was silly and sulky and had never heard of the books Jean wanted to buy.

In February 1957, it was so cold and windy Jean thought she would die. But rescue came in the shape of Selma. Seven years after first proposing that the BBC dramatise *Good Morning, Midnight*, she finally delivered. Jean was feeling sufficiently in control of her life to attend a read-through of the script in London. She and Max were living very simply and this suited her. The journey to London did not present the obstacles that had prevented her, in Beckenham, from tuning a radio to listen to an adaptation of her novel. This time she was very excited but sensible enough to scrimp some money together and organise a trip into Bude to buy a dress, a hat and some make-up. On the day itself, which was towards the end of February, she wore them all and wept with joy throughout the read-through. Max was with her, and the BBC producer gave them lunch in a nice restaurant. They stayed in a hotel that she had scrimped some more money together for. She treated herself to a facial. Selma cooked them dinner in her nice, warm house. Jean was happier than she had been in years.

She missed the eventual broadcast because she still had not worked out how to tune a radio. But she came home to Bude revitalised. She told Selma that she was finally ready to write her story of the first Mrs Rochester. Furthermore, it was all down to Selma. She was so grateful and enthusiastic in her rediscovered appetite for the life of a writer that she credited Selma with the idea for the novel that had been unsettling her for years. This was a classic mistake that Jean made over and over again. She was over-generous when someone was nice to her, trusting them utterly with everything she had to offer. When they let her down she saw them as hateful imposters – out to undermine her, rip her off, destroy her very being. Selma herself was far too ready to take the credit Jean bestowed upon her.

The broadcast she had engineered, however, did put Jean back on the literary map. Francis Wyndham, an editor at André Deutsch, read an article about her, by Selma, which proclaimed that she was writing a novel. He got in touch. He admired her work, and he hoped very much that what he had read was true. She wrote back immediately, promising him a manuscript that told the story of the first

Mrs Rochester. He could have it as soon as she had finished it. He was in for a long wait.

No matter. The important thing was that Francis Wyndham was ready to make a commitment to her. She told him she needed a 'devil' to write it. By the end of May, another editor at Deutsch, Diana Athill, had written with an offer of twenty-five pounds. She was thrilled, and told Athill she would send the novel to her 'in six to nine months' time, as a large part of it is already written'. She even discussed the titles she was contemplating: *Le Revenant* or *Creole*. On 1 June 1957 she signed a contract with Andre Deutsch. Nine years later she would deliver a manuscript entitled *Wide Sargasso Sea*.

'Phrases, sentences come and go,' like ghosts that flitted in out of her mind. She could not pin them down to the page. 'I am a tormented person, and even writing is clutching at clouds and shadows,' she wrote to Selma Vaz Dias in a letter. In letters to Peggy she said it was Cornwall's fault. There were no trees, and the house she was living in was too exposed. Passers-by would stop outside her window or knock on the door asking for directions. It drove her mad. Their enquiries were as noisome to her as flies buzzing around her head. She started drinking again to block out the noise. Peggy wrote back, suggesting that she write a notice saying, 'NO teas – NO water – NO lavatory. So bugger off.' Jean was going to amend that note to, 'No matches, No cigarettes, No sandwiches, No water. Don't know where anybody lives. Don't know anything. Now BUGGER OFF', before nailing it to the front door. Max would not let her.

This was the summer invasion of tourists but these were Jean's best months for writing. Nothing came. She ran rings round madness. She wrote another angry list:

'No privacy, No cash, No security, No resilience, No

youth, No desk to write on, No table even. No one who understands.'

Nothing and no one to help her. Nothing she or anyone could do. Maryvonne, back in Europe, visited her in November. But Jean was too mired in angry apathy to be able to respond to her daughter or her grand-daughter properly. Jean insisted on calling her grand-daughter Ruth even when the child announced she would rather be called Ellen. Jean was loyal to the baby she loved so desperately but could not help to care for. She tried to provide a brave face for her family, but the effort cost her. In December 1957 she took to her bed. She stayed there throughout the opening months of 1958.

These are the titles that she came up with for her book:

> Solitaire
> Before the Break of Day
> Speak for Me
> Before I was Set Free
> Le Revenant
> Gold Sargasso Sea
> Purple against Red
> (Across the) Wide Sargasso Sea
> I Hear Voices
> False Legend
> Dream
> Mrs Rochester
> Le Rouge et Le Noir
> Marie Galante
> Sargasso Sea (the Wide) Crossing Across
> The Image
> The Question and the Answer
> All Souls
> Three Voices

Sargasso Sea
Wide Sargasso Sea
Story of the first Mrs Rochester
Wild Sea of Wrecks
That Wild Sea of Wrecks where I was Wrecked
That Wild Sea of Weeds where They were Wrecked
There Comes a Time

At the same time as Jean was holed up in Cornwall, Lily Lockhart, her cousin from Dominica, was living alone in London. Like Jean, the girl from St Lucia was very broke and very lonely. But she was also proud and independent. She had written a poem that Jean liked a lot. It was called 'Creole Song', and began, 'Across the gold Sargasso Sea, I watch my heart come back to me . . .' Jean tried to sell Lily's poems for her, but Lily, who had been alone for so long, did not trust her. She guarded her poems jealously and finally accused Jean of trying to steal them. After a fashion, as writers do, she did.

The words 'Sargasso Sea' came to Jean like a dream and she liked them, not quite remembering where she had heard them, but when she did, it made such perfect sense. The Sargasso Sea stayed in her head. It is where the trade winds originate, where flotsam accumulates, where the sea itself looks dead, a stew of derelict ships and the *sargassum* seaweed. It is said that one can walk on its still waters.

The book remained a dream in being slightly out of reach and infuriatingly tantalising. It was there fully formed in her head if she could only transfer it on to paper. She knew she could write it but she was not sure how. Her over-riding concern was that it had to be right or it would not do. Alas, if she delayed much longer it would lose its urgency, and be no good at all. It had been too long already. Sometimes she felt it was almost there, almost ready to be put on to the page, but then something stopped her. It could be a passer-by, Max, the lack of trees, the man upstairs in his heavy boots – whatever it was, the book went away again. Like *le revenant*, it vanished, and tormented her with its absence and its promise. The lure was Dominica, her lovely, melancholy home. When she wrote of Dominica she wrote of love and her compulsion to find, again and again, the loving presence that wasn't there: her mother. Her heroine, who at the end of the novel becomes the mother she is seeking at the novel's start, personifies this longing.

She told Francis Wyndham that after writing *Voyage in the Dark*, the West Indies had been knocking at her heart. But the story that the West Indies wanted her to tell was one of betrayal: the failure of a society and a culture that creates parents who are unable to protect their children from repeating their errors. Sexual and racial exploitation were there too, as were patriarchal systems and her own oppression as a female. Like all her heroines, Antoinette would end up inhabiting a cold, ugly room in unsympathetic England, her only solace alcohol and an unquenchable yearning for the past.

In February, her friend Peggy Kirkaldy died. In March, Owen, the only sibling she considered to be 'nice', died. These deaths told her that she did not have long.

The summer and autumn of 1958 were her most intensive periods of work during which she finally made 'something from nothing'. All those years of avoiding what she feared might be the nothingness within her actually proved that in digging so deeply she had so much to tell. But it would still be eight years before she had something to show for it. The difficulty was that she had to re-create the madwoman Charlotte Brontë had turned into a monster, and then she had to write the man who married her. At the same time, she had to make her reader understand them both. She had to find sympathy in her heart for Mr Rochester. She knew that 'a mad girl speaking all the time is too much!' If it was too much for her, it would be too much for her readers. But she had to make Mr Rochester speak too. This was almost insurmountable, to present the case of the coloniser, the 'villain' of the piece. She could not find a way in.

She started writing a short story instead. 'Let Them Call It Jazz' is the fictionalised account of her time in Beckenham and Holloway Gaol. A poor, mad West Indian girl is set upon by her neighbours but still sings her song. At the same time as poor mad girls were haunting her, she dug up some stories she had already finished. She sent the story of Leslie's death and the story of her stay with Peter Warlock to Francis. He sold them on her behalf to the *London Magazine*. It was a most prestigious publication, and Jean was thrilled. She was paid as well. Most important of all, this meant she was not dead.

In August, Max had a stroke. For the rest of his life he would be dependent on her. She would have to endure endless interruptions and anxiety. Tasks, errands, chores, caring for someone, the business of living, the relentlessness of looking after an invalid, all this made her realise that all she had ever wanted, the only thing that made her life worth living, was writing. She realised this a bit too late.

In April 1958, there was no change to her situation. Flu, lethargy and depression stuck with her while she was stuck in a bungalow just outside Bude. She was resentful and bitter towards the general population, or human beings, or termites, as she sometimes called them. In dream symbolism, insects or vermin signify brothers and sisters. The illusion that parents

love all their children equally – an illusion that is essential
to good relations – is not one that Jean indulged.

She wrote to Maryvonne regarding Ruthie's 'pals':

Yes I think groups of children can be horrible. So can all
groups. I hate them and fear them like I hated termites
nests at home – Everyone used to laugh at me for this.
They don't sting like ants. They are only vile somehow –
After all, ants do walk along in the sun. But these things
build huge nests and little roads going from one nest to
the other – very nicely made and they have Soldiers, Workers, and Nurses (I believe) and a few Drones or something
– and hell to them. Well that is a Group to me.

In February 1960 she moved herself and Max to a chalet in
the south of Cornwall. She would do anything to avoid boredom, equating stillness with death; she had to keep moving
to prove to herself that she was still alive. As usual, it was a
big mistake. Perranporth was warmer than Bude but the
chalet was like a 'small horse box'. In one room she drank,
Max lay helpless in bed in the other.

Her brother Edward came to visit. He was appalled, went
home to Budleigh Salterton and found her and Max a
bungalow on the other side of Exeter. At this distance, he
could keep an eye on her without having her on his doorstep.
The village he picked, Cheriton Fitzpaine, is buried in the
Devon countryside – it's hard to get into and it's hard to
get out of: the perfect place for such a sister.

Number 6 Landboat Bungalows was squat, damp and squalid.
It was the last in a row of three farm-workers' dwellings,
and had recently been condemned. One can only assume
that Edward could not afford anything better.

It was on the edge of the village of Cheriton Fitzpaine, which is not in itself terribly pretty. The surrounding countryside is famous for its beauty, but if you cannot drive or walk very far it is easy to feel penned in by fields, hedgerows, mud and the lowering sky. Before she moved in, Jean considered this new home would be her 'new Jerusalem', 'the Ark', and the 'abode of peace'. It was to be none of these, but she was right about one thing: she would never move again.

Edward had made an effort to make the bungalow habitable, paying for it to be repainted and adequately heated. The most important thing he did was to prepare the village for Jean's coming. He approached the local vicar, the Reverend Alwynne Woodard, and told him that an extremely difficult, rather elderly woman and her infirm husband were about to come and live on the easternmost edge of the village. He did not say that the woman was a writer, or that she was his sister, only that she had caused him and his wife a lot of trouble, but that he had to do his duty by her. He asked Mr Woodard to help her should any difficulties concerning her behaviour arise. Luckily, in a village where people were watching out for something to gossip about, Mr Woodard was tolerant, broadminded and a discerning reader. He had studied the Classics at university. He understood talent and eccentricity.

'I love it here,' was the first thing Jean told Francis in a letter. She loved the green fields, she loved the black and white cows grazing outside her window, and most of all she loved the sturdy trees waving green branches. To top it all, there was hardly a person to be seen. She even loved the bungalow with its corrugated iron roof, icicles in the bathroom, wartime lino on the floor. She put a single orange light bulb in the living room to convey the impression of heat. The bungalow needed lots of red, she conceded. She would buy red velvet curtains.

Then it started raining. The Exe valley flooded, her bathroom was a shipwreck, the kitchen chimney leaked all over the floor. The bungalow was no longer 'secluded', it was 'isolated'. The village was a weary half a mile away and it didn't feel very friendly when she got there. There were no bookshops. There was no library. But there were lots of cows and wet greenery. She could not think about Mr Rochester but she knew she had to keep writing. So she continued her story about a women's prison. She could not type it herself and was reluctant to expose such a compromising story to a local typist who would, of course, assume the worst. The village had shaded into her worst fantasies. Her warm, glowing dream of a cosy refuge had blown up into 'a foretaste of hell'.

'Of all the remote and frowning places it frowns the most.'

There were icicles in the bathroom. She could hear the rain pounding the corrugated iron roof. The low walls were streaked with damp. Window panes were missing because local boys lobbed missiles at them. There was no proper heating, no telephone, no record player, no radio that she could tune. The furniture was cheap and nasty, and instead of red velvet luxury she had a single orange light bulb.

In Cheriton Fitzpaine, she was finding it increasingly hard to be reconciled to the fact that there was not a bookshop within walking distance. Equally hard to live with, there was no off-licence. To buy the only things that made life bearable, she had to hire a taxi into Tiverton where she could stock up on vodka, Pernod, 'not bad vin rouge', and Penguin paperbacks. She sent her gaol story long-hand to Francis Wyndham. He typed it for her and sent it to *London Magazine*, but not before writing to her in praise of it. His excitement raised her spirits. She was a writer, after all, not a demented old woman. But she was determined not to get excited. She had to keep calm in order to keep writing. If she became excited, despair would follow.

Alan Ross published 'Let Them Call it Jazz' in the *London Magazine* in the spring of 1961. In May she got her novel ready to work on again, but she must have got too excited because soon she was in despair. She wrote letters to Francis, Diana Athill and Selma. She told them the cows were watching her. They came right up to the window to seek her out. She told the farmer about his cows. In an attempt to alleviate her fears and stop the cows bothering her, he constructed a barbed-wire fence around her garden.

The barbed wire made her think of prison, and concentration camps, and being trapped and excluded, of being kept apart from the great horde of people who despised her and ridiculed her and whom she feared and hated anyway. She wished only that the River Exe would wash them all away, the village, the fields, the dampness of her bungalow, herself and the cows included. She got drunk and threw empty milk bottles at the fence. She screamed her fears so that all could hear. The villagers gathered round to watch a seventy-year-old woman attacking a fence, before one of them ran to fetch the vicar.

Mr Woodard took her back to the Rectory and gave her some whisky. As well as being a Classics scholar, he had once been chaplain to a mental hospital. He was accustomed to extreme states of mind. She calmed down and they had a nice, quiet chat. He was kind and she could see that. Unfortunately, she could not recognise the fact that the farmer had tried to help her by building a fence to stop his cows munching her garden. There was never going to be a meeting of minds between Jean Rhys and Farmer Giles.

Most of the villagers stopped speaking to her after the incident of the fence and the milk bottles. But Mr Woodard and Mr Greenslade, the village taxi-driver, who took her into Tiverton for supplies, became staunch allies. Mr Greenslade would chauffeur her around the Devon countryside, lulling her into peace of mind.

At some point during the autumn of 1961, Mr Woodard was the first person to read Jean's unfinished draft of *Wide Sargasso Sea*. He was stunned by its skill and passion. He knew at once that he was in the presence of a genuine literary talent. He recognised the need for concision and simplicity and the awful effort it took to make each word earn its place on the page. Each word spoke volumes of pain and yet carried its weight gracefully. But Jean was convinced that her novel had no meaning and no purpose. She could not write. Max needed a lot of care and she had persistent flu. The neighbours heard her shouting obscenities at him and finally pounding him with her fists as he lay ill in bed. Dark and howling gales, and then it was June 1963 and she still hadn't written her book, and Max had another stroke and was taken to hospital.

The little girl next door took to standing outside Jean's window. She stared at Jean with dull, empty eyes as she tried to write. Zena Raymond was what was called in those days 'mentally handicapped'. Jean was terrified of this sinister apparition outside her window. Even more hideous than poor Zena were the cabbages Zena's mother had planted in their garden. This mother was a big woman, strong, healthy and heavy and not afraid to take up space. She said that Jean was a witch and had cast a spell on her daughter. Jean told Selma and Francis that there was black magic in the village and there was a black-eyed Susan living next door to her.

The black-eyed Susan is a flower imported from South

Africa into the Caribbean by the Dutch. It has blazing orange
petals with a black stamen at its heart. It is vigorous and runs
riot throughout the islands it was brought to, stifling the
more delicate, indigenous plants. Jean wrote a poem, 'Obeah
Night'. It was about love and betrayal and it was a man
speaking, a man who was caught up in the whole hateful
business of living. He was just as helpless as any woman, and
just as angry:

> I'm no damn slave owner
> I have no slave.

By writing the poem, she felt released to write Mr Rochester's
side of the story. The clue was this: *obeah*, witchcraft, love
as magic, intoxication, disturbing beauty, his fear, her past,
his misunderstanding, her madness. Sexual hypocrisy. Sexual
repression. Fire. Lancey came to her in the night. So did
Heathcliff and Othello. She was working hard on her book,
and a bottle of whisky a day was helping her. But that little
girl would not go away. So Jean chased Zena through the
village, and in turn was chased by hordes of villagers.

One day when she had nearly finished a bottle of wine,
she pinned on all the medals Max possessed, for he had been
in the RAF in the First World War, went out of the door,
and shouted, 'Wings up! Wings up!' All the local boys ganged
up to shout taunts at her. A few days later there was a knock
at the door. She opened it and there was a young man she
did not know. When she asked his name, he said, 'Don't
you remember me? I'm your friend.' He was the boy who
had chased the other boys away. So she asked him in and
offered him a drink. After that initial visit, he would go to
Jean's when he felt her 'calling' him. He would roll joints
and they would smoke cannabis together. He told Francis

that she was a like a witch, calling him when she needed him. She loved the naughtiness of smoking joints.

When the neighbours and the fear were too much for her, the Reverend Woodard took her under his wing. She returned his kindness by behaving abominably. 'I've been seeing a lot of the collective face that killed a thousand thoughts lately. And sometimes there is blue murder in my wicked heart.' She was full of hatred and rage and fear. And she always behaved badly when someone was nice to her because she had to pre-empt their inevitable abandonment of her. She had to make them go away. But he had read her book and he forgave her.

He visited her three or four times a week and knocked out a code on her door so that she knew to let him in. She told him of her fears – that she was frightened of the badness in herself. He asked her one night if she wanted to receive communion.

The next time he came he brought the host. She got down on her knees, and he placed it on her tongue. He blessed her, and she found the strength to continue her novel.

Having been cleansed, she went back to writing. However, on her seventy-fourth birthday all she could think of was a song Jean Harlow had sung in the 1930s.

> Everything's been done before
> But it's new to me, it's new to me.

This was what gave her writing its power. It was the sense of being a newborn: that fragility on which roughness makes such a cruel impact. She told her daughter about a conversation she had once had with a publisher – it is not clear which one, but she had said to him, she told Maryvonne, that 'being soft hurt too much'. Because of this, she 'intended to grow hard.' He replied, 'If you grow hard you will not be able to write. You will lose your touch on the piano.'

She would never grow hard or lose her touch. She carried on. Max came home from hospital to be with her on 11 July 1964. She knew he was worth the sacrifice because without him she was lonely. He loved her not because she was a writer but because she was his wife. 'Whatever you call me I love you and only you and always shall,' he had told her in a letter from hospital. She loved him because he didn't like her white hair and wanted her to dye it back to its 'natural' colour: brown. This meant he wanted her. She broke off writing to make tea, buy bread, and sweep the kitchen. But she could not look after him, and he was very weak by now.

The village nurse came to see him, so did the Reverend Woodard and his wife when she dared. The nurse, and sometimes Mrs Woodard, washed Max and changed his clothes when Jean would let them near him. It was obvious to all except Jean that home was no place for him. He had to go back to hospital. Jean wrote every night in his absence.

She made Mr Rochester as passionate as Antoinette and as fearful of his passion, so fearful he needs to possess because of what he might lose. She sat up for many nights writing him. Once she heard a cuckoo in the morning and realised she had been writing all night and had been doing so for many nights. Still she worried that it had all been done before, that she had stolen passages from *Madame Bovary*, that she was mixing poems with memories or facts. She was not sleeping; she was confused. Associations were crowding in. James Joyce, grand opera, Anna Livia Plurabelle – but hers was a musical comedy. Wasn't she once in a musical comedy? – a Viennese one, too. In fact, she had nearly died of it. She remembered the song of the *siffleur montagne*, the mountain whistler. It had only one note. It was like the cuckoo, very wild and very lonely. You could only hear it high up in the forest. She hoped there were some left. She worried that they might be all trapped in a zoo for people to stare at. She remembered Rimbaud: 'We have faith in the poison. We know how to offer up our life, day after day, entire.' She remembered the 'well-washed' Stella. A lightweight. A living compromise. She remembered Ford, and thanked him for making her write. She remembered Lenglet. He was dead, her old *copain*. She thought of prison and remembered she was in Cheriton Fitzpaine which had a barbed-wire fence and staring people. There were two more years of hospital for Max and hospital for Jean, who collapsed. Two more years of loans from Francis and other friends for £100 here and there to buy food and drink and to pay for painstaking writing. Then on 7 March 1966, Max Hamer, who had once been a frightened old man in a beret who was sent to gaol, and before that had been a feckless, charming fellow who chanced his arm in any trade, died. The following day Jean delivered *Wide Sargasso Sea* to her publishers.

Chapter 25:

LA VIE EN ROSE

'No one is ever going to know what labour and torment has gone into the years of writing this book. It's going to alight in their hands as complete and natural as a bird on a bough, as though it had just come into existence by itself. Does that make you feel better, after all the blood sweat toil and tears? It ought to make you feel so proud – a rare and splendid creator.'
Diana Athill, letter to Jean Rhys, March 1966

In March 1966, Jean Rhys wrote, 'whisky is now a must for me'. She needed a bottle every day. But she kept her wits about her. The journalist Hunter Davies interviewed her for the *Sunday Times*. He described her as 'strange' and 'shy'. She had given good copy to suburban Beckenham, now she was providing the same service for literary London.

Jean Rhys was the voice before her time; the voice that did not belong to any group; a voice that was rendered speechless much of the time because it suffered alienation from language itself. Sonia Orwell, the widow of George and a patron of writers, and Francis Wyndham cherished her talent and the woman herself. Jean loved Francis. He was a literary man who not only loved and admired her books, but loved and admired her as a woman. He would drink cocktails with her during the blue hour, and leave her gay and stimulated. Unfortunately, it would be one of Jean's women friends who had to witness the descent into maudlin aggression as Jean's night darkened. But all these friends wanted this elderly woman to enjoy herself and take her rightful place in the world. They loved her books and they loved her courage. Most of all they loved what her new book contained. *Wide Sargasso Sea* had its beginnings in Victorian England, Oxford Street and the demi-monde, a big American, an Edwardian gentleman, Paris in the Twenties, an abortion and birth in the rainforest. It had fire.

It was published on 27 October 1966. Its author was an elderly woman who had lived in obscurity for years. She had kind, understanding and well-connected friends in London: Francis Wyndham, Sonia Orwell and Diana Melly, the wife of jazz musician George. She had friends in Devon: Sam Greenslade, the taxi-driver and Francis Woodard, the local vicar. Before the publication of *Wide Sargasso Sea*, Sonia paid for Sam to drive Jean all the way to Brighton. She stayed in a hotel chosen by Sonia and Francis. Sonia also bought Jean a pink dress to wear and gave her money for restaurants, hairdressers and shopping. Sonia regularly sought Jean out and gave her holidays, emotional support, financial assistance and laughter. She paid for her to stay in London flats and hotels and to go on holiday every winter. When she could not visit Jean in person, she would send her whisky, champagne and make-up through the post. When she did visit Jean she made her giggle. Sonia could be charming, frivolous and girlish to such an extent that Jean would be enlivened into telling tales of Lancelot and being a chorus girl vamping men. But still Jean could not be happy.

In December 1966 Jean won the WH Smith Prize of £1,000 plus a bursary of £1,200. She had many interviews and photographs taken. Each one brought anxiety and depression. Anxiety because she wanted to look pretty, depression because she was old.

She had many visitors who paid pilgrimage to Cheriton
Fitzpaine. To each one she said that success had come too
late. Insecurity is a habit. Loneliness and persecution become
routine. Fame and financial security had come too late to
make any difference to an old woman. She told her new
friends this over and over again. She was too old for this,
and they were far too late.

In 1970 her friends and admirers sought her views and
sounded her out on the prevailing topics of the day: 'Women's
Lib' annoyed her. Black activism annoyed her. When black
people or women started organising themselves and chanting
slogans and making a fuss they became an embarrassment
and a nuisance. Besides this, they had forgotten how kind
men like her beloved father had been to them. Not all white

men were oppressors. Only when women and blacks remained victims could she identify with them. There was beauty in suffering.

She had many correspondents. A man accused of murder wrote to her. She took up his cause. A handsome Dutchman came to visit her. They went on a drive. She enjoyed this passive interlude but her real escape was through thoughts of suicide.

In the autumn of 1970 her brother Edward died. He had accused her of alcoholism and madness; he had wanted to lock her up. She went to his funeral. Either his widow Gertrude's relations snubbed her or she snubbed them, she was not sure. There were people there who called her 'Gwennie'. Her name was Jean. She left feeling bewildered and reminded of her mother scolding her for being rude to Mr Hesketh Bell. She could not fit in. She did not know the form.

She hated being old. She wanted to be young and beautiful. She wore a Jean Muir wool caftan and spent ages putting on make-up. Diana Melly watched her once gazing at herself in a mirror. 'Found drowned,' Jean said as she turned to face Diana. These are the words she uses of her heroine, Sasha, in *Good Morning, Midnight*. They are also the words a coroner uses at the inquest of a drowned body fished up from the deep.

In early January 1971 she stayed in a hotel in Eaton Place, London. She went to see *The Mousetrap* with Antonia Fraser and shopped at Biba with Diana. She bought shoes, jewellery and hats. She raged at black people and at Maryvonne who had come to visit. Maryvonne disapproved of her, she felt. She disapproved of her new pink suit, her obsession with make-up and because she had been a bad mother. By the end of March Jean was at home again, writing *Smile Please*, her unfinished autobiography. She could not work on it in any sustained fashion so she started her final collection of short stories, *Sleep It Off Lady*. She continued to write these two books in fits and starts, assisted by a young writer called David Plante.

Time is running out, she knows that. In February 1972 she falls and damages her ribs; she has toothache, and gastric flu. Mr Greenslade has an eye operation. Mr Woodard is beginning to falter. Lily Lockhart, her lonely, proud cousin from St Lucia, dies. Lily was a *siffleur montagne*, and in Jean's imagination she becomes Antoinette. Jean's pain is still there but her fame is growing. V.S. Naipaul writes an article about her. *Who's Who* gives her an entry. The Queen gives her a CBE. In January 1973 the *Guardian* interviews her. The photo is hideous. She looks a 'complete fool with a lurid past'. At Crediton Library, she asks for Arthur Mizener's recently published biography of Ford Madox Ford. She is reminded: he called her a 'blackamoor' in *When the Wicked Man*. More newspaper articles about her; intrusions into her privacy. Didn't they know she used to be young and pretty?

In 1973 she made two new friends: Gini Stevens and Jo Batterham, young, energetic girls. They took her to London for a day out. In an antique market in Chelsea, Jo watched Jean examining rings. Her hands, Jo noted, were marvellously expressive, but large and bony. Jo watched this elderly lady with wavy grey hair and a bent back struggling to stay upright on frail legs, assessing the gems laid on a tray before her. She hovered for an age between two cheap rings. Eventually, with a sigh, she chose one. She was entering Jo's car when the stallholder ran up to Jo. The man pressed the other ring Jean had been looking at into Jo's hand: 'She has such beautiful eyes. Please give her this when you get home.' Jean still had an impact on men.

When Jo first visited the Devon bungalow it was bare. Wartime linoleum and an old electric cooker. She saw the bare orange light bulb hung from the ceiling of the sitting room, Jean's attempt to create sunshine. The garden was wild, though there were roses, her favourite flower. Selma had donated a painting of red roses for her bedroom. Jo and Gini installed heating, a cooker, and a fridge in her bungalow. In October Diana Athill wrote to the Arts Council applying for a grant. In December Jo and Gini turned the horrid old shed in her garden into a cedar hut that gave off perfume when heated. They filled the hut with Indian bedspreads and pillows. They used white paint and furniture from Habitat to make her sitting-room more cheerful. They put pink curtains in her kitchen. In November Gini started working ten days a month as her literary assistant. She did the shopping, and cleaning, the et ceteras that Jean could never manage. Jo wrote an account of Jean's living arrangements:

The kitchen table Jean sat at, with its seersucker cloth, was her desk. Wedged between the table and the sink was an old armchair, beside it a log with an ashtray balanced on the top. She kept her writing materials and notebooks with the linen in the airing cupboard. The narrow passage had a bookcase. She was sceptical and suspicious when a telephone was installed. She never understood how to work the 'beastly thing'. She stored sentimental possessions in old battered suitcases in a spare bedroom. She kept the pillow Max had used here too. Eventually the wall to the kitchen would be knocked down in order to enlarge the sitting room. It would have white walls and a white carpet, bookshelves, tables and lamps. In the meantime, Jean took pleasure from re-arranging ornaments and pictures, a few from her past but mostly chosen by herself, or given to her more recently by friends. Jo noticed that if she moved one of these ornaments, sharp-eyed Jean would replace it to its rightful place. She also noticed the instant anything, however negligible, went missing.

Jean kept a watchful eye on her precious possessions. They were like memories. Jo noted that life for Jean in Devon was quiet but she had more friends and assistance than she pretended to. She was not the helpless outcast who needed endless sympathy. She was coping rather well. A local woman came in to clean, and since she hated cooking, a neighbour provided a roast chicken once a week. The rest of the time Jean lived quite happily on vegetables, cheese, fruit and her favourite pudding, Angel Delight. Her favourite tipple every evening was a glass of Cinzano. Other treats included Mr Greenslade taking her for a drive and a meal, sipping crème de menthe and eating curry.

Jean liked Jo, and encouraged her work as a sculptor. She preferred the company of artists to that of writers, there was no competition. Jo also found Jean to be an excellent correspondent. Once, while abroad, in a moment of depression, Jo wrote with despondent irony, 'There does not seem much left but to go on the streets.' By return of post came Jean's reply: 'Please, please, dear Jo, don't do that, promise me that you won't. Try and do some more sculpture, I know you will feel better.' She cared about her friends, especially those friends who did not nag her to write or who, like her, saw through hollow flattery to the feeling person beneath the surface. She did not want to be treated as a writer, but as a woman. Jo did that.

Her other new friend, Diana Melly, took her to nightclubs, and, together with Jo, to Venice. In their company she was relaxed and often giggly. She made up a rhyme about the pink wig she sported on nights out:

> They twig
> It's a wig
> What care I?
> I am shy
> And it helps.

Jean's pink wig became legendary at Ronnie Scott's, the London night-club that Diana's husband George took her to. It was ornately curly and the drunker she got the further it slipped off her head. She enjoyed playing the part of the grande dame here and in Venice where charming Italians helped her into gondolas.

One day in 1974, she feels the presence of the Reverend Woodard beside her in her kitchen. She realises she hasn't seen him for some time. Two weeks later she hears he is dead. Mr Greenslade, the taxi-driver, retires, and is replaced by Mr Pike. He is not the same as Mr Greenslade, who had been so patient. Mr Greenslade carried her parcels for her, and made gallant compliments about her dress. Once she forgot her keys and he climbed into the bungalow through a window. He never asked for anything. He always knew when it was going to rain. When he planted something, it grew. She was never able to repay him for his constancy and kindness. It broke her heart how nice he had been to her. She calls Mr Pike, 'Mr Fish'.

In the spring she begins writing short stories. In 'Fishy Waters' Jimmy Longa is an outcast, stoned by children. Dr Cox in 'Pioneer' is like her father. On 17 March in an article in the *New York Times,* Al Alvarez hails her as 'one of the finest British writers of this century'. During the interview she had flirted with him, lifting her dirndl skirt and petticoat so that he could see her shapely knees.

'I've always wanted to live in a forest,' she tells Francis

Wyndham. In December she is in a nursing home. She complains of 'two years wasted' on short stories and an abortive autobiography: '*tant pis*', nothing to show, like her father's tombstone.

In October 1975 Mr Greenslade dies. Jean realises she has not long to go. She falls, and she cries when she sees a spider. In December she is in a London hotel that caters for old people. She hates it. Her body is twisted. David Plante visits her to talk about *Smile Please*. She talks about Ford, Paris, Dominica. She gets drunk, swears, spits, and wets herself.

The evening had started relatively well. He told her she looked marvellous.

'Don't lie to me,' she said. 'I'm dying.' She asked him to buy her a bottle of sweet vermouth.

It was clear that she was disgusted by her surroundings – all those old people and a bossy manageress. She made David take her up to her room for another drink. In his book, *Difficult Women*, David makes heavy weather of getting Jean up to her room. To be fair, she did lean on him heavily. But then, why not? He was there, he'd be gone soon, he might as well make himself useful.

He describes himself and Jean as they lurched from one piece of furniture, where they stopped for a moment for a breather, to another. At certain key moments, Jean would entangle her legs with her stick and David would have to untangle them. He had to twist himself round many times to get her into the lift. When they got out, she leaned her bent back against the wall outside her room. He unlocked the door with her key.

'The room was all pink,' he writes.

'Never mind,' she said a propos of nothing. Her feelings, which she had to make apparent to any onlooker, were, as she knew from experience, irrelevant to any onlooker. No one would make her feel better. She would not let them.

'Let's have a drink,' she said, and decided upon rum. But there was a problem: 'The manageress won't let us have ice.' David rang for some and notes that she did not seem impressed or acknowledge she had been proved wrong when the ice arrived. It is obvious why this should be: because that would destroy her myth that she would never get what she wanted from the world and its inhabitants. To destroy that myth would be to admit that she had been wrong all her life, which would be unbearable. There is a grim satisfaction to be had from being proved right. Besides, by now, there would never be enough ice.

'Jean,' he said. 'There's no rum here.'

She had forgotten that she had asked for rum. 'I must have thought I was in Dominica.' He asked her when she had last been. Years ago. Of course it had all been ruined by 'them'. The rivers that she had drunk from as a girl were polluted. Everything she had loved was gone.

Then she teased him. She knew he was interested in her writing, and that he wanted to write about her. So, just to keep him in the room perhaps, she told him she would tell him how it was she started to write. She told him about Lancey, the abortion, the bed-sitter in Bloomsbury, the Christmas tree and not being able to pay the rent. And when she told him that Lancey gave her money she cried. 'And after that I didn't care, it didn't matter . . .'

'Maybe I do have black blood in me,' she told David. 'I think my great-grandmother was coloured, the Cuban. She was supposed to be a Vatican countess. I think she was coloured. Where else would I get my love for pretty clothes?'

She told him about her dead baby son. She told him she had not been a good mother. How could she be? If she could not recognise her own needs, how could she respond to another's?

They put too much ice in her drink, she complained. They did not want her to have a large drink. But why shouldn't she?

'I took the money. I didn't care,' she said referring to Lancey again. 'I don't care about anything any more. I know how to do it now. Not jumping out a window. Not taking pills, because they just pump out your stomach.'

'I'm boring you,' she worried. He reassured her.

'Oh what a goddamn shitty business we've taken on, being writers!'

He was surprised to hear her reveal her age when she admitted to being over eighty. She complained that her work was mediocre, that the stories she had been commissioned to write were mediocre, that what she really wanted to write was her autobiography, because everything people said about her was wrong. She wanted to tell the truth, not just about her but about Dominica. Her people did not treat the black people badly. Though now everyone said they did.

'I'm becoming a fascist,' she said because she thought David wasn't listening.

'I'm listening,' he said.

'*You*,' she spat at him. What did he want from her? Besides, there must be something poor, mean and bad about him if he was listening to *her*. She told him about the proud, dignified black man who had accepted a loaf of bread and a sixpence from her as alms. She remembered his unconquerable mind. He had not been debased by taking something from her. She had been left free to admire him.

David did not know how to respond to her, her moods changed so suddenly. Everything was so complicated with Jean. She asked for so much and tried to give so much, which was unbearably moving because it cost her so much. By now, he had been with her for five hours and she was still drinking. Some more mumbled poetry recitals led to reminiscences of her first meeting with Ford Madox Ford. But the recitation was so drained of emotion, so clinical that it chilled him. He told her he had to go. This story was what he had been waiting for but now that it had come he could not take it. Before he left, he used her toilet. Then she asked him to help *her* use the toilet. He struggled to get her into the bathroom and left her leaning on the wash-basin, her hat still on. After a long time he heard, 'Help me!'

He opened the door and saw that she was stuck in the toilet, her knickers round her ankles. There was urine all around the toilet. He had to step into it to lift her out. He finally got her on to her bed and put a blanket over her. She was desperately unhappy. 'It doesn't matter. It doesn't matter. Nothing matters,' she said.

By 1976 she is too tired to read book proofs any more. Instead she sits still and listens to David, remembering every word precisely. She cannot hold a pen, so in January Sonia moves her to the Portobello Hotel where David works with her on *Smile Please*. She suggested to David that they write a short story about the toilet incident. She was so adept at distancing herself from herself that she could see the literary possibilities: the comic element inherent in an old woman wetting herself, the tragedy propelling it. The ruthlessness of the literary imagination was uppermost at this moment. She was willing to exploit her own frailty, her humiliation. It was funny, and, after all, it did not matter. And she knew that was what he wanted. It was at least part of the reason why he kept coming to see her. But she made him feel uncomfortable. This was her gift to him: she was holding up a greasy, smeared mirror in which he could just about make out his own image. His motives were less than noble, and she knew all about that. She also thought he would not be interested in her if she did not make it worth his while.

'I'll get some paper,' he said.

'Yes, do.'

So he came to see her regularly, always working on the story, feeding her drinks, listening to her talk. The more excited he became the more she receded until, finally, it was his story to do what he wanted with.

'A gift.'

When Francis brings the actress Claire Bloom and novelist Alison Lurie to visit her at this fashionable hotel she is fascinated by Bloom's beauty – an older woman, still beautiful – and takes hardly any notice of Lurie. It was like visiting an actress, not an author, said Lurie. Francis knew that she wanted to be treated as a woman, not a writer. He always took her little presents of books, records or alcohol. He knew she was confident about her writing, and that she did not need reassurance about that. Diana Athill, however, did not appreciate Jean's response to having been born a woman. She resented Jean's fretting and anger, she could not under-stand why Jean, who was so talented, should be so unhappy. She admitted to being jealous of Jean's talent but had no patience for her need to be admired as a woman. Having said that, Diana would help Jean in practical terms time and time again, and was the kindest of friends. But her response to Jean is instructive: a strong woman's impatience with one who insists on her emotional frailty and her need for men.

In February Jean falls, and breaks a rib. Her heart is enlarged. Back home in April she makes a scene with her nurse, Janet Bridger. Gini has gone the way of all the other women who tried to befriend Jean. Nurse Janet is already frightened of her.

On 21 October 1976 *Sleep It Off Lady* is published. This means more publicity and more exposure to the late-1970s world of Women's Lib, Jean Muir kaftans, bearded academics asking her silly questions about a woman's lot, hippies and activism. In December she is in a ground-floor flat near Sloane Square working on the 'Jean Book' with David. On New Year's Eve she hosts a miserable champagne party. She is in despair. In April 1977 Nurse Janet is too frightened of this paranoid, raging woman to be able to stay in the house with her. By autumn she is in an old people's home. Paranoia and depression have overwhelmed her and everyone near her. In December Diana Melly, far away in London, does a very brave thing, and invites her to stay with her in her home. She gives Jean the best room in her house and has people round to entertain her. The stay in Diana's house starts well – clothes, visits, flirting with George, trips to Ronnie Scott's wearing her pink wig – and ends badly with terrible fits of anger and paranoia. George compares her to Johnny Rotten, the lead singer of the Sex Pistols. She is an elderly punk in a pink wig. Maryvonne visits her in Diana's house and faints on being attacked by her. Jean tells lies about all the people trying to help her. But she still finds time to tell David Plante about a vision of happiness that is not just for her. There are no words to describe it 'except perhaps in a still unknown language'. She feels 'a certainty of joy, and terrific terrific happiness, not only for me, but for everyone'. Ultimately, she knows 'that the end would be joy.'

On 1 March, Diana can take no more and drives Jean home to Cheriton Fitzpaine. By the end of March Jean is in a nursing home in Exeter. In May she has a bad fall and is complaining about everyone. All through the summer she toils at *Smile Please*. Her childhood was 'peopled with fears'. And then she says, 'Ford helped me more than anyone else.'

She finally gives up her secret: she is happiest when she writes.

Back at home in the late autumn of 1978 Jean finishes the first part of *Smile Please*. She complains that the cold has frozen her body and soul. On 19 April she has a fall and fractures her hip. She is taken into Exeter hospital.

On 14 May Jo Batterham has a sudden feeling that she must see Jean Rhys.

She knows this much about her friend:

> One of the main reasons Jean held on to life so tenaciously was because she could not bear to think of the gossip that might emerge when she was gone. She feared vicious remarks and harsh judgements. She knew the cruelty people are capable of behind your back. The control they take over your life. She was very private, she never gossiped. She hated to discuss mutual friends. She could be trusted with a secret.

Jo had made two promises to Jean: that she would not die alone and that she would not allow people to say nasty things about her after her death. Jo had discussed ways of dying with her. After she broke her hip, Jean realised her favoured option, hypothermia, was out. She had wanted to walk into the snow and die of exposure.

'How long will she go on living like this?' Jo asked the doctor.

'Days or months,' the doctor replied.

Jean lay in bed mute. Many years ago she had been mocked for her foreign accent. She had started whispering. Now she refused to speak.

'Jean, I'm here,' Jo said. 'If you want to die, do it now. But first we're going to have a glass of champagne.'

Jo mimed the action of pouring a glass and then sipping from it. Jean smiled. Jo sang 'Je ne regrette rien', and Jean started waving her hand to the rhythm. Jo left her bedside

and walked around Exeter saying, 'She's got to die. She's
got to die.'

When she came back to Jean's bed she saw that Jean had
pushed the oxygen mask off her face. The nurse asked Jo to
put the mask back on. But Jo said, 'No, she doesn't want it.'

The nurse tried to feed the dying woman, but Jean pulled
her face away. Jo told the nurse to stop: 'She wants to die.'

'You'll go to a happy place,' she told Jean. 'You'll be with
the nuns.'

Jean starts to die. Jo feels a moment of happiness. Jean
knew that she was there and that her friend had not failed
her. She could go back to her realm of colours. She finally
joined Mother Sacred Heart and Mother Mount Calvary.
She had earned her rest.

On 14 May 1979 Jean Rhys, née Ella Gwendoline Rees
Williams, died, three months before her eighty-ninth
birthday.

AUTHOR'S NOTE

Research conducted by Carole Angier in her biography of Jean Rhys (*Jean Rhys: Life and Work,* Andre Deutsch, 1991) leaves no stone unturned in uncovering the facts of her life. Angier has laid the groundwork for any biographer of Rhys and I am very grateful to her for that. In my exploration of Rhys's life I have taken a different approach to Angier, who finally diagnosed Rhys as a 'borderline personality'. Rhys laid herself bare in her writing, and it is clear that she was an unconventional woman tormented by her inability to conform. It would be too easy to judge her for that and more rewarding to see how she departs from the mainstream. In doing so she shows us something about ourselves as well as her. My aim in writing this book was to present the facts of Rhys's life in such a way that the reader is left with an impression of what it was like to have lived such a life.

Throughout my book, I have touched on Angier's as a departure point for my own researches. The chapters on Dominica were inspired by my reading of *Smile Please* and *Voyage in the Dark,* as well as several of her short stories. There are many nineteenth-century texts that ponder the beauty of this island, as well as its history.

Rhys's arrival in London and subsequent career in the theatre are fictionalised in *Voyage in the Dark* and several more short stories. The London Library is well stocked with books on Edwardian theatre, interwar Paris and Vienna. I read them all, as well as contemporary periodicals and newspapers. The *Illustrated London News* was very good on women's fashions as well as publishing reviews of plays in which Rhys appeared.

Shari Benstock was particularly helpful on the circles Rhys largely avoided in Paris. Stella Bowen's *Drawn from Life: Reminiscences* (Collins,1941) was most enlightening when it came to dissecting the *ménage à trois* she entered with Rhys and Ford. But again, it is Rhys's own texts, *Quartet* and *After Mr Mackenzie*, that offer the most tantalising biographical clues to incidents and relationships I have endeavoured to depict. As Rhys grew older, lost her looks, and adjusted to the 'invisibility' of middle age, *Good Morning, Midnight* traces her despair when faced with her mortality. It is essential reading in its exploration of the female experience of urban alienation, poverty and loneliness.

Jean's adventures during the Second World War were hard to research, as her experience of it was so interior and so unique. She largely sat it out. Her diaries and letters draw a blank, but her short stories fill in some of the gaps. Along with *Good Morning, Midnight* they, too, delineate the dislocating features of profound emotional distress. But they are remarkable, too, for so precisely evoking the chilling effects of war.

In discussing Rhys's literary output, I have been influenced by the work of Anne B. Simpson (*Territories of the Psyche*, Macmillan, 1999) in particular. Her Kleinian reading of Rhys's fiction amply illustrates the importance of mother and daughter relationships that is so crucial to understanding Rhys. Similarly, her understanding of object relations is convincing when considering Rhys's difficulties with friends and lovers. In her critique of *Good Morning, Midnight* Simpson employs a Lacanian approach which emphasises Rhys's extraordinary innovations with the novel and with language itself.

The British Library has some of Rhys's manuscripts including an early attempt at *Wide Sargasso Sea*. 'English Harbour' is an unfinished drama set in eighteenth-century Barbados, and shows how Caribs, race and sex haunted Rhys. At the end of a 1964 draft of *Wide Sargasso Sea* is a handwritten note saying, 'The rest of the book can be dictated. I will get it done somehow.' It was illuminating to see her manuscripts. The pages were stained with grease, sweat and face powder. Each word had clearly earned its place on the page.

The 1950s and 1960s found Rhys struggling to survive but writing nevertheless. Her letters (*Jean Rhys: Letters 1931–1966*, Deutsch, 1984) provided excellent source material as well as entertainment. Her humour and *joie de vivre* shine though, and show her in a quite unexpected light. One can only assume that sometimes, when she was writing to friends, she forgot to be unhappy.

Alexis Lykiard is one of many who have written memoirs of Rhys. His is one of the most poignant and sympathetic. As well as his, I have used an incident from David Plante's recollections in *Difficult Women* to illustrate her torments in old age. His description of her is unsparingly candid and so helpful to anyone who wants to understand her. At the same time, I owe a debt of thanks to Francis Wyndham, Diana Melly and Jo Baterham. All three were close to the elderly Jean Rhys, and they were all generous to me. I cannot thank them enough for their support and encouragement. Jo Baterham gave me a moving account she had written of Jean's final years. I quote it at the very end.

In her biography, Carole Angier called Rhys and Ford Madox Ford, 'perhaps the two greatest artists of self-pity in English fiction'. I do not see self-pity in Rhys's work or her life. I see an angry woman who had good reason to be angry, and whose vision was bleak. She found life difficult because she found it hard to be herself. She was born into a world where she was not white enough, where she was made to feel unwelcome from an early age, and where she did not learn the social niceties to overcome such setbacks. Furthermore, whether she frequented the artistic demi-monde or conventional society, her peers were disinclined to indulge the female artistic temperament. Besides this, no one could judge her as harshly as she judged herself. This can make for uncomfortable reading. She challenges us in the very act of reading her. I felt it was important to write about her on her own terms.

I would like to thank the Arts Council of Great Britain and the Society of Authors who assisted me financially. I was, and remain, extremely grateful. Victoria Millar at Bloomsbury is an excellent editor, as is Justine Taylor. Maureen Allen at the *Times Literary Supplement* helped me in my career and I would like to thank her, as well as my friends Chris Peachment, Phil Davies, Janet Rand and Dougie Salmon.

COPYRIGHT ACKNOWLEDGEMENTS

For permission to reprint copyright material the author and publishers gratefully acknowledge the following:

Text:
Diana Athill, for lines from personal correspondence with Jean Rhys.

Lines from *The Orchid House* by Phyllis Allfrey, copyright © P Shand Allfrey, 1954. Reproduced by permission of Curtis Brown Group Ltd, London, on behalf of the Estate of P Shand Allfrey.

Extracts from *Smile Please* by Jean Rhys, copyright © Jean Rhys 1979, are reproduced by permission of Sheil Land Associates on behalf of Jean Rhys Ltd.

Lines from *The Soul of London* by Ford Madox Ford, published by JM Dent. All attempts at tracing the copyright holder were unsuccessful.

Extracts from *Jean Rhys: Letters* by Jean Rhys, ed. Francis Wyndham and Diana Melly, copyright © Jean Rhys 1984, 1995, reproduced by kind permission of Penguin Group.

Photographs:
All images are © The Jean Rhys papers, The University of Tulsa – McFarlin Library, Department of Special Collections and University Archives and reproduced by kind permission.

BIBLIOGRAPHY

Works by Jean Rhys

After Leaving Mr Mackenzie, London, Jonathan Cape, 1930

Good Morning, Midnight, London, Constable, 1939

Jean Rhys: The Collected Short Stories, New York, Norton, 1992

trans. *Perversity* by Francis Carco, Chicago, Pascal Covici, 1928

Quartet, London, Chatto & Windus, 1928

Smile Please: An Unfinished Autobiography, London, André Deutsch, 1979

Voyage in the Dark, London, Constable, 1934

Wide Sargasso Sea, London, André Deutsch, 1966

Wyndham, Francis and Melly, Diana, eds, *Jean Rhys: Letters 1931–1966*, London, André Deutsch, 1984

Further Reading

Angier, Carole, *Jean Rhys: Life and Work*, London, André Deutsch, 1990

Benstock, Shari, *Women of the Left Bank, 1900–1940*, Austin, University of Texas Press, 1986

Bowen, Stella, *Drawn from Life: Reminiscences*, London, Collins Publishers, 1941

Gates, Henry Louis Jr, *Race, Writing and Difference*, Chicago, University of Chicago Press, 1986

Howells, Coral Ann, *Jean Rhys*, Hemel Hempstead, Harvester Wheatsheaf, 1991

Hunter, Jefferson, *Edwardian Fiction*, Cambridge, Harvard University Press, 1982

Kloepfer, D.K., *The Unspeakable Mother: Forbidden Discourse in Jean Rhys and HD*, Ithaca, Cornell University Press, 1989

Kristeva, Julia, trans. Jane Marie Todd, *Colette*, New York, Columbia University Press, 2004

Le Gallez, Paula, *The Rhys Woman*, London, Macmillan, 1990

Lykiard, Alexis, *Jean Rhys Revisited*, Cambridge, Exeter, Stride, 2000

Maurel, Sylvie, *Jean Rhys (Women Writers)*, Basingstoke, Palgrave Macmillan, 1999

Plante, David, *Difficult Women: A Memoir of Three*, London, Gollancz, 1983

Simpson, Anne B., *Territories of the Psyche*, Basingstoke, Palgrave Macmillan, 2005

Staley, Thomas F., *Jean Rhys: A Critical Study*, London, Macmillan, 1979

INDEX

A NOTE ON THE AUTHOR

Lilian Pizzichini has worked for the *Literary Review* and the *Times Literary Supplement*. Her first book, *Dead Men's Wages*, won the 2002 Crime Writers' Association Gold Dagger for Non-Fiction. Until recently she was writer-in-residence in a prison. She lives in London.

A NOTE ON THE TYPE

The text of this book is set in Bembo. This type was first used in 1495 by the Venetian printer Aldus Manutius for Cardinal Bembo's *De Aetna*, and was cut for Manutius by Francesco Griffo. It was one of the types used by Claude Garamond (1480–1561) as a model for his Romain de L'Université, and so it was the forerunner of what became standard European type for the following two centuries. Its modern form follows the original types and was designed for Monotype in 1929.